SUPERVISION OF INSTRUCTION:

Foundations and Dimensions

SUPERVISION

FOUNDATIONS

MILDRED E. SWEARINGE

F INSTRUCTION:

ND DIMENSIONS

Professor of Education, Florida State University

ALLYN AND BACON, INC., BOSTON, 1962

To

the Greater Realization

of Human Potentialities

PREFACE

Supervision of instruction has broad foundations and numerous dimensions. It is the purpose of this book to explore these foundations and dimensions, and to give emphasis to the belief:

—that supervision arises from a matrix of values and conditions in our society.

—that to understand the raison d'être of supervision enables us to see its essential functions and potentialities.

—that the major functions of supervision, clearly perceived, can give organization to the field, making it possible to choose daily activities with relevancy and coherence.

—that the human dynamic for learning is enormous, with only a minute portion of it typically being realized, and that adult learning is often sharply stunted by stresses and strains, some of which could be reduced by helpful supervision.

—that the human dynamic for cooperative action is only partially understood and that supervision can facilitate its greater realization.

—that supervision is a creative enterprise, deeply rooted in the capacity of human beings for cooperation, aspiration, and continuous growth.

It is hoped that the book will be of use to persons who are beginning their study of supervision, to those who are engaged in seminars, and to those individuals and staffs who are seeking to clarify and enlarge their purposes as they carry out the daily responsibilities of supervision.

MILDRED E. SWEARINGEN

TABLE OF CONTENTS

CHAPTER 1

THE NATURE OF SUPERVISION

SUPERVISION, along with all other major aspects of the educational system, has as its ultimate goal the improvement of learning for all those who take part in educational programs. Supervision focuses upon the improvement of instruction. It is concerned with the continuous redefinition of goals, with the wider realization of the human dynamic for learning and for cooperative effort, and with the nurturing of a creative approach to the problems of teaching and learning.

The need for supervision lies deep in a matrix of cultural and professional conditions characteristic of the present time. A careful analysis of these conditions makes it possible to see clearly the reasons for the rise of supervision, the essential functions it should serve, and the scope of its potentialities. Supervision today also carries the imprint of needs felt in previous generations and the efforts made to meet those needs.

This chapter presents an overview of the professional background for supervision, the responsibilities of supervision being discharged in the contemporary scene, and the challenge to supervision that exists today. The chapters immediately following trace the evolving concept of supervision through the years and explore the conditions of today which are the bases for deriving the essential functions of supervision.

PROFESSIONAL GROWTH IN A MODERN SOCIETY

One of the significant developments of the mid-twentieth century has been the widespread acceptance of the concept of the continuation of education for the professional worker or specialist. Members of the medical profession were among the first to recognize the necessity for an on-going education. For some time they have participated in conventions, postgraduate sessions, seminars and refresher courses, and have sought still other forms of professional stimulation and association. Today many other kinds of professional workers, whose education formerly would have been considered completed at the time of their entrance into work in their field of specialization, also engage in educational activities and set up voluntary associations for their professional stimulation and advancement.

Many factors contribute to the necessity for a continuation of education. The great increase in knowledge during the past century and the increasing specialization of knowledge have been widely recognized. Almost daily, invention and discovery make some new impact upon ways of living and upon our resources for improving the quality of living. Continued contributions from research in the basic sciences open new potentialities in their own and related fields. To keep abreast of such changes calls for continued education. Furthermore, new areas of specialization come into being during a person's maturity that did not exist in his youth. New opportunities may arise which require further education. In addition, new emphases in social relationships and increased understanding of human interactions often lead to the need for further education. For instance, the concept of leadership now emerging has stimulated industrial leaders, personnel managers and others to further study of human relationships. The professional person today is a lifelong student of his work.

Professional Development and Education

The field of education is no exception among the professions. Contributions from research, new emphases in social relations, and the appearance of new areas of specialization all impinge upon educators too. It has become commonplace in recent years to speak of "in-service education" of teachers and to signify by the term, not a catching up on what should have been learned earlier, but rather the continuing education essential to a specialist for his further professional development.

While the significance of in-service education has been recognized for some years, it seems to be of increasing importance. At the same time there is a growing recognition of the variety of activities, many of them cooperative activities, which have educative value for school personnel.

Supervision and Professional Growth

Supervision, as one of the areas of education, is subject to the same forces which make continuous professional development essential in other fields. In addition, there is at least one other major factor which enhances the need for in-service education for supervisors. The concept of supervision itself has undergone a rapid evolution in the last two or three decades and is still in a period of extensive development, moving toward the idea of supervision as a creative enterprise in cooperative effort among peers. Significant values are emerging more clearly and procedures in harmony with democratic principles are in experimental use. Yet supervision has not come entirely through its twilight era. Shadows of authoritarianism and didacticism linger in some places, in some attitudes and practices, in some habits and assumptions. There is great need for supervisors to have close, vital professional association and stimulation in order that they may continue as learners, and contribute to increased vision of the function of supervision. To paraphrase a statement from Bigelow [1]—helping the supervisor to do better what he sees as his job, and to see better what his job might be, becomes the goal of the professional development of supervisors.

RESPONSIBILITIES OF SUPERVISION

Supervisors, then, have responsibility, along with other members of the school system, for fostering sustained professional development of all personnel, which in turn leads to improved education for the youth of the land. How is this responsibility discharged? A frequently cited definition of supervision offered by Barr, Burton, and Brueckner several years ago provides important clues: "Supervision is an expert technical service primarily concerned with studying and improving conditions that surround learning and pupil growth." [2] The ultimate goal is learning and pupil growth; the means involve study and action; the persons designated as supervisors should have expertness in the understandings, skills, and attitudes which enable them to render service. Definitions presented in subsequent years emphasize still other important aspects, especially leadership, creativity, and the releasing of energies of people, which will be discussed in Chapter II, where the evolution of a concept of supervision is traced.

At this point it may be helpful in gaining an overview of supervision to approach the matter by asking a few direct questions. What is supervision? Who are supervisors? What do they do? Why do they do whatever it is they do?

What Is Supervision?

In a free association situation what terms first come to mind at the mention of the word *supervision?* A group of experienced

[1] Karl Bigelow, "The Future and Teacher Education," *Teachers College Record,* Vol. 47, No. 6 (March, 1946), p. 393.

[2] A. S. Barr, William H. Burton, and Leo J. Brueckner, *Supervision,* 2nd Ed. (New York: Appleton-Century-Crofts, Inc., 1947), p. 11.

teachers, all of whom had worked in situations having supervisory service, were asked to record the first four or five words or phrases that came to mind when they heard the word *supervision*. Among the terms were: helper, advisor, resource person, visitor (to *my* classroom), coordinator, curriculum consultant, leader, dictator, fear, a place or person to consult, stimulator of creativity, overview, aid in problem solving in subject areas, developer of new programs in the county, scapegoat for failures, one who requires action of teachers, one who makes program lighter and more enjoyable, consolation when things go wrong, one who acquaints teachers with new materials and ideas, one who puts direction into activities. The term *helper* appeared more often than any other word and was followed in frequency by *advisor* and *coordinator*.

A group of supervisors at work in varied positions were asked to make a similar free association list. Helper, counselor, friend, and leader, again appeared with high frequency. Other terms were: travel, big meetings, person-to-person conferring, the negative reaction in some situations (fear of "snoopervision"), the busy butterfly (starting so many projects).

The above description of supervision, while informal, has a sense of vividness and reality, for it is expressed in terms of the perceptual world of those who daily experience supervision. Several significant points are apparent: (1) the focus of attention is upon service toward the improvement of teaching-learning conditions, just where Barr, Burton, and Brueckner indicated it should be; (2) stimulation of creativity and the initiating of new steps are recognized as responsibilities of supervision; (3) remnants of the prescriptive, coercive supervision of an earlier day are still visible (handed down in part, perhaps, by mores and unquestioned expectations, and nurtured in part by normal apprehension regarding the unfamiliar, by unfortunate mannerisms of a few supervisors, and by misunderstanding as to the nature of modern supervision); (4) the dynamic, or power of personal relationships, and the force of feelings are stated or implied in many of the terms. Supervision, as experienced by the individual, is a highly personal affair; feelings are necessarily involved; (5) aiding in establishing an awareness of purpose or over-arching sense of direction is recognized as a function

of supervision; (6) a reply to the basic question as to what constitutes supervision is shaped in part by the particular experiences and
purposes of the individual involved and by the role he holds in the
situation. However, in spite of differences of perception according to role, the common elements are predominant.

Who Are Supervisors?

Supervision is carried on by persons holding varied titles. Supervisor (general, elementary, secondary, subject area), curriculum coordinator, consultant, director of instruction are some of the commonly used titles. In large school systems, where division of labor
among many specialists and generalists is made necessary, other
titles often appear. Helping teacher, supervisor of pupil personnel
services, and supervisor of instructional materials are among them.

In addition, principals and superintendents carry as a normal
part of their work a large responsibility for supervision. It is probably unnecessary (and somewhat futile) to try to draw a sharp line
between the supervisory and administrative roles of the principal
or the superintendent, since ultimately every act is intended to
enhance the learning of children. The building principal, especially,
is in a strategic and vital position, for he is both the daily instructional leader of the faculty in the individual school and the coordinator of the supervisory services available from the entire school
system.

It is common practice to use the term *supervisor* with both a
general and a specific meaning. In the broad sense, it refers to all
persons responsible for instructional leadership. In the narrower
sense, it refers to those persons who devote all their time and energy
directly to the improvement of instruction.

The multiplicity of titles may seem confusing at first, but it usually reflects an effort on the part of the local school system to
designate the major functions assigned to a position and to clarify
lines of responsibility. The assignment of functions is usually a relative affair, a matter of emphasis rather than a mutually exclusive
arrangement. For instance, a curriculum director, an elementary

supervisor, and a social studies consultant working in the same school system would have many functions in common, but the emphasis and approach would be somewhat different for each of them. Meanwhile, the titles indicate some of the uniqueness of activity and responsibility expected of each of the three.

In different communities the same title may have different meanings. A helping teacher in one system may be called a consultant in another; the director of instruction in one city or county may perform essentially the same work that the curriculum coordinator does in another situation; the assistant principal in one school system may be an administrative aid, but in another he may be responsible for curriculum coordination and development.

The lack of neat categories of titles is understandable enough when factors such as the following are taken into account: the local history and previous organization, the increase in size of school systems which necessitates more of the familiar services, and the rapid accruing of new responsibilities in modern education which necessitates new services.

From the standpoint of a study of supervision the diversity of titles and other conditions should not prove distracting. The important point, in response to the question as to who is a supervisor, is that the person so designated should be devoting a major portion of his time directly to the stimulation and coordination of efforts to improve the conditions of learning.

What Do Supervisors Do?

Another question which is more quickly asked than answered is that of what supervisors actually do when they are at work. A look at what supervisors do on the job can provide one kind of insight into the nature of supervision, although a knowledge of what prevails in supervisory activity is not the only component of an understanding of the nature of supervision.

SUPERVISORS EXAMINE THEIR PRACTICES. An interesting study by Louisiana supervisors throws light on the question of what supervisors do.[3] Three basic questions were asked. What do Louisiana supervisors do? What practices do they employ to improve instruction? Are the things they do to improve instruction considered good practices? In seeking answers to these questions, the supervisors agreed to do four things: (1) to keep time logs of their activities on selected half-days throughout the 1955–56 school session; (2) to select one supervisory activity in which they were engaged on each of these half-days and describe it objectively in writing; (3) to analyze the time logs and anecdotal descriptions to ascertain how supervisors spent their time and what techniques were used frequently to improve instruction; and (4) to examine professional literature and research to find out if the things the supervisors were doing were considered good practice.

The data from the time logs indicated that visiting classrooms, doing clerical work, conferring with principals and teachers, working with lay groups, and traveling were the five activities which occurred most often and occupied about 63% of the time. The remaining 37% of time was divided among 17 other types of activities.

The analysis of time logs and descriptive accounts indicated that the ten most frequently recurring practices were:

1. Working with principals to improve instruction
2. Engaging in classroom visitation
3. Initiating ideas, making suggestions, and accepting responsibilities for getting a job done
4. Serving as resource persons
5. Providing help on the basis of needs considered important by teachers
6. Working with lay groups
7. Trying to foster an atmosphere of support and understanding to facilitate learning
8. Engaging in activities for their own professional growth
9. Making plans for their own activities

[3] *Louisiana Supervisors Examine Their Practices.* The Louisiana School Supervisors Association in Cooperation with College of Education, Louisiana State University and the State Department of Education (Baton Rouge: Louisiana School Supervisors Association, 1958).

10. Providing opportunities for people to share in planning and making decisions about matters that affect them

The examination of literature and research on supervision revealed ample theoretical support for each of the above recurring practices as a good supervisory procedure.

A PRINCIPAL LOGS HIS SUPERVISORY ACTIVITIES. A principal's day encompasses a variety of responsibilities. The following excerpts from a principal's log reflect some of the many aspects of his supervisory role. The events occurred over a two-day period near the opening of the school term.

From Daily Log of an Elementary Principal:
1. Planned with music consultant for the faculty study for the year—incorporating listening, rhythms, theory and fun songs. (Original planning was done with a group of teachers to determine what types of activities they wanted for their faculty study.)
2. Attended a principals' and test coordinators' meeting explaining the county-wide testing program.
3. Discussed with the test coordinator in reference to the points he will cover in his meeting with the faculty explaining the testing program in the county and in the local school.
4. Met with the county health nurse planning the implementation of the health program through the health curriculum taught by the classroom teacher.
5. Conferred with a parent, whose child has a particular emotional problem. The parent wishes to explain the problem so that we may plan student placement and use of the appropriate special services of the county in working with the child.
6. Planned with custodians for optimum use of the available television sets in connection with educational television programming.
7. Planned with committee of teachers for listening experiences in music over the school's inter-communication system. The programs will be directed to the students in grades 4, 5, and 6.
8. Introduced the visiting teacher to new members of the staff. A discussion was held with each of the new teachers as to how the

visiting teacher aids the school in improving instruction. If there are children assigned the new teacher who have had the services of the visiting teacher, the teacher is informed of the results of this effort.

9. Presented helping teachers from the county office to the total group. These teachers explain their role in the improvement of instruction, and invite all teachers to make use of their services.

10. Introduced the appropriate helping teacher to each new teacher in the school. A tentative appointment is made for the first visit and the principal acquaints the beginning teacher with the types of things he will look for when visiting and also what type of things the helping teacher looks for.

11. Conferred with a reporter from the local press who is preparing a series of articles on new developments in service to children through the schools.

12. Prepared the requisition for social studies materials requested by third grade teachers.[4]

Even a casual examination of the principal's log and of the practices of systemwide supervisors reveals the fact that supervision is a transaction among persons. Whatever the specific activity may be, people are involved. The expression, "supervision is people," has real truth in it. The exact wording of the titles of several books appearing in recent years takes on deep significance: for example, *Supervision as Human Relations, Supervision as Cooperative Action, Supervision: a Social Process.*

TEACHERS DESCRIBE SUPERVISORY AID.   It is important to know what supervisors do, in the eyes of teachers. In Appendix A are four brief cases or incidents, described in the teachers' own words, which show principals and system-wide supervisors assisting teachers with their daily problems, such as interpreting to parents a change in the kindergarten program or becoming acquainted with new co-workers and materials. Once again the person-to-person nature of supervision is apparent.

The examples cited give an overview of supervisors at work and

---

[4] Log provided by Carlos Taylor, principal, San José School, Dunedin, Florida.

lead to a further question. Why are supervisors engaged in these activities rather than some others?

Why Do Supervisors Engage in the Selected Activities?

A more intensive discussion of the question of why supervisors are engaged in certain activities rather than others will await the exploration of the roots or bases of supervision, but for the present it may be helpful to point out a few of the guidelines supervisors have available in selecting activities.

A continuing or over-arching sense of direction can often be derived from the familiar guidelines recognized in most areas of educational endeavor: (a) principles of human growth and development; (b) principles of the learning process; (c) the demands of the society in which the individual lives; and (d) the continuing effort to increase the degree of realization of democratic ideals. These guidelines are especially helpful in determining direction and ultimate goals.

A second kind of guideline, and one which is helpful in determining starting points, is a knowledge of the problems that teachers encounter and recognize. A person who has become aware of a problem has already developed momentum for working toward a solution, or, to phrase it differently, is ready to perceive the helpfulness in suggestions or opportunities being offered. The professional literature is replete with studies of what problems teachers say they encounter. Hill summarized 475 such studies and identified the five leading types of problems as difficulties: (1) in providing for individual differences; (2) in teaching method; (3) in discipline control and social development of pupils; (4) in motivation, interest, and getting children to work; and (5) in the direction of study.[5] However suggestive the general literature may be, the supervisor in a specific situation would want to make careful surveys of local needs and do thoughtful listening for clues while school personnel discuss problems and plans.

[5] George E. Hill, "Teachers Instructional Difficulties: A Review of Research" (*Journal of Educational Research*, Vol. 37, No. 8, April, 1944), pp. 602–615.

A third kind of reason for choosing certain activities in prefer-
ence to others is found often in the immediacy of on-going events
in the local, state, national or world community. A look at specific
supervisory activities of the 1930's would reveal the impact of the
Depression in such matters as the increased tempo of efforts to
expand the range of curriculum offerings and in efforts to keep
children and youth in school. A look at the 1940's would show the
effects of World War II upon supervisory activities in such diverse
matters as the constant search for replacements for teachers drawn
into the armed services and industry, and the requested organization of educational drives for one worthy cause after another. The
late 1950's saw hours of supervisory time diverted suddenly to cooperative efforts to spend wisely the funds available from the National Defense Education Act. Or a locally enacted school board
policy, such as the decision to offer foreign language in the elementary school effective immediately, can cause instructional leaders to
choose their activities along certain lines for weeks or months. If
immediacy of events were the only criterion, of course, sheer expediency could easily result and supervisory effort would have no more
consistency of direction than a weather vane. But when urgency of
need is joined with other considerations, it can help determine
priority of choices.

A fourth kind of concern gives guidance both for long range
planning and for daily choices: namely, the concern for helping
education to incorporate as rapidly as possible the findings from
research in its own field and in numerous related fields such as
psychology, child development, physiology, sociology, and pedi-
atrics. Steadily increasing knowledge from many fields and a clearer
perception of the human dynamics involved in achieving social
ideals necessitate sustained leadership if educational advancement
is to be realized.

The utilization of new insight is not an intermittent rushing
about to close the gap between theory and practice first at one
point and then another, but is rather a careful development of
avenues or ways of work built upon the glad recognition of an exciting facet of human existence: namely, that man, being man, can

use his intelligence endlessly for invention and discovery leading to the gradual improvement of human conditions and the broader realization of human potentialities.

THE CHALLENGE OF SUPERVISION

The full scope of the challenge of supervision can be understood better after a discussion of the matrix of needs from which supervision arises (Chapter III), but it is already clear that three big areas invite effort: to serve and facilitate, to stimulate creativity, and to aid in the integration of goals.

To Serve and Facilitate

To help the teacher "do better what he sees as his job and see better what his job might be," to use Bigelow's phrasing, is an essential work of supervision. To secure materials needed by teachers and children, to give support to those making changes for improvement, to coordinate efforts of those who are already striving, and to induct new teachers so that they may grow to their full professional stature are tasks which challenge supervisors to expedite educational advance.

To Stimulate Creativity

To help teachers extend their experiences in the pursuit of broader meanings, to take problems as challenges to go beyond what they already know, and to respond happily and trustingly to the nudge of new ideas are opportunities for supervision. To free vision from the confines of the too familiar, to free action from inhibiting lassitude and fears, and to help teachers feel the lift of a creative approach to the day, call for the best that supervision can offer.

To Integrate Goals

Seeing things whole gives meaning to the parts. It is not easy for any individual either to attain or to maintain a sustaining sense of the whole while he struggles for accomplishment of parts. It is an enormous challenge to supervision to help all concerned with education have such a clear vision of values and ultimate goals that they can see parts-in-relation-to whole and thereby work with a sustaining sense of purpose, and with rising energy and satisfaction vitalizing each day.

AIDS TO STUDY AND DISCUSSION

1. Develop a working definition of supervision which you can accept for the present. Be ready to explain why you regard each concept in it as important.

2. Examine the definitions of supervision found in any three of the books suggested in the bibliography below. At what points are the definitions similar? How do they differ in emphasis?

3. What is your very first awareness of supervision which you can recall? Did it occur when you were in elementary school? Secondary school? A beginning teacher? What was the feeling tone of the event? Looking back on it now, what would you judge the purpose of the event to have been?

4. When you were preparing to do your student teaching, what were your expectations regarding the role of supervision? Were these expectations modified after your first few meetings with instructional leaders?

5. Confer with two or more system-wide supervisors or principals, asking them to describe the scope and distribution of their responsibilities. In what ways are the responsibilities similar? Dif-

ferent? Is the individual's title descriptive of his major areas of work?

SUGGESTIONS FOR FURTHER READING

Barr, A. S., William H. Burton, and Leo J. Brueckner, *Supervision,* 2nd Ed. (New York: Appleton-Century-Crofts, Inc., 1947).

Bartky, John A., *Supervision as Human Relations* (Boston: D. C. Heath & Co., 1953).

Bigelow, Karl, "The Future and Teacher Education," *Teachers College Record,* Vol. 47, No. 6 (March, 1946).

Briggs, Thomas H., and Joseph Justman, *Improving Instruction through Supervision* (New York: The Macmillan Co., 1952).

Burton, William H., and Leo J. Brueckner, *Supervision: A Social Process,* 3rd Ed. (New York: Appleton-Century-Crofts, Inc., 1955).

Crosby, Muriel, *Supervision as Co-operative Action* (New York: Appleton-Century-Crofts, Inc., 1957).

Elsbree, Willard S., and Harold J. McNally, *Elementary School Adminstration and Supervision,* 2nd Ed. (New York: American Book Company, 1959).

Fox, James Harold, "What is Good Supervision?" *The National Elementary Principal,* Vol. 26, No. 4 (February, 1947).

Franseth, Jane, *Supervision as Leadership* (Evanston, Ill.: Row, Peterson & Company, 1961).

Guss, Carolyn, "How Is Supervision Perceived?" *Educational Leadership,* Vol. 19, No. 2 (November, 1961).

Gwynn, J. Minor, *Theory and Practice of Supervision* (New York: Dodd, Mead & Co., 1961).

Hill, George E., "Teachers' Instructional Difficulties: A Review of Research," *Journal of Educational Research*, Vol. 37, No. 8 (April, 1944).

Louisiana Supervisors Examine Their Practices. The Louisiana School Supervisors Association in Cooperation with College of Education, Lousiana State University and the State Department of Education (Baton Rouge: Louisiana School Supervisors Association, 1958).

CHAPTER 2

AN EVOLVING CONCEPT OF SUPERVISION

SUPERVISION has been almost co-existent with public education. Supervision had its beginning in the early colonial period and it has evolved gradually through the intervening years. Its three centuries of development show the influence of most of the major factors in education during the years. Thus the great influx of students beginning in the 1870's, the expanding curriculum, the accruing functions of public education, and more recently the knowledge gained from research in the learning process and human dynamics, have all helped shape the concept of supervision as we find it today.

HISTORICAL SKETCH OF THE RISE OF SUPERVISION IN THE UNITED STATES

Early Appearance

Supervision appeared early in some of the colonies. In 1654 the General Court of Massachusetts Bay Colony directed the selectmen of the towns to secure teachers of sound faith and morality and to continue them in office only as long as they met these requirements. Nothing was said specifically about inspection or supervision of schools, but the enactment did imply a felt need for establishing some kind of community responsibility for the success of the school.

Another step came in 1709 in Boston, when a committee of laymen was appointed to visit the schools, to inquire into the methods of teaching, to examine pupil achievement, and to formulate means for the advancement of learning. During the next hundred years or more there was apparently little change, and committees of this general type continued to function largely to see that no one, teacher or pupil, shirked on his job, and that activities distasteful to the community were not carried on at school.

It would probably be quite inaccurate to picture all schools, and certainly all children, as benefiting from the concern of such committees in formulating means for the advancement of learning. An enactment by one or several legislative bodies was often many years in being fulfilled. Numerous individuals, families and even whole villages were indifferent to the values of education or regarded the cost as prohibitive. Educational efforts were often spotty and sporadic. Yet succeeding generations owe considerable gratitude to the vision and diligence of the individuals and committees that sought the continued improvement of learning.

Dickey summarizes this early period by saying that the first attempts at supervision were characterized by three fundamental approaches: (1) authority and autocratic rule; (2) emphasis upon the inspection and weeding out of weak teachers; and (3) conformity to standards prescribed by the committee of laymen.[1]

The Nineteenth Century

During the nineteenth century these approaches continued in use. By the middle of the century, however, one trend was apparent, that of a shift from lay to professional responsibility for inspection

[1] Frank G. Dickey, *Developing Supervision in Kentucky.* Bulletin of the Bureau of School Service, Vol. XX, No. 3 (Lexington: University of Kentucky, 1948), p. 8.

of schools. Many factors in the latter half of the century encouraged and confirmed the trend. The rapid growth of villages and cities necessitated schools with more than one teacher. A head teacher or principal was named and was freed from part or all of his teaching responsibilities in order to care for the administration of the school. As the schools continued to expand, the offices of city, county, and state superintendents arose. These new officials gradually won from lay boards the major responsibility for supervision (inspection) of schools.

Meanwhile, during the latter part of the nineteenth century, school enrollments were increasing rapidly. There were far too few teachers who were prepared for their work. Yet there was the beginning of an educational "science," and hope was high that if all teachers could learn the new methods being brought back from Europe and being developed here, instruction could be quickly improved.

Furthermore, many new subjects were being introduced into the curriculum and even prepared teachers felt inadequate when asked to handle the new fields. Special supervisors were often added to the staff to show teachers how to give instruction in the new areas. These conditions—the urgent need for teachers, the slight amount of preparation for teaching, the expansion of the curriculum, and the beginning of a body of professional knowledge—all led to the growth of supervision as a function of school people rather than of lay boards. The same conditions, however, perpetuated the concept of supervision as inspection and encouraged the idea of supervision as the transmission of superior knowledge. Supervision was regarded as inspection to determine weaknesses of teachers and then the supplying of information and specific methods to correct deficiencies. Since many superintendents lacked time or technical information, or both, the work of inspection and correction was often turned over to persons who were allotted full time for supervision.

The Early Twentieth Century

Toward the end of the nineteenth century and in the first few years of the twentieth, the professional literature showed a shift in emphasis away from the authoritarian concept of supervision and toward the idea of cooperative effort and guidance. McMurray made an early statement of this concept:

> The teacher cannot do this—cannot secure self-expression in pupils—unless she herself is practicing it; unless she is clearly conscious of her own freedom to say and do what she sincerely believes in. It is the duty of the prncipal or supervisor, therefore, to surround the teacher with such an atmosphere as will encourage her to think her own thoughts, and to express them frankly; i.e., to be her normal self.[2]

Yet through the first third of the twentieth century, practice was scarcely touched by the emerging concept of supervision as a democratic, cooperative enterprise. Perhaps the discrepancy between the evolving concept and the continuing practice is understandable when it is realized that many of the factors leading to autocratic, authoritarian supervision in the 1800's continued to prevail in the 1900's: i.e., inadequate professional preparation on the part of many teachers, an expanding curriculum, and the introduction of new methods. In addition, two other factors probably played an important part. First, the rapid rise and popular acceptance of standardized testing in the 1920's was influential in leading to a brief period of "scientific" supervision which gave fresh impetus toward uniformity and toward standardization in many learning situations. Supervision of the inspection or correction-of-specific-deficiency type was thus enhanced. Second, the mechanistically conceived behavioristic psychology of the early 1900's gave almost as much sanction as the faculty psychology of the 1800's to the efficacy of models and ready-made solutions to problems. Hence again the authoritarian type of supervision was enhanced and perpetuated.

Still another reason for the perpetuation of outmoded practices in supervision may be in the relatively small amount of special training obtained by supervisors. A research project of the United States Office of Education in 1937 revealed that few universities

[2] F. M. McMurray, *Elementary School Standards* (Yonkers-on-Hudson: World Book Co., 1922), p. 178.

offered courses in supervision. Furthermore, only a few of those offered related to philosophy, purposes, or techniques of educational leadership. The majority of courses dealt with such matters as subject area supervision and measurement techniques.[3] Hence it is reasonable to suppose that if supervisors were to develop a new point of view, it would have to come some other way, possibly out of their contacts with professional literature and professional organizations.

Meanwhile, another concept of supervision was gaining some attention, that of supervision as primarily inspiration. According to this view a supervisor is one "who inspires his teachers, lifts them above themselves, reinvigorates their flagging spirits."[4] While inspiration and encouragement are undoubtedly an important part of supervision, they do not alone solve fundamental problems. A supervisor's wide variety of experiences should enable him to help teachers regain perspective lost from standing too close to a problem and to help teachers see new potentialities in themselves and in the situation. But when the supervisor relies on enthusiasm and sheer ability to inspire, he is in the presence of two subtle dangers, according to the Yearbook Committee. One is the implication that supervisors and teachers are qualitatively different, the supervisors being inspiring people and the teachers uninspired. The second danger is the ever present possibility of self-deception. The supervisor may well inspire himself through his efforts to be enthusiastic and a person of high vision, and yet never inspire anyone except himself. Because he is carried away with enthusiasm, it is easy to deceive himself as to the reactions of others.[5]

Ability to feel deep conviction and to arouse it in others was, and is, important in a supervisor's work. The ideal of inspiration, however, did not constitute an adequate conceptual framework for a theory of instructional leadership.

[3] U. S. Office of Education, *Preparation for Elementary School Supervision*. Bulletin No. 18, 1937, pp. 12, 44–45.

[4] *Leadership Through Supervision*, 1946 Yearbook of the Association for Supervision and Curriculum Development (Washington, D.C.: National Education Association, 1946), p. 117.

[5] *Ibid*, pp. 118–119.

AN EMERGING CONCEPT OF SUPERVISION

By 1935 a concept of supervision as democratic, cooperative, and creative was beginning to take definite shape. Much of the literature previous to this time had concerned itself with techniques of supervision such as classroom visiting, achievement tests, or score cards for fixed recitation procedures. Emphasis was upon efficiency of operation of what existed rather than upon growth.[6] Much of the concern after the mid 1930's was with goals, values, the nature of children, human relations, and the development of democratic processes.

Converging Factors

PROFESSIONAL NATURE OF TEACHING. Several factors converged to make the emphasis upon cooperative, creative supervision rather distinct. First, teaching began to be recognized as more of a profession than formerly. Teaching was seen as a non-repetitive act involving judgment and creativity rather than the automatic application of rules. It might appear to the uninitiated person that the fourth grade teacher or geometry teacher would obviously present his special subject year after year in the same manner to learners who were essentially the same, but many school people, sociologists and child development specialists knew otherwise. The individuality of the learners and of the teachers provided factors that actually made each day and each group of children unique. Supervisors were having to exercise situational judgments themselves and had to make room for teacher judgments that were situation-based. Furthermore the motivation or learning dynamic of the individual—whether supervisor, teacher, or pupil—was being given greater recognition. Therefore supervision could not, with consistency, remain

[6] Harold Spears, "Can a Supervisory Leopard Change His Spots?" *Educational Leadership*, Vol. III, No. 4 (January, 1946), p. 152.

highly authoritarian and prescriptive. Reeder summarized this subject saying:

> A new psychology, a respect for the period of childhood resulting from the child-study movement, a re-examination of the meaning of teaching, and new concepts of the curriculum have produced a revolution seldom or never equalled in the history of education of children. Every phase of our educational system has had to undergo basic changes both in theory and in practice as a result of this revolution. And our concepts of supervision and our definition of it have been remade in the twentieth century.[7]

In a dynamic, rapidly developing profession it would be anachronistic if supervision were to remain static or fail to react to the factors involved in change.

DEMOCRATIC IDEALS. Second, the world events of recent years have made us more aware of discrepancies between what we say and what we do. The world-wide depression, war, and conflicting ideologies have made us examine our democracy intellectually and try to analyze the components of our democratic civilization. Democracy is being recognized by an increasing number of people as a concept applicable to all aspects of living, not to the political scene alone. More people realize that democratic values and processes have to be nurtured through daily practice rather than precept alone. They see the school as a basic social force. The concept of supervision has been profoundly influenced by recent efforts to clarify the meaning of democracy. Dickey describes the democratic concept of supervision as follows:

> The democratic concept of supervision has inherent in it the idea of cooperation of teachers and supervisors upon the problems of improving instruction. The emphasis is placed upon teacher growth; upon teacher participation in the discussion of and determination of aims, plans, methods, and procedures for the improvement of teaching; and upon the development by the super-

---

[7] Edwin H. Reeder, *Supervision in the Elementary School*, Educational Research Circular No. 60 (Boston: Houghton Mifflin Company, 1953), p. 6.

visor of the teacher's powers of self-direction. The supervisor thus becomes a guide, an aid, and a co-worker of the teacher. . . . The democratic process is a means, but a means so vital and indispensable that it affects the end. In other words, the democratic concept involves a kind of perpetual growth. . . .[8]

NORMALCY OF CHANGE AND GROWTH.   Third, other areas as well as education have underscored the normalcy of change and the importance of adaptability and growth. The economic and social world daily receive the impact of scientific invention and discovery. Most philosophic positions support change as a part of the world order. Psychology and sociology show children and adults, each with his unique original nature, as "learning" their personalities from daily interaction with their culture. This idea of the normalcy of change and the necessity for growth is applied to supervision by Spears:

> Supervision is concerned with the improvement of instruction and if such improvement is seen as influencing both the material and personal aspects of the teaching situation, then the attention should be focused on the whole of teaching and not just the individual teacher as has been the case. The teachers' best contribution will come through their cooperative participation in the continual improvement of the curriculum—the curriculum being conceived in its broadest aspects. . . . Teachers have a right to grow through participation in the supervisory program of the school." [9]

Modern Emphases

The above quotations contain many words essential to a modern concept of supervision: improvement of instruction; growth; participation; democratic process; self-direction; supervisor as guide, aid, co-worker; material and personal aspects; the whole of teaching. Several other key terms are needed to round out the concept,

[8] Frank G. Dickey, *Op. Cit.*, p. 10.
[9] Harold Spears, *Op. Cit.*, p. 153.

such as: coordination, leadership, cooperation, releasing of energies, creativity, and human relations.

The converging factors just described—recognition of the professional judgments involved in teaching, alertness to the urgency of greater realization of democratic ideals, and awareness of the normalcy of change—have given modern supervision several areas of sharp emphasis. Attention is focused upon the pursuit of new knowledge in regard to learning, the study of interaction among human beings, the invention and refinement of democratic ways of working, the stimulation of creativity, and the nurturing of personal-professional development as a form of continuous growth or change. The dimensions of supervision have been greatly enlarged.

Supervision today, then, is concerned with all of the conditions of learning. It is a democratic enterprise and is rooted in the capacity of human beings for cooperation, creativity, and continuous growth. It stresses service, leadership, coordination among peers, and vision to help increase the level of aspiration for the improvement of living.

AIDS TO STUDY AND DISCUSSION

1. Visit the office of the Board of Public Instruction in your community. Ask to see the oldest available minute books from regular meetings. Skim the records looking for references to supervision, curriculum development, and professional growth of teachers. What appeared to be the role of supervision? Are there any statements that seem startlingly recent, as though they had been written yesterday? Do you see evidence of some problems in education being extremely persistent?

2. Browse through recent issues of several periodicals such as *Educational Leadership, Education, Educational Administration and Supervision, National Elementary Principal,* and *Adult Leadership.* Judging by the scope of titles included, what do you find to

be some of the major concerns in instructional leadership today? Select two articles to read, and be ready to share with your classmates a short statement of the central points in each. Among you, you should have a timely survey of on-going concerns in supervision.

3. Go back to the earliest available issues of the periodical you used above. What were the concerns when the journal first began publication? Do the early issues of the periodical reflect expectations of supervision or of the nature of learning different from the expectations of today?

4. Talk with teachers or principals in your school system who began their teaching careers before 1940. How much supervisory help did they receive in their early years of work? What was the nature of the help?

5. Read the opening chapters of *These Happy Golden Years* by Laura Ingalls Wilder for an account of how a fifteen-year-old girl left her own classroom in the frontier village on a Friday to begin her teaching career in a remote cabin on Monday. How would the supervision that might have been helpful to her differ from (or resemble) the aid which professionally prepared teachers in urban centers desire today?

SUGGESTIONS FOR FURTHER READING

Ayer, Fred C., *Fundamentals of Instructional Supervision* (New York: Harper & Brothers, 1954).

Burton, William H., and Leo J. Brueckner, *Supervision a Social Process*, Third Ed. (New York: Appleton-Century-Crofts, Inc., 1955).

Dickey, Frank G., *Developing Supervision in Kentucky*. Bulletin of the Bureau of School Service, Vol. 20, No. 3 (Lexington: University of Kentucky, 1948).

Douglass, Harl R., Rudyard K. Bent, and Charles W. Boardman, *Democratic Supervision in Secondary Schools*, 2nd Ed. (Boston: Houghton Mifflin Company, 1961).

Edwards, Newton, and Herman Ritchey, *The School in the American Social Order* (Boston: Houghton Mifflin Company, 1947).

Leadership Through Supervision, 1946 Yearbook of the Association for Supervision and Curriculum Development (Washington, D.C.: National Education Association, 1946).

Mackenzie, Gordon N., "Role of the Supervisor," *Educational Leadership*, Vol. 19, No. 2 (November, 1961).

McMurray, F. M., *Elementary School Standards* (New York: Harcourt, Brace & World, Inc., 1922).

Reeder, Edwin H., *Supervision in the Elementary School* (Boston: Houghton Mifflin Company, 1953).

Spears, Harold, "Can a Supervisory Leopard Change His Spots?" *Educational Leadership*, Vol. 3, No. 4 (January, 1946).

Spears, Harold, *Improving the Supervision of Instruction* (Englewood Cliffs, N.J.: Prentice-Hall, Inc., 1953).

U. S. Office of Education, *Preparation for Elementary School Supervision*, Bulletin No. 18, 1937.

CHAPTER 3

BASES OF NEED FOR SUPERVISION

SUPERVISION has a history which helps determine its present role in education in the nation, state, and local community. But whatever its remote or recent past may be, supervision also has deep foundations in the present way of living. Careful analysis reveals in current American civilization basic needs which supervision in education can help meet. Some of these needs have their origin in the nature of American culture; some arise from the philosophic positions of the times; some stem from psychological discoveries and understandings; some have a social setting and others come from a professional background. It is well to examine the roots or bases of supervision, for it is largely from such an examination that it is possible to estimate the legitimate functions of supervision, judge the appropriateness of activities and techniques, and arrive at principles which can give a consistent sense of direction in a developing program of supervision.

At least six bases of supervision are discernible: cultural, philosophic, psychological, social, sociological, and professional. An exploration of these bases reveals the firmness of the foundation on which supervision rests and permits a projection of what it *should* be.

THE CULTURAL BASIS

American culture is the product of rapid but evolutionary changes and is characterized today by an increasing tempo of change. Where many older civilizations and most primitive ones prize conformity and pride themselves on transmitting their culture unchanged, most Americans prize the new and anticipate doing something different from and often "better" than what their parents and grandparents did. In the American culture there is expectation of change and a firm belief in progress. Americans take the expectation of change so much for granted, as being so "natural," that it is a little hard for us to be sensitive to its influence upon our attitudes and actions. But foreign observers are aware of it. The Swedish sociologist, Myrdal, in referring to Sumner's theory of the binding effects of folkways (a theory based largely on studies of primitive societies) pointed out, "Sumner's construction conceals what is most important in our society, the changes, the conflicts, the absence of static equilibrium. . . . The valuation spheres, in such a society as the American, more nearly resemble powder magazines than they do Sumner's concept of mores." [1]

In an anthropological sense, American culture is attuned to change. It has a forward reference. The school, as the intentional agency of society for education, has its share of responsibility for orienting children to the normalcy of change in a complex society which is perpetually trying to improve the lot of its members. Furthermore, unless changes brought by scientific and social invention and discovery are to be accepted haphazardly, there must be cooperation and planning among men.

Meanwhile, it should be noted that change is not the only value Americans prize; they also cherish the familiar. Hence value conflicts frequently arise. The comfortableness of continuing to do what is already thoroughly known often deters an individual, either

[1] Gunnar Myrdal, *An American Dilemma* (New York: Harper and Brothers, 1944), p. 1032.

in private or professional life, from attempting the new or launching into the partially unknown or untried. In addition, it is actually difficult for an individual to grasp a new set of relationships regarding partly familiar objects, events, and people. In recent years, from work with perception and from the field of phenomenal psychology, has come a better understanding of why this difficulty is so persistent and how previous experience limits, shapes, and even distorts the perception of a new situation.

In a culture that expects change, but also prizes the familiar, value dilemmas are inevitable. Since choices are possible, decision making is a necessity. It takes courage and confidence to live with change, and a constant vigilance in appraising the worth of proposals. Change must be based on evaluation and advance must consider the contingencies in specific situations.

There is need for coordination of efforts and a clear sense of goal. In the realm of education, here are the grounds for two major functions of supervision: the coordination of effort and the development of a sense of direction so strong that it can help discriminate as to which changes may be beneficial.

THE PHILOSOPHIC BASIS

In simple terms philosophy may be regarded as a self-consistent set of principles which men, individually and in groups, use to guide their conduct of living.

Educational theory is closely allied with philosophy or ways of viewing the world. Both education and philosophy have been greatly influenced in the last three-quarters of a century by developments in the field of physics and other sciences. The early nineteenth century assurance regarding the nature of reality and truth has been modified. Brim points out that laws are now regarded as human constructions, not pictures of reality; that the universe is now conceived to be in a process of "becoming" not in a state of "being": i.e., emergent evolution is a general characteristic of the universe. He observes further:

> "Increasingly, philosophy is discarding its concept of superimposed and fixed values. Man, under the guidance of and by means of his intelligence, is viewed as responsible for conceiving and achieving his better tomorrow. Ability wisely to select values, to think, to plan, to execute, are held to be the very essence of good life." [2]

The concept of the world as open and evolving, and the interpretation of experience as the interaction of organism and environment in which both are modified, lead to a realization of the potential creativeness of every moment and situation. Also, if human beings are dynamic and every experience then potentially creative, it is clear that there is need for coordination of creative efforts and for the arranging of opportunities for the interaction of persons. Here, again, is a basic need for supervision in providing for interaction and coordination.

The significance of the openness or evolving nature of the world and its consequent impact upon the role of man are emphasized by scholars in many fields. Huxley, the zoologist, speaks of evolution as the realization of ever new possibilities by the stuff of which the earth is made, and points out that "during the last few ticks of the cosmic clock" man has appeared with his capacity for thought, awareness, purpose, and pooling of experience. Then Huxley adds that the new understanding of the universe amassed by scientists in the last hundred years "has defined man's responsibility and destiny —to be an agent for the rest of the world in the job of realizing its inherent possibilities as fully as possible." [3]

Gardner Murphy, the psychologist, in writing of human potentialities, speaks of the three natures of man. The first human nature is that of biological endowment. The second is the mold of culture

[2] Orville G. Brim, *The Foundations of Progressive Education* (Columbus: Ohio State University, 1936), pp. 1–2.

[3] Julian Huxley, *New Bottles for New Wine* (New York: Harper and Brothers, 1957), p. 13.

with its transmission of man's accomplishments, accompanied, however, by rigidities which tend to stultify thought. The third human nature Murphy describes as the thrust to understand, the effort to break through the mold, the freeing of intelligence and the yen to discovery.[4]

The major consideration here, from the standpoint of a basis of need for supervision, lies in the fact that the evolutionary nature of the universe and the human potentialities of man which are now glimpsed more clearly than formerly, indicate an ever larger role for man as a creative, thinking, intending creature. Man has ability to improve his conditions of living through his creative efforts. The encouragement and coordination of such efforts constitute a function of supervision.

THE PSYCHOLOGICAL BASIS

Nature of Experience

Supervision has a psychological basis in the very nature of experience itself. Experience is sometimes described as a "trying and an under-going." It is an effort to attach meaning to an object, event, or situation in order to know how to react now and on subsequent occasions. It is the basis for greater awareness of and control of future events. "To grasp the meaning of a thing, an event, or a situation is to see it in its relation to other things: to note how it operates or functions, what consequences follow from it, what causes it, what uses it can be put to." [5] Broad experience makes it possible to bring a wealth of meanings to new problems and thereby increase the possibility of their solution.

From the standpoint of Gestalt psychology, broad experience means varied "fields" against which a "figure" (problem) is seen.

[4] Gardner Murphy, *Human Potentialities* (New York: Basic Books, Inc., 1958).
[5] John Dewey, *How We Think* (New York: D. C. Heath & Company, 1933), p. 137.

With each extension of experience, the potentials of ground and figure are changed. Since teaching is largely a non-repetitive act involving many variables, a rich "field" is necessary. Widening the field, thereby increasing the bearings of experience, enhances the possibilities of a teacher's effectiveness and the success of reflective thinking. The need for extension of experience, including interaction among peers, is a matter which can be met in part through supervision.

Nurturing Conditions Conducive to Creativity

Culturally and philosophically, as indicated in the preceding sections of this chapter, creativity is a desideratum. Furthermore, the fundamental nature of man—biologically and culturally—not only permits but also stimulates some creativity. But the conditions which are conducive to creativity are not automatically present. Many of the conditions which promote or hinder creativity are largely psychological in the sense that they involve ways of feeling, perceiving, judging, and acting rather than residing primarily in the objective aspects of the environment.

On the negative side, for instance, it is often easy to see that fear, prolonged anxiety, ridicule, and distrust of self and others inhibit creative solutions to problems. In panic situations, individuals and crowds sometimes even develop such "tunnel vision" that they are blind to familiar meanings, let alone new relationships, that would help them solve their problem. On the positive side, mutual trust among peers and respect for individuality, apparently promote the fluency of ideas, the flexibility of approach and the sustained curiosity which are the seed beds of creativity. The need for the nurturing of the conditions conducive to creativity gives rise to an important function of supervision.

Providing of Support While Learning

One of the more recent insights coming to education from the field of psychology relates to the importance of emotional support for the person who is learning; i.e., making changes in his familiar procedures. Emotional support appears to expedite learning. An obvious example of support for the learner is seen in the aid given a child trying to walk. Either with or without an extended hand or finger to sustain the child, mother or father gives numerous signs of vigorous emotional support: approving words, encouraging sounds, smiles, triumphant cries, sympathetic consolation in case of trouble, suggestions for another try. An adult, prepared for his professional role, does not crave such overt, extreme signs of approval, but he does have a basic need for more subtle signs of assurance, concern, and helpfulness from those whose opinion he values.

In the last analysis, making changes involves some degree of uncertainty, some sense of risk (often acute), some threat to a sense of adequacy, or competency, or even survival (personal or professional). The providing of emotional support for the adult learner constitutes one of the functions of supervision.

Perception and Behavior

Another fairly recent insight from psychology, social psychology especially, relates to the nature of perception. A person reacts to a situation in terms of the way he perceives it, really the only way he can act, since that is the way he is receiving, recording, and assessing the events in the situation. It has long been recognized that the actual angle of perception has much to do with what is perceived, as both umpires and spectators at a sports event can testify. What is being realized now with greater clarity is the extent to which such factors as previous experience, purpose, and emotion determine what an individual sees. Thus each year hunting accidents occur in which the eager hunter, intent with purpose and acting on the basis of previous experience with movement in the bushes meaning the desired game, fires his gun and then is horrified to find that he has hit his companion.

More detailed discussion of the implications of perception for teaching and supervision follows in Chapter 12, *Frontiers of Supervision*. Here it is perhaps sufficient to say that the nature of perception is often involved in the analysis of learning problems in the classroom, in the preventing or dissolving of misunderstanding, in the collaborating toward achieving immediate and long-range goals. The nature of perception creates a need for assistance in seeing a situation from all possible angles, a need which supervision can help meet.

Goals, Integration, and Energy

Reference has been made earlier to the importance of goals or a sense of direction as a basis for estimating the probable worth of a proposed change. A second reason for attaching high significance to having a keen awareness of goals lies in the fact that clear perception of the goals sought "structures" or organizes the field, to return to the terminology of Gestalt psychology. When an individual can hold his values and long range goals at the conscious level, he then can array in proper relationship the intermediate goals and their myriad enabling activities. In addition, when goals are perceived and activities are carried out in relationship to one another, they reinforce one another instead of moving in cross currents or at tangents. The individual therefore can move toward the goal more rapidly. At the same time he develops an invigorating sense of moving one-directionally, instead of the devitalizing feeling of going in circles or being on a treadmill.

This concept of rising energy accompanying the clear perception of goals is a third reason for recognizing the essentiality of defining and re-defining goals. Probably human energy is at its highest when a goal, which has been dim, becomes clear or when the enabling steps, which have been obscure, are recognized or invented. The energizing quality of goal perception is enormous. Almost everyone has had the experience of being jerked from semi-sleep into full wakefulness by the impact of an idea, i.e., by the grasp of a new set of relationships, often one which resolves some persistent problem. An individual can be empowered for hours, days, or even a lifetime by a sharp awareness of goal. Purpose and goal pack power.

To help teachers raise their values to the level of consciousness, to set and reset goals, to integrate their diverse activities, and to feel the empowering energy rising from such integration becomes a function for supervision.

THE SOCIAL BASIS

Our society is committed to democracy as the most desirable system of social arrangements. Democracy has many definitions or statements of principles. Common to most definitions are these four elements: (1) respect for the worth and dignity of the individual; (2) faith in the improvability of society; (3) faith in the method of intelligence, together with the use of reason and persuasion rather than violence; and (4) faith in cooperation as a way of work. Each one of these tenets of democracy leads to the need for the encouragement (stimulation and release) of creative efforts toward improving the quality of living. Each of the tenets also leads to the need for coordination of such efforts. Meeting this need is a validation of supervision.

In a democratic social order the nature of leadership is of special concern. The imposition of an authoritarian, autocratic concept of leadership upon a democratic situation has led to many incongruities. Much study has been devoted to the nature of leadership in a democracy, in recent years, and considerable research is under way at the present time. There is rather wide agreement on the idea that democratic leadership results in the releasing and coordinating of the creative energies of the members of a group. It is not a *laissez-faire* matter nor an attempt merely to take the group where it appears to want to go. Leadership has a responsibility for helping the group reach valid commitments cooperatively and for following through on the commitments.

Mackenzie suggests that six functions of democratic leadership are: (1) contributing to unity (through clarifying values the group wishes to accept or act upon); (2) enriching thinking; (3) aiding in the development of new skills; (4) helping to provide confidence and security; (5) helping define the limits of autonomy and interaction; and (6) encouraging an experimental approach.[6] The exercise of these functions would lead to the further development of leadership within the group.

A helpful distinction is sometimes made as to kinds of leadership, the two terms often used being "shared" leadership and "status" leadership, although the two ideas are closely intertwined. In shared leadership, responsibility passes from member to member of the group as each makes his contribution. Even when leadership is widely shared, however, group work seems to be facilitated by status leadership. A status leader (chairman, president, principal, teacher in her classroom) takes special continuing responsibility for the security, growth, and accomplishments of all members and for carrying through the commitments of the group. According to Miel, functions for status leaders are: (1) improving human relations in the group; (2) providing expertness along certain lines; (3) generating or evoking leadership in others; and (4) coordinating the efforts of others.[7]

In the authoritarian concept of leadership, authority resides in the leader; in the democratic concept authority resides in the group and is delegated to the leader by appointment or election, and provision must be made for the orderly re-delegation of this authority. However, even in sincere efforts to use the democratic concept, difficulty sometimes arises, since many common organizational forms tend to pyramid authority upward to one or a few persons and to isolate the leader from close contact with the group. The maintaining of communication becomes difficult. At present considerable effort is being expended to try to analyze the nature of the dynamics of group effort and the relationship of group dynamics to leadership. Since a supervisor usually holds status leadership because of his position, the responsibility for releasing group potentialities makes the problem of group dynamics and shared leadership a

[6] Gordon Mackenzie, "Curriculum Leadership," *Educational Leadership*, Vol. 6, No. 5 (February, 1949), pp. 264–271.

[7] Alice Miel, *Changing the Curriculum* (New York: Appleton-Century-Crofts, Inc., 1946), pp. 157–159.

matter of immediate and continuous concern to him and to his way of work.

In summary, it may be said that supervision has a social basis, since both the tenets of democracy and the nature of leadership in a democracy call for individuals who can devote time and talents to stimulating creative efforts toward improvement, to coordinating such efforts, and to following through on group commitments.

THE SOCIOLOGICAL BASIS

As pointed out previously, American culture has a forward refer- ence and democracy assumes the improvability of society. Sociolo- gists, in analyzing human relationships and the factors in our cul- ture which influence peoples' judgments and actions, place great emphasis upon the area of childhood and the formation of per- sonality. The sociologist and psychologist point out that personality is not merely inborn but is acquired or achieved; that, on the basis of the individual's innate physical equipment, human personality develops through social conditioning. In other words, human beings "learn" their personalities out of interaction with all their surround- ing culture, as represented in members of the family, peer groups, school associates, and the social and economic structures of their communities. Bossard and Boll state, "Human personality is a prod- uct of social contact and communication, and its scientific study leads directly and inevitably to the study of the background situa- tions to which behavior is a response." [8]

It might also be added that realization of some background fac- tors leads straight to social action. Many social agencies exist today to ameliorate conditions unfavorable to wholesome personality de- velopment and to take positive action for the improvement of the conditions of childhood. Schools are usually mindful of other agen- cies dealing with children but lack of personnel has often prevented

[8] James H. S. Bossard and Eleanor Stoker Boll, *The Sociology of Child Develop- ment*, 3rd Ed. (New York: Harper and Brothers, 1960), p. 11.

effective cooperation. There is need for school representatives to work with other social agencies in improving conditions under which children develop their personalities. Supervision can render great service in this connection.

As a part of the general concern for personality development, school and community have a specific interest in the intellectual and emotional growth of children and youth. Contributions to knowledge are sorely needed in this area, and supervision should assist in the search for understanding.

The nurturing of intelligence and the development of emotional health have been the subjects of extensive research in recent decades. Study after study indicates the great signfiicance of what happens to children in their early years. Full intellectual development appears to be partially dependent upon a stimulating environment during childhood, and considerable emotional stability is a necessary condition for optimum learning. Hence the school has an important stake in the conditions under which children live their pre-school years and their out-of-school hours. The need for continuous study of community conditions and for school collaboration with social agencies creates a function for supervision.

THE PROFESSIONAL BASIS

Education is increasingly a profession. It exhibits most of the characteristics associated with a profession, although it is still deficient in some. Thus education, like other professions, according to Rorer: (1) possesses a specialized body of knowledge and a specialized group of techniques; (2) requires a broad cultural background of preparatory education plus specialized intellectual and practical training; (3) is constantly evolving a growing body of knowledge and techniques of which its members must be informed through continuous organized study, individual reading and group conference; (4) recognizes its social obligations and its humanitarian potentialities; (5) maintains some solidarity of interests, education, and purpose among its members and organizes them for mutual stimulation and advancement. Education has not yet achieved full professional status with regard to such characteristics as an effective code of ethics, setting its own standard of admission, tenure and advancement, or disqualifying members for gross incompetency or unethical practice.[9]

It is in the third and fifth aspects above that supervision in education can play a highly significant role. The fact that education, as a profession, must keep drawing upon findings from the background sciences such as psychology, biology, and sociology, as well as from research in education, means that in-service learning on the part of school personnel is a normal and continuing process. Furthermore, if the "growing body of knowledge and techniques" is to evolve at more than an agonizingly slow pace, much analysis of learning situations, application of principles, action research, and basic research must be carried on. While the utilizing of new findings and the contributing to new knowledge may be regarded ultimately as the individual responsibility of any person who enters a profession today, it is also clear that the individual can assume and discharge this responsibility more effectively where opportunities to learn and to contribute to knowledge are accessible and inviting.

Fortunately, many school boards and administrators have, in recent years, come to see the providing of opportunities for professional development of their staff and for contribution to knowledge as a legitimate and desirable function of the school system. The planning for a rewarding program of professional growth calls for much coordination and continuity, frequently on a school-wide and system-wide basis. It also calls for zest, imagination, and sustained effort on the part of those carrying leadership. Hence there is a need for personnel in education whose responsibility is to use their time and energy in filling this role.

The fact that a profession "maintains some solidarity of interests, education, and purpose among its members and organizes them for mutual stimulation and advancement" indicates another need

[9] John A. Rorer, *Principles of Democratic Supervision* (New York Teachers College, Columbia University, 1942), pp. 93–99.

which supervision can help meet: namely, the promotion of and coordination of the daily work of the numerous professional organizations within education. As active members of some groups and as representatives filling a liaison function in others, supervisors can help the work of professional organizations move forward.

Another characteristic of a profession relates to the gradual induction of its new members into their full professional responsibility. The person who is well prepared to enter his chosen profession brings a large body of knowledge, together with its theoretical and philosophical underpinnings; but the judgments expected of him involve complex situations with constantly new, and often locally unique, factors present. A gradual induction into full responsibility, and guidance from an experienced person during the induction, can facilitate the proper assessing of relevant factors in a situation and the making of sound judgments with increasing confidence. Gradualness of induction and provision of guidance as the novice gains facility and reliability in judgment-making are areas where education as a profession has been quite lacking until recently and where, even now, much remains to be done. Here again is a need which supervision can help meet.

The increasingly professional nature of education, then, through its several aspects of in-service learning and contributions to knowledge, of stimulation through interaction of individuals and teamwork of groups, and of recognition of the importance of gradualness of induction, gives rise to a host of needs which delineate a role to be filled by supervision.

THE MAJOR FUNCTIONS OF SUPERVISION
IDENTIFIED

Out of the matrix of need arising from the nature of man, the nature of learning, and the nature of our society and its ideals, emerge the major functions of supervision. These major functions give supervision its scope and direction, in much the same manner that the shape of the hand and purpose of the glove determine the nature of the glove designed to fit it.

If supervision had not already evolved gradually through the years in response to needs discernible in past generations, the educators of today would be busy designing, *de novo*, a service to fit the educational needs as they are perceived in the latter half of the twentieth century.

The educational needs of today, as analyzed in this chapter, have cultural, philosophical, psychological, social, sociological and professional bases. The functions of supervision arising from these needs are numerous, but for purposes of discussion are summarized as eight major, continuing functions:

Coordination of Efforts
Provision of Leadership
Extension of Experience
Stimulation of Creative Effort
Facilitation and Evaluation of Change
Analysis of Learning Situations
Contribution to a Body of Professional Knowledge
Integration of Goals

It has been the purpose of this chapter to probe deeply the nature of the educational field in order that the broad, firm foundation of the on-going functions of supervision can stand plainly revealed. An awareness of the major functions can, in turn, provide a stabilizing, invigorating sense of direction through the hundreds of specific activities performed in the name of supervision.

AIDS TO STUDY AND DISCUSSION

1. Read in such books as *The School in the American Social Order* for a glimpse of how the cultural aspirations and the social and economic conditions of a period influence what people want from the schools, and of how these expectations, in turn, influence the kind of supervisory help needed.

2. Consult periodicals outside the immediate field of education but related to it, to locate some of the newer developments or major concepts in these areas. Can you identify any concepts that are, or should be, influencing supervision?—for instance, the nature of leadership in democratic situations, or the conditions under which people change old habits and attitudes.

3. Go to two or more industries or large business establishments in your community, and find out what supervisory help is available. What are the objectives of supervision in industry? How do the background conditions shape the kinds of help needed from supervision?

4. In relation to the above visits, compare education and the selected organizations with regard to such specific matters as:
   a. the end product or goal
   b. the level of preparation of the workers
   c. the proportion of the end product for which each worker is responsible.

SUGGESTIONS FOR FURTHER READING

Allport, Gordon W., *Becoming* (New Haven: Yale University Press, 1955).

Bossard, James H. S., and Eleanor Stoker Boll, *The Sociology of Child Development*, 3rd Ed. (New York: Harper & Brothers, 1960).

Brim, Orville G., *The Foundations of Progressive Education* (Columbus: Ohio State University, 1936).

Dewey, John, *How We Think* (Boston: D. C. Heath & Company, 1933).

Huxley, Julian, *New Bottles for New Wine* (New York: Harper & Brothers, 1957).

Mackenzie, Gordon, "Curriculum Leadership," *Educational Leadership* (Feb., 1949).

Miel, Alice, *Changing the Curriculum* (New York: Appleton-Century-Crofts, Inc., 1946).

Murphy, Gardner, *Human Potentialities* (New York: Basic Books, Inc., 1958).

————, *Freeing Intelligence through Teaching* (New York: Harper & Brothers, 1961).

Myrdal, Gunnar, *An American Dilemma* (New York: Harper & Brothers, 1944).

Rorer, John A., *Principles of Democratic Supervision* (New York Teachers College, Columbia University, 1942).

CHAPTER 4

MAJOR FUNCTIONS OF SUPERVISION

THE major functions of supervision, clearly perceived, can give organization, structure, and meaning to the activities of the day and of the year. Countless forces push and pull at the supervisor on the job, with the element of time pressure often turning a frenetic situation into a frantic one. Hence the achievement of wholeness or integration of activities is no small accomplishment.

Awareness of the whole gives membership character to the parts. The specific task of the moment takes on greater significance when it is seen in relation to its larger context. The activities, when related, reinforce one another and hence have optimum impact. The multiple values inherent in a situation also have a greater chance of being realized.

The supervisor is able to work with satisfaction and with energy renewed by way-station accomplishment toward distant goals. Thus a supervisor who spends a morning in the following rush of activities may feel disintegrated and exhausted by the rapid succession of responsibilities:

(1) conferring with a committee of principals,
(2) writing a short newsletter to junior high teachers,
(3) discussing with the superintendent a proposed research project, and
(4) meeting a visiting consultant at the plane and having an early lunch with him in order to brief him on the expectations for an afternoon conference.

However, if he sees in the diversity of specific tasks the "thread that doth run through all and doth all unite," namely, the continuing functions of coordinating of efforts, contributing to a body of knowledge, and facilitating of professional growth, he can work with a sense of sustainment and freedom from wearying confusion.

A close look at the major functions of supervision is in order, to see sharply their origins, to observe their appearance in the process of fulfillment, and to examine some considerations for enhancing their successful achievement.

COORDINATION OF EFFORTS AS A FUNCTION OF SUPERVISION

In the analysis of conditions which create a task for supervision, the need for coordination of efforts appeared frequently. The need for coordination was found in the American cultural expectation of change, in the philosophic outlook that regards the universe as open to change and man a force in the changing, in the democratic tenet of the improvability of man and society, and in the psychologically based need for extension of experience and the integration of effort. It was also found in the sociological need for coordination among man's institutional efforts, and in the professional need for continuous study, stimulation of thinking, and cooperative attack on problems.

Examples

INDIVIDUAL EFFORTS. The fulfillment of the function of coordination of efforts takes many forms. There is the coordination of individual efforts, as when the principal makes it possible for two or more teachers to work together on a common concern for concept building in the arithmetic program, or when a supervisor and principal arrange for teachers in different schools to pursue a common interest such as alerting the community to the need for a junior museum. There is also the coordination of diversified individual efforts, as when instructional leaders help teachers unite their separate talents and concerns into a true team effort in such a matter as total faculty evaluation of the school program.

SCHOOL EFFORTS. There is the coordination of the efforts of many schools, as when representatives from several faculties form committees, at the request of the superintendent or supervisors, to formulate proposals for system-wide policies, to plan a program of interpretation to the public of school procedures, or to appraise the usefulness of expensive instructional aids. Committee representatives from different schools constitute gate-keepers of ideas, for they transmit committee decisions and concerns to the faculties and take faculty opinions and concerns to the committee.

COMMUNITY EFFORTS. There is also the coordination of efforts within the community, as when a supervisor represents the schools on a youth council, children's commission, or other community agency concerned with planning for services for children and youth. The supervisor is often called upon to assist principals with information or telephone calls in securing welfare, health, and psychological services for individual children. A supervisor needs to know community agencies and organizations well, from the standpoint both of scope of services and of personnel responsible for different phases of work.

Instructional leaders also help coordinate community efforts when they serve as the medium for an exchange of information and concern between civic groups and schools, interpreting school policies and procedures to the public and, in turn, receiving from the agencies and civic organizations an expression of their understandings, worries, and aspirations regarding schools.

PROFESSIONAL GROWTH EFFORTS. The efforts toward professional growth involve many people and many degrees of complexity of organization. The effort may be as direct as the instructional leader himself being the means for a person's professional growth through an individual conference or through serving as a consultant for a committee; or it may be as remote as his calling a soloist for a banquet program or bargaining with janitors for extra service in boxing books to return to an extension division after a workshop.

Instructional leaders are usually responsible for surveys to ascertain the felt needs of teachers in regard to areas of work for pre-school conferences, workshops, extension courses, and other large undertakings intended to promote professional growth. The extent to which the instructional leader functions as a coordinator often determines a large part of the satisfaction participants experience in feeling that their planning has been productive and their needs met. He also carries out the function of coordination when he helps project a long-range plan that can give continuity to several years of systematic efforts.

An important part of the forward momentum of a school system is provided by its professional organizations. These organizations, with their local, state, and national ties, usually have a number of concerns in common, as well as each having its own area of special emphasis and contribution. If the professional organizations are to team their efforts effectively, avoiding both duplications and gaps, there must be a high degree of communication among them and frequent planning for joint action. Instructional leaders can often provide constructive service as liaison persons and information expediters, as well as serving as active participants in one or more of the organizations, since their normal range of responsibilities keeps them in close contact with the entire program.

Considerations

UTILIZATION OF EXISTING ENERGY.   In the work of a supervisor as a
coordinator of efforts several considerations are discernible which
may be designated as working principles. One relates to the fact
that, in many cases, efforts of individuals or groups are already on-
going at the time the supervisor enters the situation. Momentum is
already up. A coordinator's contribution is to help interrelate the
energies so that there can be maximum forward pull instead of
colliding and overlapping. Since there can be no standard harness,
as for a twenty-mule team, for linking human energies together, instructional leaders and all others involved need to be conscious of
factors which are helpful.

Flexibility.   There is the need for flexibility, for willingness to
recognize that there are many roads to Rome, and that varied procedures can have a common goal. There needs to be willingness to
revise an approach when a better plan evolves or when new circumstances alter the situation, without an emotional, defensive attachment to the first plan creating a barrier to change. There should be
glad expectation that good ideas will beget still other ideas, some of
which will necessitate revisions in original planning.

Foresight.   There needs to be foresight of consequences. A
change in plans in one place impinges on commitments in perhaps
a dozen other places. There is foresight of the mechanics of operation needed to expedite group work. For instance, if the dates for
system-wide meetings are publicized in the school calendar, then
special committees will not find that they have unwittingly called
meetings on the same dates. Or, where information has to be
gathered and exchanged among several groups, the time lapse necessary for organizational or committee meetings and action must be
accurately calculated.

Mutual Trust and Respect.   An instructional leader should
be worthy of the respect and confidence of others and should do all

in his power to create a climate of mutual trust and respect among all those whose efforts he is seeking to help coordinate. Belittling remarks, innuendoes of doubt, even a depreciating shrug of the shoulders can destroy in minutes attitudes that may have taken months to build.

Clear communication is not always easy. It is actually very difficult to summarize group planning accurately and transmit information from one committee or group to another. But occasional distortions of perceptions or lapses of understanding are readily surmounted if there is a great backlog of mutual trust and respect among those who are trying to work together.

Good Humor and Poise. In like manner, good humor and poise can bring co-workers through minor mishaps. The full expectation that group undertakings, whether involving a few members or hundreds of persons, will encounter some misunderstandings and rough spots will help a leader keep proper perspective on a situation. Patience is sometimes defined as the proper estimation of the hazards and difficulties involved in an undertaking. A person who has a true estimate of the difficult nature of group work can afford to be patient when delays and minor mishaps occur.

Caustic remarks, irritability, or worried frowns tend to inhibit a person's own freedom of thinking and, through interaction with others in the group, blight their openness of thinking and action. On the other hand, a quick smile, a joke made from the incongruities or irony of the situation, or ready recognition of the ultimately minor nature of the mishap, enables people to be resilient, and to proceed to fresh solutions of problems.

Insight. If coordination of efforts is to proceed at all smoothly, it is important for the supervisor and others concerned to become accustomed to looking for principles behind practices, to seeking the kernel of a problem whatever the outer shell may be. An instructional leader can often expedite group efforts by helping individuals or committees rediscover the commonness of the goal that has become obscured by the diversity of plans offered for reaching the goal. In fast moving discussions, for instance, with numerous proposals being made for action and tested in the imagination for workability, it is exceedingly difficult for leader and participants alike to maintain insight as to the real nature of the problem under discussion. To the extent that a leader can promote such insight he facilitates group work.

STIMULATION OF ENERGY. In contrast to the above, where the major concern was coordinating efforts which were already on-going, there are many situations which are static; the problem is primarily that of *stimulating* cooperative effort. Sometimes individual energies are already somewhat aroused, but channels or means for coordination are lacking. Hence the task for supervision becomes one of organizing committees or councils that can enable the efforts to come to fruition. Occasionally, it happens that new organizations are not needed, but only new functions perceived or active participation encouraged for committees and groups already existing. Instructional leaders new in a system would want to be especially cautious about hastening to organize new groups, and then belatedly discovering that other groups were, or could have been, carrying out the desired function.

In other situations, activity is almost entirely lacking and the problem is one of helping individuals or groups become sensitive to a desirable goal, or free themselves from chronic discouragement and lassitude which have put the brakes upon earlier efforts. When persons seeking improvement in a situation are faced with indifference, or even resistance, it is sometimes profitable to remember the push-pull principle often noted in history in the movement of people. It takes the force of dissatisfaction with something in the current setting (push) and the force of a new goal (pull), if action is to occur. For instance, the political unrest and strife in the German states in the 1840's created a push; the possibilities of freedom and economic success in the United States created a pull; a wave of German migration to the United States ensued. In like manner, junior high teachers who have been deaf to suggestions for more varied ways of teaching parts of speech as a means to language improvement (pull), suddenly can hear once they have begun to doubt (push) the efficiency of the time and energy consumed in their customary approaches.

The development of a push-pull energy system usually takes time, for it is based on the broadening of understanding and the questioning of familiar assumptions, but once in operation it is powerful and self-propelling. Certainly, the long tried alternative of direct assault on a problem is seldom productive. Individuals or committees that feel themselves accused of doing the wrong thing or not doing anything are immediately thrown on the defensive; and threatened persons can rarely extend themselves creatively or trust themselves to try new approaches.

SATISFACTION IN GROUP EFFORT.   A third consideration in connection with coordination of efforts is the role for supervision in helping people feel the satisfaction of group effort.

Montagu, among anthropologists, has emphasized the biological naturalness of the principle of cooperation within the organism and among organisms.[1] Psychologists and other social scientists have stated from many viewpoints the basic necessity for human association if the individual is to realize his potential. Yet group efforts do not always yield the energy-renewing sense of satisfaction that is inherently there. This lack of felt satisfaction is partly traceable to the fact that the actual product of group effort is often remote enough in time or place that there is no immediate evidence to the senses that the goal has been reached. When members of a professional organization, for instance, assess themselves an extra fee to help establish a scholarship fund, the good that is to be realized from their action is far in the future. Or a committee on revision of curriculum or statement of philosophy may spend hours in deliberation and investigation, but yet present recommendations for change that to a casual glance seem trival, since immediate, visible change is not involved. In addition, group work has its natural strains and irritations which greatly dilute the sense of reward in cooperative effort.

[1] Ashley Montagu, *On Being Human* (New York: Henry Shuman, 1950).

There are several ways in which supervision can enhance the sense of satisfaction in cooperative work. One is to contribute to the sheer efficiency with which a group operates. Getting out notices for meetings in ample time, controlling of ventilation, noise, and light during the meeting, and making arrangements for secretarial help are of this type. A second way is in helping with the follow-through from each meeting so that promised reports or actions are carried out swiftly, thus increasing the awareness that the group is accomplishing something. A third way is in helping spread responsibilities among many members. This spreading of responsibilities means that a few persons are not depressingly burdened, that specific tasks are reduced to manageable size, and (most important of all) that the wide involvement of members utilizes talents and creates an understanding which then not only accomplishes work but also precludes or reduces thoughtless criticism.

Another important way is in nurturing the expression of appreciation and satisfaction in group efforts. In the hurry typical of group meetings, the expressions of gratitude for work well done are often neglected or at least deferred. Appreciation toward individuals and committees may be genuinely felt but rarely put into words or gesture. Supervision can make a real contribution to the spirit of group work by giving expression to feelings of appreciation and making it easy for others to do likewise. In like manner, there is need to nurture the expression of satisfaction and joy in group work. The sense of enlargement that accompanies cooperative effort is a deeply satisfying experience for most people, and the expression of some of that satisfaction can increase the warmth of human association and the anticipation of future efforts.

PROVISION OF LEADERSHIP AS A FUNCTION
OF SUPERVISION

The need for leadership as a function of supervision is deeply rooted in the extent of change in our culture, in the democratic faith in the improvability of society and in the school as a social agency, in the stimulation and utilization of creative efforts, and in the need for an extension of experience for professional workers and for a concerted attack upon professional problems. In mid-twentieth century, leaders in many areas—industry, business, labor, military, government, social agencies and school administration—have given much attention to the nature of leadership. An examination of several issues of such a magazine as *Adult Leadership*, published by the Adult Education Association, reveals something of the variety of groups interested in the subject and a sampling of its many facets. Instructional leaders have to join others in becoming life-long students of the nature of leadership in a democracy.

Some of the attributes of leadership which evolved through generations of an autocratically organized society are anachronistic in a democratic society, while other behaviors are partially usable but simply inadequate in discharging the responsibilities of democratic leadership. For instance, in a democratically organized group the ultimate authority lies with the group, not with the leader, and is only delegated to the leader. Orderly, recognized procedures for delegating and redelegating the authority have to be devised and provision made for a two-way flow of ideas. Viewed historically American society, including the school system, is in the creative process of inventing and perfecting procedures for democratic living.

At least five facets of leadership in a democracy are of great significance to supervision: (1) assuming initiative; (2) aiding in goal setting; (3) stimulating and releasing talents of group members; (4) supporting members while change is in progress; and (5) following through on commitments.

Examples

Supervisory personnel fulfill the leadership function when they take the initiative in such matters as proposing problems for fact-finding investigations and experimental research, or organizing a system-wide curriculum council. They aid in goal-setting as they work with faculties engaged in curriculum revision. They stimulate and release talents of group members when they help structure committees so as to involve all persons, or when they help new members of a faculty contribute their special abilities in the new situation.

They provide emotional support for those making changes when they take an interest in the special hopes and projects of individuals or encourage an experimental approach to problems and share in the necessary appraisal of progress and outcomes. They fulfill the follow-through function when they perform such a simple task as duplicating and mailing a short committee report, or such a complex one as carrying out arrangements for a week's pre-school conference for two thousand participants.

Considerations

In fulfilling the function of leadership a supervisor or principal often needs to take the initiative unhesitatingly. He must remember, however, that he is not the only one charged with responsibility for initiative. He must anticipate it in others, look for it, and go to meet it gladly. For instance, superintendents, school board members, and principals have a very specific responsibility for exercising initiative in both the administrative and supervisory phases of their work. Teachers, as professional workers, and as leaders in the classroom, must exercise initiative; children as learners can use initiative to their own and their classmates' advantage; citizens take initiative in relation to school matters. An instructional leader needs to develop a welcoming attitude toward initiative in others and be sure that he does not chronically express a negative slant toward ideas that were not originally his own. He also needs to examine his own actions from time to time to make sure he is avoiding the extreme, on the one hand, of taking the initiative so frequently and rapidly that he precludes the opportunity for it in others, and, on the other hand, always expecting the other fellow to provide the extra energy and courage that initiative usually entails.

In shared leadership a supervisor has to cultivate the art of being quiet and listening. Members of a group will often look to a system-wide supervisor or principal, even if he is not currently the status leader, to see if he is going to offer an opinion. If he consistently comes forward at once with vigorously expressed ideas, group members may soon fall into a habit of deferring their own thinking until after he has spoken; then there follows the subtle temptation for members not to think at all, or not to express ideas and assume initiative.

Instructional leaders who have an unusually high energy level or who have a life style of quick articulateness must exercise diligent self-control. It is all too easy for them to monopolize time or dominate without intending to do so. A leader who finds himself talking too much can sometimes prevent much of the ill effect of the moment by using a rising inflection in the voice, thus decreasing any dogmatic overtones, by laughing at his own talkativeness, or by suggesting that there must be other ideas to be heard.

A supervisor or principal, as a status leader, also needs to remember that unless he takes action at expected times, other people may be prevented from functioning effectively. Other persons who might act in the situation hesitate to do so for fear they will appear presumptuous or aggressive, or they wait so long for the leader to act that insufficient time remains for efficient work. For instance, if a county-wide testing program has been agreed upon and the tests are to be selected by representative teachers and principals, the program is temporarily blocked if the system-wide supervisor does not complete the committee organization for selection.

In the carrying-through phase of leadership, it should be clearly recognized that an instructional leader usually needs help, often of a secretarial nature. The correspondence, telephoning, compiling and reproducing of reports that are a normal part of follow-through on group commitments necessarily involve quantities of time. Superintendents and school boards should be quick to see that if the supervisory time is to be consumed extensively in this fashion, then other vital functions cannot be well served.

In order to carry out obligations efficiently, it is often important to make notes, while the group is still in session, regarding the responsibilities to be assumed. Otherwise, a particular obligation might be overlooked entirely, or some detail of information be forgotten which would then absorb valuable time to locate again.

EXTENSION OF EXPERIENCE AS A
FUNCTION OF SUPERVISION

The extending of experience as a function of supervision is deeply rooted in the nature of human learning and human satisfactions. A characteristic of living matter is that it tends to elaborate itself to its full capacity. For human beings this elaboration means a life-long desire to understand, to grow, and to gain control of their surroundings. A person with broad experience brings more meanings to novel situations and therefore has greater chance of success in evolving solutions to problems. Furthermore, an adult learner feels enlarged by new experience and from that feeling gains one of the most abiding of human satisfactions. An instructional leader performs a significant function when he helps school personnel gain new experience.

Examples

An instructional leader is fulfilling his function of extending experience when he engages in such in-service education activities as arranging for consultants with specialized knowledge to work with interested individuals or large groups, when he locates films or printed material to help teachers enlarge their acquaintance with effective procedures, or when he helps teachers carry on intervisitation among several classrooms and schools. Principals and system-wide supervisors often work together in discharging the responsibility for extension of experience when they make it possible for individual teachers to attend professional meetings, serve on local or state-wide curriculum or textbook selection committees, or participate in bulletin production committees. Taking interns and beginning teachers on tours of selected classrooms and central offices is another form of extension of experience. Keeping the superintendent and school board informed of pertinent research findings, new procedures, and changes in local efforts to meet the needs of children and youth is an important form of extension of experience for those whose decisions are strategic in improvement of instruction.

Considerations

Several factors enter supervisory work in extending experience. First, new experience usually has to be analyzed if it is to have maximum effect. It is probable that subliminal perceptions are more significant in influencing action than is now commonly realized; but, in general, new experience has to be analyzed and evaluated if generalizations are to be formed and carried forward as meanings or expectations which will have application in new situations. For instance, intervisitation, films, and demonstrations lose much of their effectiveness unless analysis brings to the conscious level significant points and relates them to previous understanding. Hence, it is important for a supervisor, principal, or experienced teacher to discuss what has been observed, noting principles that underlie the specific procedures witnessed and often clearing up inadvertent misconceptions. The principles and generalizations thus derived then have a chance to enter the goal and value system of the individual in a non-threatening situation and really influence his subsequent actions.

Second, the extension of experience must be recognized as an inner process. To speak of the instructional leader as extending the experience of others is not entirely accurate; the reorganization of meaning or grasp of new relationships is within the learner. But the supervisor can play a vital part in creating opportunities for the learner to achieve new experience and, over any long period of time, interaction of human beings is essential.

Third, arranging for the interaction of persons is a time-consuming, even though fundamental, activity of supervision. An instructional leader needs to recognize fully its importance and have confidence that time and energy spent in this direction are productive. He often has to help others build confidence in the process too. Administrative arrangements are not simple. Released time for teachers is often awkward to arrange and costly. Therefore, all people concerned need to understand the necessity and worth of continually providing new experience.

STIMULATION OF CREATIVE EFFORTS
AS A FUNCTION OF SUPERVISION

In addition to being a phase of leadership, stimulation of creative efforts is a function of supervision in its own right. The need for creative effort is deeply rooted in the philosophic position of the openendedness of the universe and man's responsibility for aiding in its evolution. It is based on the psychological need to extend understanding, to feel the satisfaction of using potential resources, and to experience the energy achieved through closure of the field, i.e., grasping a fresh solution to a problem. It is also based on our cultural and professional expectation of creativity on the part of the individual.

According to Taylor the creative person is characterized by flexibility in his approach to problems, both a spontaneous flexibility which suggests more than one solution and an adaptive flexibility which enables him to think of another route when the first attempt is blocked. There is a fluency of ideas, along with willingness to revise his own ideas without a close attachment to his first effort. The creative person has capacity to be puzzled, sometimes about the obvious and familiar, and to keep wondering after others are satisfied with an explanation. He often displays playfulness with ideas, and is willing to throw ideas into an arena without undue personal defensiveness and apprehension. He has keen foresight of consequences, but he can tolerate a considerable degree of temporary ambiguity or uncertainty while he works toward an ultimate goal.[2] Supervisors and principals, indeed all school personnel, may

2 Calvin W. Taylor, "The Creative Individual," *Educational Leadership*, Vol. 18, No. 1 (October, 1960), pp. 7–12.

well ask themselves how they can nurture the development of creativity in children, in one another, and in themselves.

Examples

An instructional leader often stimulates creativity when he explores a classroom problem with a teacher and they have, through their interaction, arrived at a proposed solution with the clear understanding that if this line of effort is not successful a second one can be devised, or that after the teacher has started along the agreed upon line he will surely notice new factors that will suggest modification in the original plan. A supervisor often stimulates further creativity when he notices and genuinely commends the early or on-going efforts of individuals and faculties.

Supervisors, principals, and teachers stimulate others on the faculty when, by their own fluency of ideas and flexibility of planning, they form a living example of the effectiveness of and satisfaction in a creative approach to teaching. When the example of supervisors and principals causes teachers to support one another, appreciate another's efforts, and trust themselves to try, then a climate exists which stimulates creativity.

When a supervisor brings material assistance to a teacher who is partially interested in something he has not tried before, creativity is often stimulated. For instance, a pamphlet on role-playing at the junior high level, placed in the hands of a teacher whose interest had already been piqued, could provide the lift that starts him on the productive use of that and related media. Or if the supervisor actually helps a teacher and committee of children make the first set of figures for work in puppetry, a host of effective ideas for dramatic and language arts activities may follow. Literally helping the teacher make the initial effort unbinds his imagination and energy.

Considerations

The systematic study of creativity is perhaps still in its exploratory stages. Much has been learned and much remains to be learned.

Some of the dynamic for creativity undoubtedly lies well within the individual, beyond the ordinary reach of events at school: for instance, the individual's energy level, his habits of perception, his life style (some of which may be constitutionally based), and his self-concept, which is derived in part from childhood experiences. Some of the dynamic is in the environment in such matters as paucity or profusion of materials and degree of opportunity for interaction of persons. But some of the dynamic may also be in the expectation of creativity and the daily nurturing of the conditions that are conducive to it. In this phase supervision should be able to assist teachers and children to become creative.

INHIBITING FACTORS. Perhaps it is easier to see at first what inhibits creativity than it is to speak with assurance of what conditions are conducive to it. Prolonged, intense anxiety usually limits the free flow and use of ideas. Whether the source of the anxiety is personal or professional, the feeling is pervasive and intrusive, often impinging on activities and moments of the day that are not directly connected with the cause of anxiety. It is not readily amenable to reduction by reasoning through the problems involved. Anxiety preoccupies time and energy, thus usurping the opportunity for creativity. In its more extreme forms this preoccupation with anxiety leads to what psychologists sometimes call tunnel vision, in which the individual is so absorbed with his anxiety that he is insensitive to the periphery of vision and events and is aware only of what is immediately in front of him or immediately connected with the subject of his anxiety. The teacher, child, or supervisor who is heavily preoccupied with anxiety would seldom be sensitive to the nudge of a new idea, a prick of curiosity or the freshness of a new slant of perception; he would seldom feel free and confident enough to be "playful with ideas" or exhibit "fluency of ideas," as Taylor indicated was characteristic of creative people.

Quite aside from the more extreme personal and professional problems, there are frequent sources of anxiety in a school situation which are strong enough to exert a debilitating force. The limits set by a rigid course of study, the real or assumed necessity for completing certain texts or materials, and the expectations of the next teacher or unit of the school often are a source of anxiety to a teacher, or at least are offered by the individual as the reason for not venturing beyond a routine procedure. That the supposed limits and expectations may be imagined rather than real does not prevent their having the impact of reality for a long time. A supervisor can often free teachers in a significant way by helping them look for the limits and restrictive policies they genuinely suppose exist and discover that the limitations are matters of imagination or hazy tradition. In the search teachers often discover, too, that a written policy has cushioning or qualifying phrases that not only permit, but actually invite, some experimentation and deviation from the stated policy.

New materials of instruction, new patterns of organization within the classroom or school, and new areas of work introduced into the curriculum are frequently a source of crippling anxiety. When a supervisor helps teachers become familiar with new media, arranges in-service education opportunities for them, and helps them see new proposals not as great burdens or "one more thing to do" but as new vehicles or means for reaching desired goals, he frees teachers to work in a resourceful, imaginative way: i.e., creatively.

Another factor which often inhibits creativity is the normal press of the day's activities. Many school situations involve crowded classrooms and a wider range of services than a staff has been provided for rendering. There are multitudes of choices to be made and time-consuming routines to be completed. Such conditions do not preclude the possibility of creativity; indeed, many individuals find themselves at their creative best when they are busiest and when the demand in the situation is high. But to the extent that teachers become numb with fatigue in a crowded school day and drained of perceptiveness and response by the kaleidoscope of students and activities, creativity can be dampened. Supervisors can sometimes help teachers directly through increasing their sense of goal and long-range purpose, thus bringing coherence out of fragmented activities. Sometimes the help is indirect, through such matters as interpreting the program to school board members and the public so that they see the need for broader financial support for the total school program.

CONDITIONS CONDUCIVE TO CREATIVITY. As just indicated, freedom from preoccupying anxiety and freedom from chronic fatigue and stultifying routine are usually prerequisites to creativity. Another factor which can aid is access to materials. If on a day-in and day-out basis, every suggestion for improvement or innovation is blocked because no materials are available to carry it out, then the suggestions tend to stop flowing. Not all innovations need money in order to be accomplished, and ingenuity can sometimes provide alternates where materials are needed; but a constant attitude of "no money" can dampen the zest for experimental approaches.

The really important factors in nurturing creativity are probably the more subtle ones of manner, attitude, and expectation. When a teacher notices a child's questioning look and takes time to explore the by-path his question opens; when a teacher delays his own observation on a problem until others have suggested possibilities; when pupils and teachers in the primary years or graduate school speculate about the things not yet known; when the teacher and supervisor confer unhurriedly and the words "I wonder why" are frequently heard; when pupils, teachers, supervisors and community alike cease to expect a single all-time answer to a problem involving dynamic, variable human beings, then some conditions exist which are conducive to creativity.

FACILITATING AND EVALUATING CHANGE
AS A FUNCTION OF SUPERVISION

The need for facilitating and evaluating change is thoroughly rooted in the cultural, philosophic, psychological, democratic and sociological conditions described earlier. The professional basis is broad and varied, for it includes the incorporating into practice of a constantly evolving body of new knowledge from educational research and from numerous contributing sciences, and the making of new judgments in situations that involve variables. Supervision can do much to expedite the making of necessary changes and to evaluate the effectiveness of specific changes.

Examples

MATERIALS.   Supervision is facilitating change when it hastens the securing of materials in a situation where the teacher is already eager to try some different approach. It is facilitating change when it involves teachers in the thoughtful selection of textbooks, library books, films, models, and other teaching aids, since a better understanding of the specific contribution of the materials is then assured and their intelligent use enhanced.

VALUES AND GOALS.   Supervision is facilitating change when individual teachers or groups are aided in bringing values to the conscious level and reaching commitments with self or others regarding goals. The sharpness of goal perception apparently allows three important things to occur: a rise in the energy for work, a recognition of intermediate, enabling steps which are of small enough size that the individual feels he is capable of taking them, and flexibility in approach. When the goal is truly clear, unexpected developments do not panic the traveler; he can use detours and alternate routes to reach his destination. A large part of a principal's contribution to improvement of instruction often lies in the day-to-day help he gives teachers in clarifying goals and remaking plans for achievement.

EMOTIONAL SUPPORT.   Supervision facilitates change when emotional support is given to a teacher in the process of attempting a new step. This support is sometimes simply and quickly given through a smile, an interested inquiry as to progress, or through a request for a subsequent report on outcomes of the attempt. Often the giving of support entails encouraging a teacher to try a new venture, with both teacher and supervisor recognizing that the trying will be without expertness at first and with much learning coming out of the early attempts. For instance, a teacher who is attempting to use more small committee work in his social studies class may find a number of awkward moments arising from his own clumsiness and lack of foresight. If the instructional leader assures him of confidence and even shares some of the difficult moments with him, the teacher will be in a position to learn rapidly from his own experience rather than simply be embarrassed and disgusted by it.

INTERPRETATION OF PROGRAM. Supervision expedites change when it keeps each of the numerous parts of a school system informed as to modifications and their purposes. The timely interpretation of change in long established procedures can forestall much misunderstanding. For instance, when manuscript writing was introduced in the primary grades as a desirable way for children to learn to write, supervisors and principals who interpreted the change to the community and to intermediate grade teachers, fully explaining the reasons (the resemblance of manuscript letter forms to the printed symbols children were learning to read, plus freedom from fatigue, and the early attainment of sufficient command of writing skill for real communication), usually found ready acceptance of the change. But in other communities, where little explanation was made, there were sometimes resistance to the procedure and complaints to the school board.

IN-SERVICE EDUCATION OPPORTUNITIES. Supervision facilitates change when it helps plan for and carry through the details of arrangements for professional growth activities. It is sometimes easier for an individual to make a change if his peers are also making similar changes. A faculty studying together toward an improved science program for the entire school, or a group of teachers from many schools in the same system studying a foreign language together, give one another zest and confidence in making the change. Well-planned professional growth activities also have the advantage of giving a systematic quality to some of the change.

Considerations

MATERIALS. Making changes in classroom procedures often involves the use of additional material as an enabling agent. Without the materials the anticipated change cannot be fully realized, and teachers and children become discouraged in their efforts. Sometimes the idea itself seems to be at fault and the whole concept is discarded as unworkable when, in reality, the idea was sound but could not be realized because of lack of appropriate media. In some situations the person trying to make a change loses confidence in himself, ascribing the failure to his own ineptness, when the trouble really lies in the paucity of material for children to use. For instance, teachers who attempted to develop broad units of work with children in situations without varied textbook and library resources, often became discouraged and blamed the concept or themselves or the children, when the experience was not rewarding. Yet readily accessible material would have changed the outcome. There is some irony in the fact that *after* a teacher has become expert in the use of a new idea, he can usually find ways of substituting or abridging when a desired material is unavailable; but while he is in the process of initiating change, he needs the help of superior materials. Hence the securing of materials is a significant way for supervision to facilitate change.

APPRAISAL OF OUTCOMES.   An important phase of facilitating and evaluating change is the early planning for appraisal of outcomes. Changing for the sake of changing usually turns into a profitless and wearying affair. The goal or purpose of a proposed change should be clear; but equally important, some means must be anticipated and established for ascertaining whether or not the desired goal actually is being reached. Occasionally, proposed changes come to school personnel fully developed and verified through laboratory or test case trials. However, the great majority of proposed changes spring from new understandings derived from education, psychology, and other sciences where the application to each classroom involves some new factors requiring modification of a plan and constant judgment on the part of teachers and others. When a faculty or individual teacher undertakes a new procedure, a plan for appraisal of outcomes needs to be developed at the same time. Helping with the plans for appraisal is a significant part of the work of supervision.

TIME AND ENERGY FOR CHANGE. Changes take time and energy. Sound professional change is a form of growth and, like other growth, is gradual although not even-paced. Adults smile indulgently when a six-year-old returns from school the first day and announces his surprise and disappointment over not learning to read in one day. Teachers, principals, and supervisors need to be knowing and sophisticated enough about themselves and the nature of change to recognize that most changes take time: that gradualness is not a cause for faint hearts and discouragement.

Change takes energy. There are no units of measure for the energy needed for change: no foot-pounds, no ergs. But making changes requires energy. Decision-making, weighing factors involved in a choice, and making careful judgments regarding new situations consume energy. It takes less energy to proceed in a familiar routine where few new choices are needed. Also there is the energy needed to overcome the inertia of the individual who is entirely comfortable with his present set of habits. System-wide supervisors, principals and others responsible for initiating change need to remember humbly that extra energy is needed for making changes. Somewhat paradoxically, and fortunately, change can beget energy: i.e., when a new goal is perceived and a way to it glimpsed, it is a normal part of the human dynamic that energy rises, sometimes with amazing speed and force.

CHANGE AS PERSONAL DEVELOPMENT. Many understandings drawn from social and perceptual psychology underscore the fact that change, even in professional affairs, is primarily a matter of personal development: that is, change for an individual is dependent upon his achieving a new perception of familiar facts or the admitting of additional facts to his perceptual field. A change in his actions often awaits a prior change in his self-concept, in what he expects of himself or can trust himself to attempt. In the 1930's school systems sometimes employed curriculum directors to bring drastic reorganization to the total curriculum or some phase of it. In most cases the results, in spite of sincere and enormous efforts, were small, since teachers themselves had little opportunity to become involved to a point of changing their perceptions of goals and means.

A person entering a profession today should expect to be a life-long learner, i.e., changer. Most of the changes will be evolutionary rather than revolutionary. They will not involve a total rejecting of what has gone before, but a building upon it and an enlargement to accommodate more insight and new media for learning. To change a procedure is not to assume that the previous way was all wrong, nor that a person who changes is now necessarily disloyal to former ideals and co-workers. Change often stems from a refinement or a greater differentiation of a general principle that had been grasped earlier. If instructional leaders can help themselves and others view change evaluatively, understanding the *why* of proposals, they can do much to facilitate smooth growth. They can also help teachers experience satisfaction in growth on the one hand, and avoid, on the other hand, the disappointment of turning to change itself as a simple panacea for complex problems.

ANALYSIS OF LEARNING SITUATIONS
AS A FUNCTION OF SUPERVISION

The need for analysis of learning situations as a function of super-vision is deeply rooted in the nature of experience, in the nature of perception, and in the complexity of a teaching-learning situation. When a person undergoes a new experience, whether successfully or unsuccessfully, he must examine the situation carefully and gen-eralize from it, if he is to profit from it: that is, if he is to gain greater control of similar events in the future. Often another person can help an individual grasp significant relationships, verbalize them, and carry them forward as generalizations for future use. Sometimes this is possible because of the other person's broad knowledge and familiarity with similar experiences, and sometimes because another angle of perception has been achieved. In either event, an instructional leader can often help a teacher analyze a teaching-learning situation so that the next steps can be planned effectively.

It should be remembered too that teaching-learning situations are exceedingly complex systems or fields with many sub-systems, related factors, and variables. To discern important relationships and to generalize soundly from them are both intricate undertakings. No one should underestimate the size of the task.

Examples

An instructional leader is carrying out the function of analysis of learning situations when he helps a teacher hunt the causes of a specific trouble spot. For instance, Kay B——, who had had several years of successful teaching in the primary grades prior to teaching kindergarten for the past three years, took a position in the second grade. Within a few weeks the children were becoming unruly and Kay was having a serious discipline problem for the first time in her career. She asked the supervisor to come to study the children in the classroom for an afternoon and go over the records of some individuals with her. After examining together the events of the afternoon, they came to the conclusion that the children were finishing their common and individual undertakings much more rapidly than Kay anticipated, and consequently had time on their hands which they did not yet have the self-direction to use wisely. Apparently Kay's sojourn with slower-working kindergarteners had disrupted her sense of timing for seven-year-olds. When she made the necessary adjustments in frequency and length of activities in subsequent days, the discipline problems declined and then disappeared. It is true that eventually Kay might have succeeded in analyzing the situation by herself, but probably only after a longer period of time during which the problem would have become compounded to the point that the original cause was obscured and the essentially simple solution no longer adequate.

A supervisor and principal can also help teachers analyze successful ventures and bring to the conscious level, available for future use, generalizations about the reasons for the success of an undertaking. Thus a field trip that had been especially fruitful for a civics class could be examined from the standpoint of pre-planning, pupil involvement, clarity of purpose, level of complexity of the events witnessed, and follow-through for refinement of understanding and correction of misconceptions.

Instructional leaders can also help teachers analyze the status quo in situations where teachers themselves have become sensitive to a general problem but have not yet pin-pointed the trouble. For instance, middle grade teachers in one school were well aware of the great amounts of time and effort that children and teachers expended upon spelling; yet parents were dissatisfied with their children's spelling and the class achievements were actually slightly below national norms. Just increasing the time and effort still more did not seem to be an efficient procedure. A supervisor and the principal together helped the faculty devise a study to ascertain what kinds of mistakes children made (not just how many) and the conditions under which the best spelling and poorest spelling occurred. Armed with this information about types and frequency of errors, especially omissions, phonetic substitutions, and reversals, children and teachers subsequently could use learning time more productively.

Sometimes supervisory personnel can help in ferreting out remote or indirect causes in a troublesome situation, as when they join with others, such as a visiting teacher, guidance counselor or psychologist, in trying to discover why a certain child has extraordinary fear of teachers or school.

Considerations

RIGOROUS SEARCH. Adequate analysis of a situation involves a rigorous search for relevant factors and complex relationships. Occasionally a situation may yield to rather quick examination, since the supervisor's broad experience or habits of probing for principles behind practices may enable him to perceive almost at once the nature of the problem. More often, however, the analysis calls for careful study and fact-finding. The fact-finding often goes outside the classroom and school to seek cooperation from other agencies such as welfare, health, and child guidance centers. The fact-finding is frequently time-consuming or must be extended over a period of weeks, but superficial or premature judgments might well be worse than no effort at all.

NATURE OF THE HELP. The help in analysis can be of several kinds. Sometimes another angle of vision is enough to enable a supervisor or principal to see factors not noticed before. Sometimes a detached view, free from the distortion of emotional involvement, is sufficient to discover a significant relationship. Often the person closest to the problem has begun to think in circles, either through mounting anxiety or through the fact that his own previous experience limits or "blinds" him in the range of his interpretation of the scene.

Sometimes the supervisor helps by serving as a sounding board or a shoulder upon which to lean. If the troubled person can first unload his tension by giving expression to his concern and frustration, he can begin to think clearly again. As he describes the situation, he analyzes as he goes, seeing new relationships and often arriving at solutions while he talks the matter out. It is in this connection that system-wide supervisors often help principals, since principals are rarely free to talk through all their problems with members of the faculty or community.

Very often the instructional leader helps by engaging in thoughtful, unhurried discussion with the teacher, with time for probing, exploring, and speculating. The interaction of ideas and personalities is frequently conducive to new insights and is productive of creative solutions. Sometimes the sheer relaxing of the pressure for an answer seems to let people become aware of nuances and subtle clues that have actually been present for some time but unnoticed as a possible solution to the problem.

ATTITUDE TOWARD HELP. It is clear from the foregoing paragraph that, if analysis of learning situations is to be effectively carried out as a function of supervision, an attitude toward problems needs to prevail which is far different from the feeling that has existed until recently. In earlier years the presence of a problem was usually considered a sign of weakness or inadequacy on the part of the teacher; hence it was natural for the individual to want to cover up the situation. With the professional side of teaching being constantly developed, however, it is possible to admit the complexity of situations with which a teacher deals. It becomes respectable to have problems. Instead of covering up a problem, the teacher can open up the situation for analysis, calling for consultation service from other school personnel who then work with the teacher in a peer relationship in studying the problem. Under these conditions, the seeking of help is no longer a sign of personal or professional weakness; the giving of help is no longer the dispensing of bits of wisdom from an inexhaustible supply of superior knowledge. The helping relationship is more nearly a hard-headed, emotion-free attempt to solve a knotty problem. Just as opera stars and Olympic Games athletes have need throughout their careers for the services of teachers and coaches, classroom teachers have need for someone to assist them in the frequent analyses of efforts in a situation, with the expectation of achieving a continuously better and more satisfying performance.

To open up problems for analysis where he himself is an intimate part of the situation requires a considerable degree of professional competence and a healthy self-esteem on the part of the teacher. Teachers today have much more professional preparation than formerly and continue their study while they work; therefore, they have good reason to develop an increasing degree of confidence in their professional judgments. It is the privilege and responsibility of supervision to help a teacher grow in competence and confidence, achieve respect for himself and others, and develop a self-concept that permits him to function at his optimum.

CONTRIBUTING TO A BODY OF KNOWLEDGE
AND TECHNIQUES AS A FUNCTION
OF SUPERVISION

The need for contributing to an evolving body of knowledge and techniques as a function of supervision is based both in the philosophic position of the evolutionary nature of the universe, and in the psychological recognition of the thrust to understand as an essential phase of human nature. It is also clearly rooted in the nature of education as a profession. To achieve an even greater degree of professionalism, education must develop an increasing body of knowledge and techniques.

Examples

Supervision discharges this function of contributing to knowledge when it helps individuals and faculties engage in fact-finding investigations regarding their own school systems and then categorize the findings in such a way that they can be useful to other people as well as those involved in the study. An instructional leader can contribute to knowledge when he helps individuals and faculties analyze related incidents and formulate guiding principles for future use; when he helps find the extent to which a generalization is true or the kinds of conditions under which it is true; or when he helps adapt laboratory findings to classroom situations. He may also help when he collaborates with professional organizations in making surveys, in publicizing findings of such surveys, and in formulating recommendations that modify former practices so that new knowledge is accommodated and then tested further.

He often contributes to knowledge when he establishes a factual basis for causing people to challenge assumptions they have held so long they are unaware of possessing them. The supervisor also helps in the development of knowledge when he aids school faculties in their participation in national or state studies, when he encourages school boards to sponsor or take part in studies, and when he helps delineate the areas in which new knowledge is needed.

Considerations

New knowledge in any field is usually hard-won. Significant findings in any area, from archeology to zoology, typically are achieved only after prolonged effort. Education is no exception. Much has been accomplished by individuals working independently or in small groups; yet relatively little has been attempted in large scale, systematic, well-financed research. It is tantalizing to the imagination to speculate what could be learned, what break-throughs in the present limits of knowledge achieved, if education and psychology could pour manpower and money into research for the next twenty-five years the way such fields as medicine and communications have poured in effort in the past twenty-five years. Meanwhile there is much that supervision can do to aid in the development of new knowledge.

STATUS STUDIES. Status studies and fact-finding investigations related to specific school systems are needed to provide information for many kinds of choices by school boards and superintendents, by faculties, and by individual teachers. For instance, knowledge of subject matter achievement, of resources for learning, and of ranges in individual needs are necessary if good planning is to occur. If records from studies of similar design are kept for several years, gains and losses can be detected. Objective data can be used to supplement subjective judgments in planning for improvement.

Records need to be kept regarding experimental efforts, the failures as well as the successes, in order that costly repetition of unrewarding procedures can be avoided. Not infrequently a school system finds itself "experimenting" with an idea or procedure that was tried and found inadequate in previous years. Such repetition may indeed be justifiable if conditions have changed or a modification in the tested procedure proposed. But unless records of the first attempt are kept and made known, the new experimentation cannot profit from the earlier experience. Instructional leaders, because of their over-all picture of the school system, have a responsibility to help schools engage in fact-finding studies and formulate the knowledge gained into records and reports that will help all parts of the school system, from superintendent and finance officer to guidance counselor and classroom teacher, in their decision-making.

IMPLICATIONS FROM NEW INSIGHTS. Long before certain new insights from theoretical and experimental work in education and its contributing disciplines have been completely analyzed and substantiated, implications for classroom work may become apparent. Supervision can help put these implications to work. For instance, from psychology has recently come some insight regarding: (1) the inhibiting effect of intense anxiety upon learning; [3] (2) the crippling effect upon mental development of extreme deprivation of experience in childhood; [4] and (3) the possibility of a relationship between brain wave patterns and styles of learning as being characteristic of the individual learner.[5] It may be some years before these concepts are fully understood, but in the light of the gross understanding now achieved, school people should be able to take some steps to reorganize classroom living in such a way as to: (1) reduce needless anxiety in personal relationships and in presenting demands for new learning; (2) enrich the range and quality of daily experience for children; and (3) provide classrooms with a real variety of learning media in order to capitalize upon different styles of learning.

ACTION RESEARCH. It is clear that education is both a consumer and producer of research. One phase of research, commonly designated as action research, is of special concern to supervision. It is characterized by the fact that: (1) it typically starts with the detection of a problem in a real situation; (2) the projecting and carrying out of the study is a cooperative venture performed primarily by the people who are going to be influenced by the findings; and (3) the outcome of the study is expected to be put to immediate use in resolving the felt problems.

The role of the instructional leader in action research is a significant one. He is often instrumental in turning a casual moment of curiosity or mild dissatisfaction on the part of the teacher or faculty into the beginning of an important study; he is sometimes the one who first becomes sensitive to a specific problem; he usually aids in

[3] Seymour B. Sarason, "Anxiety and Learning," *Human Variability and Learning* (Washington, D. C.: Association for Supervision and Curriculum Development, National Education Association, 1961).

[4] Walter B. Waetjen, "Developmental Knowledge and Needed Curriculum Research," *Research Frontiers in the Study of Children's Learning* (Milwaukee: University of Wisconsin, 1960).

[5] W. G. Walters, *The Living Brain* (New York: W. W. Norton & Company, Inc., 1953).

the difficult step of formulating the exact questions or hypotheses for systematic study; he is of endless value in obtaining materials for work, securing consultant help, and compiling data; his assistance is essential in implementing the recommendations coming from the study, especially if more than one school in a system is influenced by the recommendations.

PERSONNEL FOR RESEARCH. The amount and kinds of research needed by school systems go well beyond what could be accomplished by faculties and instructional supervisors. Even well prepared teachers, principals, and supervisors do not have the degree of specialization in research procedures nor the time for the sustained, controlled, systematic research needed in education. Supervision should work constantly to interpret to the superintendent, school board, and public the basic need for new knowledge, and hence the need for financial support for programs and personnel for research.

INTEGRATING OF GOALS AND ENERGY BUILDING
AS A FUNCTION OF SUPERVISION

The need for integrating of goals and building of energy as a function of supervision is deeply based in the psychological aspects of human nature. Goals, clearly perceived, are temporary destinations that enable a person to move with an invigorating sense of purpose. They are the centers around which small daily activities can be organized meaningfully. They serve as milestones by which to measure progress and feel the satisfaction of achievement and the rise of new energy.

Examples

Supervision aids in the integration of goals when it helps individuals or groups become conscious of values, clarify long-range goals, and reach commitments about immediate next steps. For instance, an instructional leader working with an elementary faculty in the appraisal of the school's library program: (1) assisted a sub-committee in preparing a single-page statement of purposes an ideal library would serve in the lives of children; (2) secured a library consultant who helped analyze the changes needed to obtain broader utilization of existing materials; (3) compiled data for the superintendent and school board to show what a full-time librarian's services could mean to the children; and (4) helped the teachers evolve a plan for developing an extensive picture file in the ensuing three months.

Instructional leaders often help integrate goals and build energy when they can be articulate about goals or make a general value vivid and specific. Sometimes familiar values are held at the level of unanalyzed assumption or semi-awareness. To have the values stated explicitly, vividly, even a little dramatically on occasion, enables people to feel anew the worth of the goals toward which they have been striving somewhat haltingly.

If supervision can help teachers relate specific, small acts to larger purposes, integration of activities is enhanced and energy increases. For instance, the listing of names and addresses of children who appear by teacher observation to need referral for eye examination, may seem a tedious and annoying task; but if a few comments from the principal or consultant can help the teacher relate this task to the larger concepts not only of better health for the child but also of the cooperative effort among social agencies, the act takes on greater significance. Listing the names still requires time and effort, but there seems to be a greater reservoir of energy for doing it and there is no futile expenditure of precious energy in petty annoyance.

Considerations

At least two general considerations regarding integration of goals need to be mentioned. One relates to the naturalness of difficulty in maintaining perspective, i.e., integration of goals and awareness of values. A person deeply involved in his work is not only caught up (sometimes entangled) in varied enabling activities; he is also subject to being driven off course by thwartings, unexpected delays, and temporary failures. Keeping a sense of direction is not easy for anyone. Principals encounter a special hazard in this connection from the conflicting demands from different segments of the community and in the urgency and immediacy of many of the decisions they are called upon to make. Folk language abounds in sayings that reflect the problem of keeping perspective. A person, referring to any area of living, may speak of "standing too close to the grindstone" or of "not being able to see the forest for the trees."

The second consideration relates to the fact that all instructional leaders themselves have to cultivate vision. They are by no means immune to loss of perspective. They have to seek deliberately ways of maintaining and further developing the long view. Attendance at national conventions often helps, as do unhurried travel, and reading outside the immediate field of education. Achieving some kind of rhythm and balance in the week's work can help prevent physical exhaustion and distortion of outlook. Occasional periods of solitude, contemplation, or speculative conversation with colleagues, are beneficial for most people in maintaining perspective.

AIDS TO STUDY AND DISCUSSION

1. In retrospect, examine some of your own experiences in which supervision was of help to you (or could have been of help). In approximately one page describe the situation, the needs present, and what was done and by whom. Then in an additional paragraph, make an analysis of the functions of supervision served and the general principles involved.

2. Examine the short incidents in Appendix A which describe, in the words of teachers themselves, cases of supervisory help. What elements do you find in common among the incidents? What variety of problems and approaches do you note?

3. Study carefully the single-page Statement of Beliefs issued by the Association of Supervision and Curriculum Development. What are some points which might have been different if the statement had been prepared in 1910? From the implications of this statement, how would you phrase the major functions of supervision?

4. List a sampling of decisions you have made in the classroom or elsewhere in your work in the last week. With what kinds of decisions could you have used supervisory help? On which problems did you seek help?

SUGGESTIONS FOR FURTHER READING

Hicks, Hanne J., *Educational Supervision in Principle and Practice* (New York: The Ronald Press Company, 1960).

Lawler, Marcella R., *Curriculum Consultants at Work* (New York: Bureau of Publications, Teachers College, 1958).

McNerney, Chester T., *Educational Supervision* (New York: McGraw-Hill Book Co., Inc., 1951).

Montagu, Ashley, *On Being Human* (New York: Henry Shuman, 1950).

Peckham, Dorothy, *Principles and Techniques of Supervision* (Dubuque: William C. Brown Company, Publishers, 1953).

Sarason, Seymour B., "Anxiety and Learning," *Human Variability and Learning* (Washington, D.C.: Association for Supervision and Curriculum Development, 1961).

Taylor, Calvin W., "The Creative Individual," *Educational Leadership*, Vol. 18, No. 1 (October, 1960).

Waetjen, Walter B., "Developmental Knowledge and Needed Curriculum Research," *Research Frontiers in a Study of Children's Learning* (Milwaukee: University of Wisconsin, 1960).

Walter, W. G., *The Living Brain* (New York: W. W. Norton & Company, Inc., 1953).

CHAPTER 5

PLANNING FOR SUPERVISION

S INCE supervision is primarily a matter of working with people, the way of work is important, as well as what is attempted and accomplished. Successful planning is dependent not only on clear vision of goals and foresight of consequences, but also upon the involvement of the thinking of many persons and upon sensitivity to the thoughts and feelings of others. Several factors which influence planning for supervision, much of which is cooperative planning, are: the nature of a program in a democracy; a concept of method; the working relationships among the staff; a knowledge of the community; and the problems arising from the nature of communication.

THE NATURE OF A PROGRAM IN A DEMOCRACY

The need for some kind of organization of desired experiences, a program, necessitates a consideration of the nature of a program in a democracy.

In an authoritarian concept of living the nature of a program is clear-cut, partly through its relative simplicity as to origin and partly through familiarity with it after long usage throughout the world's history. The authoritarian program is simply a design for getting done efficiently what one or a few persons deem important to be accomplished. The flow of authority is one-directional, from top to bottom or from planners to workers. The democratic concept of a program must provide for a two-way flow of authority and ideas, with authority recognized as residing in the group ultimately, but being delegated and redelegated constantly to individuals for execution of specific tasks. A democratic program is based upon values arrived at cooperatively. For the plan of action devised, there is common understanding, with commitments and mutual acceptance of responsibility, albeit division of labor in the execution of the plan. This theory of a democratic program is applicable whether the planning is with a group in a local school, in a county, or on a state-wide project.

The very concept of democratic planning is relatively new in the history of man; hence it is small wonder that some needed procedures are still in a formative stage and that some individuals lack skill with known procedures. In practice this theory of planning leads to the evolving of a program which has several distinguishing characteristics.

Structured on the Needs for Improvement

A democratic program is structured on the needs for the improvement of living. The needs are derived from the particular situation in which planning is occurring, but all planning is not limited to the needs felt at a particular time and place. Good planning goes beyond the current scene and serves to lift the level of aspiration; otherwise accomplishment might be limited by a low level of awareness of possibilities. Thus, a community might not aspire to the elimination of slums because it does not fully realize the effect of slums upon the personalities of the inhabitants or because it has not realized its own potentials for social action. A good program is based upon immediate needs but is directed toward the best imaginable goal. A good program is indigenous but not provincial.

Contingent upon Agreement on Values

A democratic program is contingent upon a series of agreements on values; it is not a blueprint or a prescription or a map. The values, cooperatively arrived at and accepted, serve as guidelines and as goals. The means of goal seeking are submitted to criteria or values, but are varied and flexible to allow for adjustments to situational and individual differences.

Commitments Reached Cooperatively

In a democratic program agreements are arrived at cooperatively. All members of a group affected by a plan are involved in the planning. With large groups such as in a city, county, or state situation, this involvement often has to be by the republican principle of representation; but the two-way flow of authority, commitment, and responsibility is observed.

Flexibility for Revision

A democratic program has flexibility in regard to revising goals as new factors and values emerge in a situation. Media for registering and making such changes are a part of the program. The program has flexibility with regard to means of goal seeking. Differences in individuals, differences in situations, and modification through impact of invention and discovery call for a high degree of flexibility in planning.

Provision for Growth and Accomplishment by Members

A democratic program provides for growth and accomplishment by its members as the program moves forward. The talents of individuals are utilized and opportunities provided for the development of new talents. The energy and vigor of persons with diverse skills are brought into a team relationship so that the impact of the effort can be felt.

In democratic planning every member of the group has responsibility for initiative, for work, and for evaluation of outcomes and proposals for next steps. Members cannot be passive, placing all blame on others when planning goes awry or accomplishments are less than expected. Continuity and integrity of group effort are matters of voluntary, whole-hearted commitment to common value concerns.

As members engage in democratic planning and the carrying forward of the program, they should support one another in their thinking, venturing, and extending of experience. Each member should be aided in growing toward maturity: that is, toward the full use of his resources for constructive living.

In summary, it may be said that a good program: (1) gives orientation and direction; (2) coordinates efforts toward goals, giving a framework for cooperative effort, and thereby increasing the intentional rather than fortuitous achievement of goals; (3) provides multiple suggestions as to means; (4) provides for interaction of individuals and groups; and (5) provides for the personal and professional growth of those participating.

A CONCEPT OF METHOD

Of great significance for planning in supervision is a concept of method, whether the method refers to classroom instruction or to ways of organizing for educational improvement in a community.

For many years method was regarded as a fixed procedure, a known route for reaching a goal, a pattern easily repeated. The search was for ideal (constant) solutions to problems, with the expectation that a successful solution could be used again and again by any number of teachers, pupils, and supervisors. It was assumed that children exposed to the same instructional method would learn the same things or amounts. It was noted, to be sure, that the same amount of learning did not take place for each child, but the general assumption was that the child had not applied himself or that the teacher had not used the method well. The fault was not recognized at first as being partly, at least, in too narrow a concept of method.

Findings from child development and from field psychology began to give insight as to the complexity and variability of each child as a learner and of each teaching-learning situation. The total behavioral field of the individual (including his physical status, purpose and past experiences) was recognized as bearing upon what he could and would learn from a day at school. Therefore, the search for single procedures whose outcomes could be guaranteed began to be seen as an illusion.

Method as an Act of Judgment

Rather than being a fixed procedure, method is more nearly an act of judgment, or series of judgments, in choosing appropriate means for reaching a selected goal. It is a creative quandary. With goals and values clearly in mind, the individual seeks the most efficient means for reaching them. He watches for outcomes along the way, and incorporates new evidence into the choice of next steps. He assesses and re-assesses a situation, searching for all the factors discernible to him, and draws upon his background of professional knowledge in selecting appropriate means. Judgment is brought to bear upon the problem.

Actually the "problem" (the immediate goal toward which a teacher is trying to find routes) does not remain static even when superficially the situation appears the same. Hence the same method used day-in and day-out in spelling, arithmetic or any instructional field is sure to be inappropriate for some persons some of the time.

The charming folk-story of Epaminondas has significance for a discussion of method. A little boy, Epaminondas, visited his auntie on a succession of days and each time was given a parting gift: the first time a piece of cake, which became a fistful of crumbs by the time he reached home. His mother gave careful instructions for carrying cake, whereupon he applied the procedure to bringing home the gift of butter the next day, then the butter-carrying instructions to a puppy on the following day, and puppy-carrying instruction to a loaf of bread on another day, each time with disastrous results, of course.

The story retains its appeal through the years, for each reader can quickly identify himself with Epaminondas through moments in his own experience when he too failed to assess the current situation properly, when he too tried to use in a new situation a method that would have worked perfectly just a few days before, or when he too did just what he was told to do, yet came to grief.

Methodology needs to be conceived broadly and flexibly in education as a general plan, subject to modification to accommodate new factors in the field, rather than as a single procedure for all look-alike situations. In teaching and in supervision there is no escaping the constant exercise of judgment.

Choice of Method Influenced by Situation

In the ordinary transactions of life adults and children make countless situational judgments. For instance, three members of a school system planned to attend a professional meeting in Chicago, 500 miles from their city, and at first spoke of traveling together: that is, using the same method to reach the goal. The three eventually chose different means, however, when it developed that: one decided to take his family and therefore needed to drive his car, leaving in the morning preceding the meeting day; the second, who needed to attend a local staff meeting in the afternoon before leaving, but who was to appear on the program during the first session of the conference, took an evening plane; the third, a principal who needed to be at a P.T.A. meeting in the evening, took the night train, arriving at the conference as the presiding officer opened the session.

All three reached their goal, using different methods. The choice of a different method made it possible for each person to respond productively to the complex of factors impinging on his life at the time the trip needed to be made. Had the three straight-jacketed themselves by insisting on using an identical method, their level of accomplishment would have been lower for the day preceding the convention, and very probably their sense of frustration would have been a destructive factor in itself.

The rightness or goodness of a procedure, then, is relevant to the time, place, persons and purposes involved. Epaminondas' procedures for bringing home gifts were not wrong in themselves and therefore to be discarded as "bad." They were only highly inappropriate to the occasion in which he tried to use each one. Of the three ways for reaching Chicago, one was not permanently good and the others bad; each was appropriate for the person who used it at that time.

There is another aspect in which judgment has to be exercised with regard to procedures in a situation, and that is in terms of amount or degree. For instance, a third grade reading group might profit from five minutes of use of a certain procedure for word analysis, a few individuals might profit from another five minutes, but a third five minutes right then would be unproductive for almost everyone. What was good a few moments before is now not good for the time being. Or, a ceremony used in the school assembly on several occasions has impact and meaning, but if used for every assembly becomes routine. Teachers and instructional leaders cannot ask simply, "It this procedure good?", but must think more specifically, "Is this procedure productive for this child or group and for how long?"

Theory as a Guide for Practice

A concept of method as a creative quandary in which a person seeks routes to a goal makes it possible to see how theory serves to guide practice. The teacher has a broad body of knowledge (theory) and of possible techniques derived from his study of child development, learning process, cultural demands upon children and youth, and democratic ideals. Each day as he works he must assess countless situations in an effort to choose wisely the most relevant intermediate goals leading to long-range objectives and select the means most appropriate to the children, time, materials, and community.

Continually making judgments is not easy. Supervisors can help with their knowledge and their active support. Both teachers and supervisors need skill in assessing the teaching-learning act and sensitivity to small but significant factors in a complex situation. For example, even after immediate goals and procedures have been wisely chosen for a group of juniors studying Spanish, the bleakness of many secondary classrooms would have a depressing effect on the learners, until the teacher becomes sensitive to the needless loss through sensory deprivation and takes steps to enrich the surroundings.

At times the reliance upon judgment-making, i.e., the application of theory in constantly new situations, is far from comfortable. Each choice is in some degree a risk; it is a testing of the individual's competency in perceiving, selecting, and acting. Furthermore, many decisions have to be in the form of running judgments, made on the basis of a swift appraisal of a shifting scene and an instantaneous rehearsal of possible means. Some of the choices may prove inadequate and others turn into clear failure. A person then may be tempted to seek the security, false though it may be, of repeating familiar patterns indiscriminately. One of the most challenging responsibilities of supervision is to help teachers develop sound judgment, trust themselves to make professional judgments, and meet occasional disappointments with resilience.

Import for Supervision

A broad concept of method has further import for supervision in at least three respects: teacher expectation regarding supervision, the supervisor's own judgments, and the making of system-wide policies.

TEACHER EXPECTATION. The idea, prevalent for many years for historic reasons as pointed out in Chapter 2, that supervision was for the purpose of dispensing superior knowledge, led to the expectation of prescription, directives as to method, specific answers, and of "finding out what the supervisor wants me to do." It has taken nearly a generation to move into the realization that supervision is for the purpose of helping study the teaching-learning situation in order to work out better and better solutions to educational problems. To see method as a creative quandary means that teachers and supervisors together are engaged in analyzing, seeking, trying, and in judging outcomes. Conforming to an illusive "right way" is not the ideal. While teachers and supervisors do not have unlimited freedom in making choices and adaptations, the degree of freedom is often far greater than realized.

Furthermore, it has become respectable for teachers to have problems or fork-of-the-roads choices. A teacher need not feel guilty or weak when he seeks help. The seeking is, rather, an evidence of professional sensitivity and a rising aspiration for the accomplishment of the learners in his care.

SUPERVISOR'S JUDGMENTS. The supervisor's own judgments, of course, must be based on the same broad concept of method that the teacher is using. Such diverse activities as individual conferences with teachers, planning for a county-wide meeting, and preparation of newsletters must reflect the same concern for the individuality of people and the uniqueness of situations as the teacher is expected to show in dealing with children and youth.

When a supervisor sees the full significance of method as a creative quandary in which sound judgments are situationally based, he may grasp for the first time the reason for the truth of something which he has observed frequently: namely, that procedures used with great success by one teacher can rarely be copied by another teacher with equal success. But if the procedure is treated as an adaptable idea instead of a rigid blueprint, it can often be useful to the borrower.

The folly of expecting all teachers to profit equally from the same suggestions becomes clear. Also the need becomes clear, in the formulation of programs, for provision for latitude and variety of approaches. Opportunities for revision need to be planned from the beginning, to take advantage of new personalities and other new factors entering a scene.

POLICY STATEMENTS.   In view of the need for flexibility and variety, the supervisor will usually want to be extremely careful about the forming and perpetuation of system-wide policies. Some fairly fixed policies are necessary, of course, for the efficient operation of an organization that is as intricate and closely geared as a school system. Most of these are of an administrative nature. In the area of curriculum and instruction absolute conformity is rarely a necessity. The existence and wide recognition of broad policies often expedites decision-making; but problems arise when the policy is invoked or slavishly followed in inappropriate situations. For example, a frequently found policy in county or city systems relates to the time at which children will begin to add cursive writing to their skill in manuscript writing. If the policy is stated narrowly and establishes a highly specific point, such as the "seventh month of Grade Two" or the "second month of Grade Three," it is almost sure to impose unrealistic demands upon some children and cause some teachers to fly in the face of their own observations and judgments. If the policy is broadly stated, such as the "latter part of the second or beginning of the third grade," the situation is relieved of some of the strain.

Another way of preventing irrational situations from developing in the use of policies that are perfectly sound most of the time, is to be sure that qualifying phrases accompany the statement and that these phrases are fully appreciated and used by teachers. In the above example, for instance, if the phrase "for most children" preceded the statement, then the child who was unusually slow in physical development or low in language arts background would be protected from undue pressure through the teacher's earnest desire to conform to a policy.

While written statements for some policies are desirable from the standpoint of making certain expectations explicit and readily known to parents and new teachers, provision should be made for frequent review of policies, in order that necessary revisions can be made and that all concerned may understand the reasoning behind the policy. Sometimes a written policy is superfluous. It is all too easy for an originally desirable policy to become a rigidity with which school personnel persecute themselves and the children. Actually the commonness of approach, which many a policy is meant to achieve, is usually attained through the wide dissemination of knowledge and the exercise of professional judgment, rather than through the existence of the policy itself.

TEAMWORK: RELATIONSHIPS AMONG THE STAFF

In planning for supervision, an understanding of the working relationships among the staff is essential. True teamwork, not just specialization of labor, is involved. Lines of responsibility need to be delineated and made readily recognizable if effective work is to be done; but even more important, perhaps, is a keen awareness of common goals, a grasp of the diverse but vital functions fulfilled by the different members, and a high degree of trust and confidence in one another.

System-wide Supervisors and Superintendents

The relationships between the superintendent and supervisor will differ considerably from one school system to another, depending upon the size and organization of the system. In very large systems it may be that the superintendent will see the supervisor only rarely, since responsibility for instructional leadership has been delegated to an assistant superintendent or director of instruction. In any event, the superintendent or his representative has an opportunity for at least four kinds of service to supervision. The supervisor, in turn, can help the superintendent.

PRESENTING THE SUPERVISOR. When a supervisor is employed, the superintendent should make some kind of introduction of the supervisor to his own staff, to principals and teachers, and to the school board and community. The introduction may take the form of an announcement, a letter, a newspaper item, or a personal presentation at a large or small group meeting. The introduction should include the supervisor's title, the general scope of his work, and the most relevant of his qualifications for holding the position. Without such an introduction, the supervisor is in the awkward position of having to explain himself or account for his presence. Meanwhile, other school personnel will not know how to ask for his help; indeed, in a large system they may go for months before stumbling on to the fact that a supervisor is available.

DEFINING THE SCOPE OF WORK.   The superintendent needs to make clear at the outset what major responsibilities are envisioned for the position. Certain needs must have been felt or a supervisor would not have been employed. The superintendent should share this thinking as fully as possible with those persons most closely involved, usually principals and other supervisors. Clarity at this point not only gives the supervisor a sense of direction, but enables others to see where he can help serve their purposes. It also prevents needless apprehension and confusion.

It should be noted that any supervisor, whether the first one to be employed in a system or the fortieth, joins a going concern. Other people are there before him, and the newcomer may appear to be a threat to familiar patterns and to individuals unless the lines of old and new responsibilities are made clear. It is not always easy to be clear about the exact responsibilities, for sometimes the role has to be lived for a time, usually with an increasing scope of work, before the supervisor and others can see just where he serves best. Sometimes, however, fairly general statements are helpful. For example, in a county which was employing a system-wide supervisor for the first time, the principals were uncertain and uneasy as to where the supervisor fitted in. When the superintendent stated directly that the supervisor was not his administrative deputy but a consultant, not a line officer but a staff officer, the principals could see how to proceed to use the supervisor's help.

MAINTAINING THE LONG VIEW.   The superintendent has a unique responsibility for helping his staff see the total picture of the efforts being made. Each supervisor is close to one or more phases of the school program, but the superintendent is in a position to see all aspects of the system. He needs to keep members of the team informed of accomplishments and new developments in the areas outside their own fields and to help keep attention focused on the larger objectives. In turn, supervisors have a responsibility to help the superintendent maintain his sense of direction and his awareness of ultimate values, since superintendents are almost daily subjected to pleas of enthusiasts or pressure groups and to demands for hasty, often expedient, action.

Setting the tone of personal relationships. The superintendent plays a vital part in setting the tone of working relationships in the immediate staff and even throughout the system. His own enthusiasm, energy, and creativity (or lack thereof) tend to shape the image of what others around him expect of themselves. His confidence in co-workers, his resilience and resourcefulness under discouraging circumstances, his ability to handle criticism constructively instead of merely defensively, are all important to the zest and vigor with which those around him carry on their work. Especially significant to the free flow of ideas is his ability to give respectful, appreciative consideration to suggestions, to differ with people while yet maintaining respect, and to help members of the staff have confidence in the integrity and motives of one another even though there are clear differences of opinion among members.

Supervisors help the superintendent. Supervisors, in turn, have certain responsibilities to the superintendent if the working relationship is to have optimum effectiveness and reward. They must plan with the superintendent, not just present a completed plan for his nominal approval. Since the superintendent cannot possibly devote unlimited time to planning with supervisors, plans usually have to be discussed in terms of large goals, general procedures, priorities among activities, and points of possible trouble or disagreement. Details of procedure usually have to be worked out elsewhere.

Supervisors have to keep the superintendent informed regarding developments in instruction: successes, failures, and on-going at-tempts. The superintendent needs to have such information to think clearly himself; but he also needs it promptly in order to prevent embarrassment and the appearance of inefficiency. When citizens, for instance, ask him about the progress of an experimental program in reading instruction in a certain school and he cannot respond, indeed may not even be aware of the experiment, he ap-pears in a poor light. System-wide supervisors and principals need to prepare brief reports for the superintendent on their own activ-ities and on the status of programs, so that he may know the essence of what is underway in instruction. There is no magic, no intel-lectual osmosis, by which he can automatically gain accurate in-formation.

Another way in which supervisors can promote effective working relationships is for them, when in doubt about a responsibility or what is expected of them, to take the initiative and ask. Not infre-quently members of a staff, in all good faith, wait for specific direc-tion in a matter, while the superintendent, absorbed in other con-cerns, remains oblivious to the fact that anyone is awaiting specific instruction or commissioning. When in doubt, a supervisor should take the initiative by making courteous inquiry, and not feel that he is being either aggressive or ignorant.

Still another way in which supervisors can contribute to good working relationships is in connection with public speeches, pub-lications and announcements. Since, ultimately, the superintendent is held responsible for what occurs in the school system, supervisors would want to be sure that whatever they say or write is not only professionally sound in their judgment but also accurately worded and timely from the standpoint of the superintendent. Hence, there may be frequent need for conferring over public statements.

Principals and System-wide Supervisors

Supervisors and principals are allies with a continuing responsibil-ity for instructional leadership. In matters involving the entire sys-tem, supervisors usually carry the initiative; in matters concerning an individual school, the principal usually takes the initiative. Supervisors are the means of a two-way flow of concern and information between the principals and the superintendent or central staff. Supervisors can transmit to the superintendent from the principals their perception of in-school and inter-school problems, and bring to the principals the concerns of the superintendent. Supervisors are often the strategic link in involving principals or their ideas in system-wide instructional planning.

The principal individually, or the entire faculty, usually initiates the request for consultant service, although there may be times when a supervisor volunteers services. In either event, when a supervisor first enters a building, even for a drop-by call to leave requested materials, he stops at the principal's office to confer with him if the principal is available, or leaves word that he is in the building. If the supervisor is present for more than a few minutes or for more than one specific purpose, he plans to confer with the principal again before leaving. It is only when supervisors and principals plan together closely and keep one another well informed as to needs which are developing that much progress can be expected in solving problems.

A faculty sometimes extends to a given supervisor the courtesy of inviting him to attach himself to that school for all social and professional occasions during the year. Then in another year, a different supervisor is invited to "join" the staff. The closer acquaintance and cordial relationships that usually ensue are mutually beneficial.

Supervisors and Teachers

Conferring with individual teachers about classroom situations is usually one of the most satisfying activities in which supervisors engage. They have, with rare exceptions, had extensive classroom experience themselves and know both the rewards and difficulties of working with children. The degree to which the supervisor can feel and transmit his feeling of empathy will have much to do with the warmth and genuineness of his relationship with the teacher.

Some visits will be brief and informal and primarily for the purpose of leaving promised material or obtaining a reaction to a question. Other visits, usually made at the request of the teacher or principal, will be longer and for the purpose of analyzing a problem or carrying forward a project together. In both situations the working relationship needs to be friendly and informal, yet businesslike and purposeful, with a clear sense of moving forward in connection with goals. Supervisors and teachers need to be free enough with one another, too, to share the burden of difficult moments and to share the lift and joy of successful undertakings.

Relationships among Supervisors

As school systems become larger, and especially as education is charged with responsibility for a greater variety of services to children and adults, the problems of coordination among staff members also increase. A system-wide supervisory staff which numbers only a few members can often carry on its planning in a highly informal, although purposeful, manner. In large systems, however, the general and special service supervisors may number from a dozen to more than a hundred. Here the task of planning together becomes a complex undertaking in itself. Whether a staff is large or small, certain factors are significant.

TIME FOR BECOMING INFORMED.   It takes time for members to become informed about the current work of one another. Yet one cannot afford to be ignorant of what the others are doing. Obviously, coordinated planning and real teamwork cannot be going on if some members of the team do not even know what others are attempting to accomplish. If this lack of information exists, it is almost immediately apparent to principals and teachers as they talk with supervisors about system-wide undertakings, and a certain loss of confidence and enthusiasm can scarcely help ensuing. The inference should be plain that if a program being urged by some supervisors isn't worth knowing about by others on the central staff, then it is hardly worth the support and active effort of principals and teachers.

Some of the informing can be done through office memorandums, copies of bulletins and newsletters, and brief reports especially prepared for the staff. Some of it can come informally through normal conversation about what is absorbing the individual's attention. Some of it can come about as supervisors seek one another's help in a project. Some of it has to come intentionally, in time deliberately reserved for staff meetings for the sharing of information.

TIME FOR COORDINATING AND PROJECTING. It takes time for true coordination of planning and for the projecting of general plans far enough into the future so that creative, resourceful thinking can be done. Here again it becomes evident that if people can be explicit about the values involved and the ultimate objectives to be attained, then the specific methods selected for reaching way-stations can be varied and numerous. Furthermore, procedures chosen can be modified when exigencies occur, without a devastating degree of disorganization. As indicated earlier, a traveler who has a clear destination can make even lengthy detours without anxiety or fear of being seriously lost.

Supervisors can supplement one another's efforts. The general supervisor and the physical education coordinator, for instance, can often expedite each other's work. This supplementing can be achieved to an optimum degree only when carefully and imaginatively anticipated. Hence time to think together is essential to coordination of effort. Staff members should not feel guilty or apologetic when they take designated mornings, afternoons, or days in the month from "being in the schools," in order to plan together as a system-wide group of supervisors.

One aspect of well-coordinated planning involves the wise use of time in the schools, not only with regard to clear purposes and preplanning with the faculty, but also with regard to avoiding the chagrin of unintended duplicate timing of visits from the system-wide staff. When several supervisors find themselves at the same school and each expresses surprise at seeing the others, an impression of poor planning and information-sharing is created, even though presence of each one was requested by the school in relation to legitimate needs. Indeed, there may be times when a large staff feels that it needs a choreographer to keep its members moving in relation to one another and in relation to the total design of their work. Permenter provides a helpful description of how one large staff (Montgomery County, Maryland) organizes for work.[1]

TIME FOR INDIVIDUAL PLANNING.   Instructional leaders also need to take time for individual planning and projecting of work. Without some time for quiet looking back and looking forward, with a careful analysis of what is occupying his attention, a leader can easily lose balance and proportion in his work. He finds himself pushed first one way and then another by the exigencies that almost hourly arise in a school day. Building principals often report that in daily practice it is difficult to keep the immediacy of the administrative phases of their work, such as internal accounting, plant maintenance, and ordering of supplies from absorbing their time and energy to the point that leadership in instructional advance becomes a wistful dream. System-wide supervisors too are bombarded with unexpected assignments and sudden calls for help. But if an instructional leader has taken time to formulate a well-balanced plan and has made clear commitments to himself and others, he is not likely to be blown very far off course by the winds of chance and he can soon resume his intended direction.

MUTUAL SUPPORT AND SATISFACTION.   It is clear that members of a system-wide staff need to work together with the greatest possible respect for one another. It is primarily when they are mutually supportive and open to one another's thinking that they can, individually or collectively, be at their best in creativity and vigor. Persons who feel defensive with one another and suspicious of motives

---

[1] John A. Permenter, "Who Does What in Instructional Supervision?" *Educational Leadership*, Vol. 16, No. 8 (May, 1959), pp. 480–484.

seldom can think together resourcefully or venturously with regard either to the school program or to their own roles in the planning.

It should also be clear that supervisors need to give expression occasionally to their satisfaction in working together and to their respect for one another's judgments, accomplishments, and ways of work. In the press of daily activities it is very simple to let warming words of recognition of worth and of appreciation go unexpressed. To work daily in a situation where mutual trust and confidence are high is one of the most rewarding of human experiences and is one of the sustaining satisfactions in supervision.

82942

KNOWLEDGE OF THE COMMUNITY

Knowledge of the community is also essential to effective planning for supervision. It is not easy for a newcomer to become acquainted with the many facets of community life which have significance for supervision, but it is perhaps even harder for a person who has grown up in a community to become aware of the extremely familiar, of the many things he assumes to be universal, and of those things which he takes for granted.

An instructional leader needs to be familiar with the economic bases of the community, the historical and other factors which led to its early settlement and later development, the general political structure of the city government, and the relationship of the city to the county and state governments. The social organization of the community, the degree of participation of churches and of civic clubs in community life, and awareness of those people and agencies that especially influence people's thinking are also important.

As an instructional leader studies a community he would want to note the persons, places, and organizations that constitute useful resources for teaching. He can assist numbers of teachers with the ideas thus gained. He would also want to note the variety of situations which exist in the different school centers in the community.

All schools would have as their goal, for instance, the improvement of oral and written expression of the children and youth, but among the schools there might be distinct differences as to what constitutes the next needs of the students as to oral language usage patterns and out-of-school demands for writing.

Another kind of variety to be noted by instructional leaders is the basis for there being more than one *public* when matters of public opinion are concerned. Many times educators, along with others, discuss public opinion as though it were a singular rather than a plural affair. In reality the different segments of a community may see quite different qualities as desirable in a school program, and some persons and groups may find themselves holding conflicting values regarding education and, perhaps, taxation.

Probably one of the most important, and yet subtle, aspects to supervision is the prevailing temper or atmosphere of the community. Does the community reflect a conservative or a liberal approach to problems? Does it look to the past or to the future? Are the people in the habit of taking cooperative action about civic problems? Do they look within or always outside for help? How do people express their interests, grumblingly or constructively? Where would instructional leaders look to find expressions of concern for education?

PROBLEMS OF COMMUNICATION

Essential to good planning is a recognition of the problems of communication. Most of these problems arise from the very nature of communication and not primarily from ill-will or inefficiency on anyone's part. Communication contains more hazard than is commonly assumed. The wonder is not that people fail one another sometimes, but rather that they communicate as clearly as they do most of the time.

There are, to be sure, mechanical problems and a supervisor

should not reckon without the delays they can cause. Broken machines, storms, secretarial absences or misunderstandings, or short-
ages of supplies can cause delays of several days in the sending or
delivering of messages. Mislaid notices and reports, or notices that
fail to arrive, are commonplace.

Another hazard relates to the truism that, "You cannot tell a
child (or adult) what he is not listening to hear." If a person is not
anticipating information about a meeting or project, he is likely to
overlook or disregard a notice, or fail to register its significance sufficiently to reorganize his activities in relation to the notice.

Of still greater significance is the difficulty inherent in the nature
of language itself. A word, at best, is a shorthand symbol for a whole
host of previous experiences and feelings. The same symbol is sure
to have slightly different referents (sometimes drastically different)
for different people. An individual has to hear or read through a
screen of his own past experiences. He has no choice; he cannot do
otherwise. Therefore the possibility of divergent understandings is
ever present. 371.2

Instructional leaders who have a healthy respect for the normal
difficulties of communication allow extra time for the clearance of
messages, review their letters and reports for points of ambiguity,
or for unlikely but possible angles of perception. They verify crucial
arrangements or understandings with the persons directly involved.
They also need to be ready to accept with as much poise and humor
as possible the inevitable misadventures that occur.   S w e

AIDS TO STUDY AND DISCUSSION

1. Keep a record for two days of decisions made in classroom situations. Then try to analyze the basis for the decisions. Were
   choices made out of habit? Were there alternatives? Was any
   imagination involved? Were possible results anticipated? Were
   there any moments of "calculated risk"? Could another person
   have helped you think through the problem?

2. Consult a book on semantics or language, such as Hayakawa's *Language in Action* or Walpole's *Semantics, The Nature of Words and Their Meaning*, and report to the class some of your findings regarding the difficulties of clear communication.

3. Consult several books on language or speech, and be ready to share with the class some examples of the way human beings communicate feelings and attitudes, often unwittingly, through voice tone, gesture, postures, and head movements. For instructional leaders, what is the significance of this kind of communication? (See Hall, *The Silent Language*.)

SUGGESTIONS FOR FURTHER READING

Adams, Harold P., and Frank G. Dickey, *Basic Principles of Supervision* (New York: American Book Company, 1953), especially Chapter 4, "Planning for Supervision," and Chapter 5, "Developing the Supervisory Program."

American Association of School Administrators, *The Superintendent as Instructional Leader*, 35th Yearbook (Washington, D.C.: National Education Association, 1957).

Burton, William H., and Leo J. Brueckner, *Supervision: A Social Process*, 3rd Ed. (New York: Appleton-Century-Crofts, Inc., 1955), especially Part I, "Definition and Organization of Modern Supervision."

Edwards, W. T., "Charting the Supervisory Course," *Educational Leadership*, Vol. 4, No. 8 (May, 1947).

Hall, Edward T., *The Silent Language* (Garden City, N.Y.: Doubleday & Company, Inc., 1959).

Hammock, Robert C., and Ralph S. Owings, *Supervising Instruction in Secondary Schools* (New York: McGraw-Hill Book Co., Inc., 1955).

Haskew, Laurence D., "The Principal's Role in Instructional Improvement," *The National Elementary Principal*, Vol. 35, No. 7 (May, 1956).

Language and Concepts in Education, Edited by Othanel Smith and Robert H. Ennis (Chicago: Rand McNally & Co., 1961).

Melchior, William T., *Instructional Supervision* (Boston: D. C. Heath & Company, 1950).

Permenter, John A., "Who Does What in Instructional Supervision?" *Educational Leadership*, Vol. XVI, No. 8 (May, 1959).

Reeder, Edwin H., *Supervision in the Elementary School* (Boston: Houghton Mifflin Company, 1953).

Thompson, Ethel, "So Begins—So Ends the Supervisor's Day," *Educational Leadership*, Vol. X, No. 3 (November, 1952).

CHAPTER 6

SUPERVISORY ACTIVITIES: WAYS OF WORKING

THE role of supervision in educational advancement has been indicated, the values and conditions giving rise to supervision have been explored, the major functions of supervision have been delineated, and certain aspects of democratic planning have been described. A consideration of the choice of activities for reaching overarching goals is now essential. Numerous possibilities for actions and demands for attention abound in almost every educational setting. What activities are chosen and how they are carried out will influence not only the amount of forward advance, but also the creativity, zest, and satisfaction with which people work and live.

Eight major functions of supervision are discernible: coordination of efforts, provision of leadership, extension of experience, stimulation of creative effort, facilitating and evaluating change, analysis of learning situations, contributing to a body of knowledge and techniques, and integration of goals. These functions are omnipresent. They also constitute a set of criteria for choosing among the abundance of possible ways of using supervisory time and effort. If a proposed activity contributes to the achievement of one or several of these purposes, there is good reason to include the activity; if, at the same time, the proposed activity can be seen in relation to other selected ways and means of working, there is reason to assign it high priority and to expect maximum impact from it. When activities are seen in relation to one another and as contributors to the same ultimate purposes, it is also often possible to work out a kind of rhythm or pacing among activities, so that all facets of a program are served, but without apprehension regarding equality of time and energy among them.

In this and the succeeding two chapters, ten activities commonly used by supervisors, or types of responsibilities assumed by them, are set forth. For each one there is a description of: (1) the purposes which it serves especially well; (2) some of the operational principles or procedures which may enhance the cooperative effort, individual initiative and creativity, and sense of satisfaction; and (3) some of the frequently used variations of that form of activity.

LARGE GROUP MEETINGS

Large group meetings are called for many purposes, frequently out of administrative need. Sometimes the same large meeting serves both administrative and instructional purposes, in which case it is a truism that the administrative matters must be handled with unusual dispatch or they will engulf the entire meeting. Many faculty-wide or system-wide meetings are called primarily for the purpose of informing people about events that have occurred or are about to occur, as when a principal, superintendent, or supervisor at the beginning of a new term describes developments which will influence instruction. This gaining of information is an essential step, of course, in cooperative effort. Cooperation in a democratic school situation assumes a well informed body of peers who can formulate judgments on the basis of values and relevant facts.

Hence the importance of becoming well informed should not be belittled, nor the time for doing so granted grudgingly.

A second purpose, closely related to becoming informed, concerns those large group meetings which help create a common background of experience. When an unusually forceful or provocative speaker, or an unusually entertaining one, addresses a large group, he does more than provide information, important as that information may be. He also evokes a feeling reaction from the group. If the feeling reaction is a common one, the group often achieves a high sense of solidarity and united purpose. Even where reactions are diverse in nature and the amount of feeling varied in degree, the members of a large group now have something in common that they did not have before: namely, the undergoing of an event together, even though each one experienced the situation somewhat differently. Thus, when the faculties of an entire school system hear an effective speaker in one of the sessions of a pre-school conference, the members of the system have at least one common reference point for the year, both in the information he provides and in the feeling he arouses. The so-called "common experience" or common background of experience lays a basis for some cohesiveness of feeling in subsequent situations in being members of the same family or group.

A third purpose served especially well by large group meetings is the fundamental matter of the transaction of business which concerns the professional, and sometimes personal, living of the members of the group. The large group meeting gives the opportunity to receive reports from investigating and study committees, to make decisions and formulate policies officially if the subject under consideration is within the province of the group for action, and to empower small committees to undertake studies. In both the initial and culminating phases of a particular program or project, the large group plays a crucial part even though most of the fact-finding for tentative formulation of choices is carried on through sub-committees. A large faculty, for instance, or an entire school system engaging in an appraisal of its ways and means of meeting individual differences among learners would want to initiate a large scale study only after the total group had considered the project, had expressed genuine concern or interest, and had had a chance to suggest procedures for conducting the study. During the study, progress reports would be made to the total group for information of the members, and for needed re-direction to sub-committees; at the conclusion, appropriate action would be taken by the entire group.

A fourth purpose for large group meetings is to give opportunity for members who typically are at work in separate rooms, buildings or communities to see one another and to feel their united strength. The opportunity to be together should actually be a highly valued one, for it enables people to interact, to think together, to discover their common concerns, to find their areas of agreement and disagreement, to broaden horizons, and to take constructive action. The ultimate action taken often becomes the realization of the evolving aspirations and dreams of the contributing individuals, most of which could not have been realized fully by individuals working separately. Murphy regards man's capacity for cooperative action as one of his great and unique attributes.[1] Fromm also regards man's need for union with others as a basic part of his nature, and the fulfillment of this need as necessary both to his sanity and to the realization of his humanness.[2] When human beings can work together constructively, they live with greater zest and satisfaction. Therefore, supervision renders a genuine service when it creates needed opportunities for people to work together productively.

Working Principles

Since the large group meeting is of great significance from the standpoint of individual fulfillment and satisfaction, as well as from the standpoint of expediting the cooperative efforts of large numbers of people, it is well for supervisors (coordinators, principals or

[1] Gardner Murphy, *Human Potentialities* (New York: Basic Books, Inc., 1958).
[2] Eric Fromm, *The Sane Society* (New York: Rinehart & Company, Inc., 1955).

instructional leaders by whatever name) to give thought to procedures and factors that may help or hinder the progress of the meeting. Instructional leaders constantly find themselves in strategic
positions regarding the planning and conducting of meetings, sometimes because they are responsible for initiating the meeting, and
sometimes because their advice is sought by chairmen of program
committees charged with making arrangements for meetings. Experienced supervisors have found it helpful to consider the following
factors:

CLARITY OF PURPOSE.   Be sure the purpose of the meeting is clear
to all who attend. The purpose may be quite clear to the planners
of the session, but not made explicit for those invited. If the purpose is derived from expressed needs of teachers, let the fact be
known. To understand the immediate background or provocation
for a meeting often gives significance to the session. The relation of
a particular meeting to other activities often needs to be pointed
out. School personnel are busy people, and unless the purpose of a
meeting is clear and valid, participants arrive reluctantly, even re-
sistantly, instead of enthusiastically seeing in the meeting a chance
to move toward desired goals.

NOTICES FOR MEETINGS.   Unless the meeting has been included in
the annual school calendar, notices should be sent well in advance
of the session. The notice should, of course, give the vital statistics
of the meeting as to place, date and hour, including the probable
time of dismissal, so that individuals can plan efficiently for their
other personal and professional activities. While a notice needs to
be concise, since it will usually be read by busy people, it should be
full enough to indicate the scope and specific purpose of the meeting. Persons who come to a meeting with a clear expectation of the
subject to be discussed and with relevant experiences in mind are
likely to be constructive participants. Notices, although concise,
need to be phrased in a personalized and friendly manner. Conciseness that merges into curtness is costly in human energy in a subtle
way. Abruptness in a notice causes the recipient to feel slightly

jolted or shoved, and his natural reaction is one of irritation with the writer or meeting. Hence the emotional tone he brings to the session tends to be a depressing one of annoyance, rather than an accelerating one of positive concern for the subject.

MECHANICS OF THE MEETING. The mechanics of a large group meeting deserve attention both before and during a session. While smoothly operating mechanical aspects of a meeting will not assure its success, it is often true that an otherwise well-planned meeting does not achieve its potential because attendant factors mar the situation. Consequently, human satisfaction in a meeting is lessened, and the zest for like meetings in the future is decreased rather than increased. Therefore supervisors should feel that their time is well spent when they pave the way for smooth-running meetings. (Some few supervisors may have to guard themselves against an over-weening concern for small details. The major factor in the success of any meeting is the vitality of its purpose. If the purpose is high, then it does not matter much whether there is one too many chairs on the platform or the potted palms are symmetrically placed, although a rasping loud-speaker system or glaring lights would make a difference.)

Matters of heating, lighting, ventilation, air-conditioning, noise, and seating of latecomers should be noted. While the meeting is in progress, it is well for someone other than the presiding officer or group leader to be specifically responsible for adjustment in such factors, since the leader is preoccupied with other concerns, and most participants would hesitate to take the initiative, at least until a condition had become extremely uncomfortable or distracting. If loud-speaker equipment, stage lights, or audio-visual materials are involved, the necessary technical help should be secured well in advance. If the meeting place is unfamiliar to him, the supervisor should make a preliminary visit to investigate the conditions of cleanliness, appropriateness, and appearance. Where a very large meeting is concerned, he should check on such affairs as parking space and nearby eating facilities.

Once the advance arrangements have been made and responsibility delegated for the conditions during the meeting, then the leader should try to relax and not exhaust himself with a constant mental rehearsal of details. Actually, helping with the conducting of meetings is one of the most practical and constructive ways of inducting additional personnel into some of the responsibilities of leadership. Many a participant in large group meetings has had no occasion to take note of the management of a session until he himself carries some responsibility for a small phase of it. Through helping with first one phase and then another, he can grow in experience, appreciation and skill.

When things of a mechanical nature go wrong, it is often well to share the reasons with the group. Humor, as well as knowing the reason, may help relieve tension resulting from delays and blunders. For instance, if the main speaker's plane is still circling the airport ten minutes before he is to appear on the program, the leader might well take the group into his confidence while he replans the order of the program, and even laughs over the incongruities of the situation.

PRESIDING OFFICERS.   The success of a meeting, and especially the current satisfaction people feel in having attended the session, are greatly enhanced if the presiding officers are competent and relaxed. If the person in charge is uncertain and tense, some of his nervousness is communicated to the group. Some participants begin to feel nervous along with the leader and hence less free, perceptive, and receptive toward the speaker and toward one another. In large group situations where discussion is involved, the serenity, poise, humor, and quickness of perception of the leader are positive forces in helping members of the group communicate with one another to the point that they can really formulate ideas together and evolve policies. Ideally, where formal decision-making is involved, the presiding officer should know parliamentary procedure so thoroughly that he not only can use it efficiently and comfortably, but also can use it as a positive, intentional means of facilitating the intricate, difficult process of group decision-making.

Instructional leaders need to develop their own skills as presiding officers, for they are often called upon to serve in that capacity, sometimes with little or no warning. Fully as important, however, is the responsibility of instructional leaders for providing opportunities for others to cultivate the skills essential for leading large group meetings. If supervisors and principals are watchful, they can usually help a number of teachers start with small responsibilities in meetings, and move along a ramp of experiences to the competency, graciousness, and even artistry of an excellent presiding officer.

VARIETY IN LONG MEETINGS.   When group members have driven long distances to attend the meeting, economical use of time and energy demands that as much as possible be attempted within the session or day, since the expense of repeated drives is prohibitive. The tendency is to crowd many activities into one day. Many things can actually be accomplished in one day, without a sense of crowding and undue fatigue, if several vital factors are observed.

Member involvement is essential. To listen continuously without opportunity to react in a discussion period, buzz session, or informally over coffee cups, produces a kind of brain numbness before the end of the day. *Pacing* or varying the kind of activity is another essential. A dynamic, emotion-arousing speaker, for instance, should not be followed immediately by another speaker of the same kind. *Continuity* in the activities needs to be apparent, and can often be seen clearly in the statements and titles on a printed or mimeographed program. Coffee and lunch intermissions should be brief enough that forward momentum is not lost. The factors just mentioned are achieved primarily through careful pre-planning. Since instructional leaders usually participate in the advance planning for large group meetings, they carry a big responsibility at this point for the successful arrangements for the day's meeting.

EVIDENCE OF COOPERATIVE PLANNING.   Large group meetings are usually the product of the planning of many persons over an extended period of time. Yet for every one who participated in the planning directly, there may be ten or more who had no contact with the evolving plans. Therefore, it is worth some effort to let the participants know the extent of the cooperative planning, lest some individuals assume that key decisions were made arbitrarily by one or a few persons. If the meeting is the outgrowth of needs originally expressed by individuals or sub-groups in the school system, let it be said explicitly. The presiding officer, in opening the session, can usually sketch briefly the reason for the meeting, the selection of topics for study, and the kind of cooperative planning that has gone on. In recognizing and thanking various working committees, the presiding officer can not only express the gratitude of the group, but also show something of the structure and extent of the planning necessitated by the large meeting, something to which many participants remain oblivious.

FOLLOW-THROUGH.   It is clear that much of the effectiveness of a large group meeting will be lost unless there is follow-through on all significant agreements reached, and the persons involved know that tasks or assignments have been completed. Here instructional leaders usually have a large responsibility. They are often the ones charged with transmitting reports and recommendations, or in some way following through on actions taken by the group. Sometimes others have the technical responsibility, but the supervisor assists in the mechanics of discharging the responsibility. A short progress report to the participants a few days or weeks later, a single page often sufficing, lets people become aware of what their cooperative effort achieved, and forestalls feelings of futility or disappointment.

Types of Meetings in Frequent Use

Three types of group meetings are in such frequent use as to warrant special attention. They are pre-school and post-school meetings, workshops, and curriculum councils.

PRE-SCHOOL AND POST-SCHOOL MEETINGS.   One of the encouraging developments of the last two decades has been the increasing recognition on the part of communities and school boards of the significance of teachers having time for professional planning within the scope of a normal school year. Many school boards now employ teachers for periods when pupils are not present, varying in length from a few days to a whole month or more. A considerable portion of this time is devoted to system-wide or school-wide planning, for it is also recognized that professional planning involves a large measure of cooperative effort. A good school program is not achieved merely by adding separate classrooms together. Hence teachers must have time together to plan, if there is to be a truly coordinated program.

Instructional leaders are usually charged by the superintendent with the specific responsibility for pre-school and post-school planning. While part of the time is reserved for administrative needs, the major portion of the time is regarded as the opportunity par excellence for system-wide and school-wide instructional planning. At least four points in connection with pre-school and post-school sessions are worth observing.

Long-range nature of the planning. Successful pre-school sessions are planned long in advance, usually in the spring before the fall session. It takes time to secure effective speakers and to prepare materials for distribution. More important still, it takes time prior to the selection of speakers, for planning committees composed of teacher-representatives and others to meet, develop tentative plans, confer with the groups they represent, and refine plans.

A broad base for planning. Detecting the real concerns of teachers, and choosing topics and experiences around recognized needs, are usually essential aspects of successful pre-school and post-school planning. Hence the broader the participation by teachers, the greater is the chance for finding the vital, crucial concerns. Even where direct teacher participation is extensive, individuals may need to make building or area surveys to get at the scope and depth of interests. If pre-school and post-school sessions are planned in a sequence for several years, there can be balance, concentration, and a cumulative effect.

Variety in place and type of sessions. Where the size of the group to be accommodated permits, it is often helpful to vary the place and style of meetings. Being in different schools in different parts of a city or county can be educative in itself. Some faculties have enjoyed the benefits of a retreat to mountain or seaside resorts and camps for the giving of concentrated attention to professional planning.

Protection of time for individual planning. Sometimes the opportunity for large group work in pre-school and post-school session has been embraced so enthusiastically that there has been little time left for teachers to do individual planning or work in their own classrooms. It takes time to plan for incorporating new perceptions, new research findings, and new materials into classroom procedures, and perhaps change long-standing habits. Program-planning committees would do well to protect a generous amount of time for individual work.

Wide use of extensive periods of pre- and post-school planning is a relatively new venture in the improvement of instruction, but enough experience has already been obtained to yield valuable suggestions for further work. Reports from specific school systems, such as contained in *Extending the School Year*, reflect procedures that have been found successful in actual practice.[3]

WORKSHOPS. Another type of large group meeting for which supervisors have responsibility is the workshop. While the term is freely used, and sometimes carelessly used, the workshop does have certain emphases which give it uniqueness among meetings. It may be of almost any length, from a few concentrated hours to several weeks, and it may involve a few persons or several hundred. But if it has the following features, it is usually identified as a workshop: (1) The participants have a genuine conscious concern for the problem or subject under study; often they have initiated the request that the problem be studied. (2) The participants bring relevant

---

[3] Association for Supervision and Curriculum Development, *Extending the School Year* (Washington, D.C.: National Education Association, 1961).

prior experience and knowledge to the sessions; they expect to learn from consultants and also from fellow members, and to contribute from their own thinking. (3) The participants involve themselves deeply in varied activities of the session, and what the individual undergoes gives him new skills or understandings which he can use soon in his own situation.

Kelley has summarized pertinent ideas regarding the principles and purposes of workshops as follows:

Principles

1. The most important thing about any person is his attitude toward other people.
2. The primary need in the building of people is to learn better human relations.
3. Every individual has worth, and has a contribution to make to the common good.
4. Learning leads to more learning and the human organism is infinitely curious.
5. The most crucial learning at any given time has to do with the individual's current problems.
6. Cooperation as a technique and as a way of life is superior to competition.

Purposes

1. We want to put teachers in situations that will break down the barriers between them so that they can more readily communicate.
2. We want to give teachers an opportunity for personal growth through accepting and working toward a goal held in common with others.
3. We want to give teachers an opportunity to work on the problems that are of direct, current concern to them.
4. We want to place teachers in a position of responsibility for their own learning.
5. We want to give teachers experience in a cooperative undertaking.
6. We want teachers to learn methods and techniques which they can use in their own classrooms.

7. We want teachers to have an opportunity in collaboration with others, to produce materials that will be useful in their teaching.
8. We want teachers to be put in a situation where they will evaluate their own efforts.
9. We want to give teachers an opportunity to improve their own morale.[4]

A particularly interesting facet of workshops is the high degree of impact they have upon subsequent actions of the people who have participated. A comment offered half-humorously and half-seriously by persons who serve as consultants for workshops is that "You better be careful what you advise in a workshop; somebody will go do it." A study of the elementary school principalship included a question on the source of new ideas in experimentation. Two qualifications were placed upon the question as to the source of new ideas: one was that the idea resulted in a change in action, and the second was that the change had taken place in the past three years. The principal was asked to mark one among six possible choices as his main source. The replies showed the following in descending order:

Conferences or workshops
Contacts with other principals and teachers
Administrative or supervisory personnel
Professional reading
Parents or other community contacts
College courses [5]

Perhaps in the light of what is known about adult motivation, it should be no cause for surprise that workshops make a difference in what people do. Two vital factors are present: high awareness of purpose to start with, and close involvement throughout the workshop. Supervisors should count their time well spent when they

---

[4] Earl Kelley, *The Workshop Way of Learning* (New York: Harper & Brothers, 1951), pp. 4–11.

[5] *The Elementary School Principalship—A Research Study*. Yearbook, National Elementary Principal, 1958 (Washington, D.C.: National Education Association, 1958), p. 23.

engage in the careful pre-planning needed for workshops, and in the countless activities related to conducting them.

CURRICULUM COUNCILS.   A third type of large group meeting is the curriculum council. In some cases the curriculum council may be a small group, but in school systems of any size, the membership may run to a hundred or even several hundred. Perhaps the major purpose of a curriculum council may be stated as that of giving faculties a recognized *continuing* channel or round-table for communicating about curriculum development and the improvement of instruction. In a large school system it is scarcely expected that curriculum development would move forward on an even front, but unless schools plan with one another and keep one another informed of innovations and efforts, disharmony, contradictions, and misunderstandings can easily occur.

Curriculum councils are usually constituted of representatives from each school. These representatives are in a strategic position to bring problems and concerns *from* faculties to a central place where cooperative action can be devised, and to take recommendations *to* the faculties regarding curriculum needs and proposals. For details of the organization and functions of a curriculum council in a large system (Pinellas County, Florida), see Appendix B, where excerpts from the council's statement of purposes and structure are included.

Curriculum councils are often the first place for the discussion of new proposals, the detecting of emerging needs, the formulating of recommendations, and the giving voice to felt needs in such a considered way that school boards and superintendents can know what is desired or can take appropriate action. Curriculum councils can also be helpful in making fact-finding investigations related to curriculum. Members of the council may be the first to feel the need for certain kinds of information. The council may also be responsible for instigating research projects or collaborating with others in conducting research.

Again, instructional leaders who spend time, effort, and imagination in helping develop a curriculum council should feel that their energy is well invested.

SMALL GROUP AND COMMITTEE MEETINGS

The distinction as to size between a large and a small group is not a sharp one, although the small group rarely exceeds 20 to 25 persons. The important distinction lies in the greater degree of participation and direct involvement that is possible for members of a small group. Almost constant interaction can occur among members, as well as between designated leaders and members. Since the individuals are usually seated in a semicircle or around a table, eye contact can be maintained, and facial expression and posture can therefore aid in communication. If an attitude of good will and intent to understand is also present, then communication is at its peak, and fluency of thinking is evoked and enhanced.

Small groups or committees are usually formed within a faculty or system for a specific purpose. Sometimes the total faculty or large group charges the committee with a specific task of fact-finding or formulation of a policy for recommendation. Sometimes the assignment of responsibility comes from the superintendent or other leader. The task may be a short one accomplished with a few hours' work, after which the committee is dismissed, or it may take several months or years to discharge. It may be a continuing responsibility of a general nature, such as the detecting of emerging needs in secondary education, or a highly specific one such as the assigning of priorities in purchasing instructional aids, in a given semester, from a highly limited budget.

Whatever the charge may be, it is within the small group or committee that certain purposes can be served unusually well. It is here that careful weighing of values can take place, the seeking of evidence that must go into decision-making, the deferring of judgments while evidence is sought, the projecting of solutions to see what the consequences of action might be; in brief, the reaching of mature judgments. In the small group exploratory thinking can be welcomed and imaginative ideas considered. It is characteristic of creative work that closure must not come too soon, lest subsequent good ideas or variations of first ideas be denied a chance to come into existence. The small group is usually the place to get out new thinking, and for individuals to present cherished ideas and to respond to one another spontaneously. Since the degree of personal involvement is high, and the emergence of ideas a delicate affair, human relations and communication need to be at their best. Hence instructional leaders find it productive to plan carefully for committee or small group meetings.

Working Principles

Most of the observations made about large group meetings (clarity of purpose, notices, mechanics, presiding officers, variety, evidence of cooperative planning, and follow-through) are also relevant to committee and small group work. In addition, there are at least three major considerations.

ARRANGEMENTS.   Since a sense of freedom, latitude, and informality is usually conducive to constructive thinking (especially exploratory thinking), the physical setting for a meeting has significance. Seating arrangements that permit members to see as well as hear one another easily are helpful. Relative freedom from noise and from interruptions from telephone calls or messages for individuals is desirable. Advance, quiet arrangements for simple refreshments before, during, or after an extended meeting can be helpful. Friendliness, sometimes evidenced in the use of first names, and positive expressions of confidence in co-workers and in the worth of the project at hand are extremely important. Leaders and participants who can be articulate about their sincere faith in human capacities to deal with problems often render a tremendous though subtle service to the quality of thinking in a group, for many people are thereby released to become open to one another and open to their own relevant experiences.

FORMULATION OF THE COMMITTEE. The members of committees are sometimes appointed or elected formally, and other times are named swiftly, almost casually, by a leader. Appointment by a superintendent or head of a large system, whether a city, county, or state unit, carries a certain dignity or prestige. Election by a group has its own important kind of authority or validity. Sometimes members are nominated by a local leader and appointed by a county or state official. In any event, members of a small group usually have a representative function: i.e., they are standing for a larger group; hence time must be planned for members to communicate, to take ideas to and from their groups. The pressure for immediate action is sometimes so great that it is hard for a committee to form its plans to take this representative function into account.

When a commitee meets for the first time, the leader needs to plan for the unhurried introduction of each member, unless all members are extremely well known to one another. The introduction may be made by the individual himself, by the leader, or by someone designated by the leader who has had an opportunity to know the persons or their backgrounds previously, such as the supervisor. The introduction should be full enough to give some idea as to why each person is well qualified to serve on the committee working with the current problem. This knowledge is actually the basis for the confidence in one another so necessary to group action, and which was just described.

TIME FOR MEETINGS. The typical committee has to meet rather frequently in order to discharge its functions; therefore, arranging adequate and appropriate time for meetings is a persistent problem. Many plans and combinations of ideas are in use. Some schools have an early dismissal hour for pupils on certain afternoons in the month, dates being regularly scheduled and made known to all concerned, including parents, through the school calendar or other means. The time thus obtained is reserved for large group meetings on some dates, and small group work on others. Some schools arrange a partial release of teacher-time during class hours by having a few substitutes available for designated periods. Frequently committee work is carried on in the limited time just before and after the pupils are present.

A new attitude toward work to be done when pupils are not present is in the process of developing, both inside and outside the teaching profession. Just as the public has come to realize that much of the significant work in banks has to go on when the customers are not there, so it is that communities increasingly realize that teachers have much to do that cannot be done while the pupils are there. Meanwhile, the professional nature of teaching, i.e., primarily judgments being involved rather than repetitive routines, is more apparent both to teachers themselves and to lay people. Many school boards, and even some entire state systems, have already recognized the need for time for professional planning by teachers, and have provided the "tenth month" or its equivalent for individual and cooperative work. Rochester, Minnesota is representative of school systems which have developed extensive and varied summer programs of learning opportunities for teachers.[6]

As changes produced by technological advances and by better understanding of the learning processes accelerate, the need for personal adaptation and for curriculum revision also increases. The time needed for making change, much of which will be accomplished in small group work, should be regarded by teachers and public alike as a normal expectation of professional work.

Types of Small Group and Committee Meetings

There are many types of small group meetings, most of which are so familiar as to need little elaboration, but it is well for supervisors to be aware of the variety of small group sessions which can be helpful, and also aware of the possibility of improvising still other forms. Probably the most frequently formulated committee is one chosen *within a single faculty*, with grade level, subject matter, or special interest being the basis of selection. *Inter-school* committees serve many purposes in large school systems, as well as

[6] *Ibid.*, pp. 39–45.

system-wide groups. There are also many *state-wide* committees, such as Curriculum or Courses of Study Committees, or Textbook or Teacher Education Advisory Councils. When committees are to be appointed by a state official, he often asks the local or county superintendent for suggestions as to members. The local superintendent, in turn, consults the supervisors and principals as to what persons among the faculties have indicated special interests or abilities that would enable them to make real contributions to the proposed committees. For this reason, among others, instructional leaders need to be familiar with the concerns and work of individual teachers.

Small group activity is an important phase of work within and among professional organizations and community agencies. Here a steering committee, coordinating council, or clearing center is important, and the liaison and representative functions of supervision are again especially significant.

INDIVIDUAL CONFERENCES

Individual conferences, which for the purpose of this discussion include classroom visits, constitute one of the most immediately fruitful and rewarding activities of supervision. One of the major purposes served especially well by this form of activity is the knowing first-hand about the learning situation for children. During a classroom visit when pupils are present, or an individual conference with the teacher in the room when students are not present, the instructional leader can become aware directly of such important factors as: (1) the physical setting, with its particular advantages and limitations; (2) the materials the students and teachers have to work with; (3) something of the scope of work attempted and the ways of organizing for work; (4) the experience background and language facility of the pupils; and (5) something of the rapport with one another and with the teacher.

A second important purpose is served in ascertaining what specific help is needed by the teacher. The help needed may be in the direction of developing still further a good idea already under way; it may be the detecting of a distracting factor which had gone unnoticed by those enmeshed in the situation, but which is visible to another person; or it may be in the discerning and overcoming of a deficiency in materials, information, or approach on the part of the teacher.

A third purpose is found in the opportunity for encouragement of experimental work. It is usually difficult for an individual teacher to carry on experimental work in a strictly go-it-alone situation. Through the individual conference, teacher and principal or teacher and supervisor can often devise, carry out, and evaluate ideas that could not have been accomplished by one person alone.

A fourth purpose served is that of permitting two people to become genuinely acquainted. As they discuss and analyze problems and follow natural by-ways of conversation which open up, the two persons who are engaged in an unhurried conference discover their common concerns and values, comparable experiences from the past, and common interests for the future. They have a chance to find each other's present and potential strong points, and to build a foundation for mutual respect.

Working Principles

Considerable experience with individual conferences as a way of work has led to observations about effective procedures. Some are positive findings and some are cautions.

SPECIFIC PURPOSE AND OCCASION.   The individual conference, especially the classroom visit, needs to have a specific purpose. When the supervisor comes on invitation of the teacher, the outcome is usually high. The teacher's purpose may be to have the supervisor see a particular phase of work, analyze a learning problem, or watch a certain child's reactions. The purpose may also be that of securing the supervisor's help in initiating or carrying forward an activity new to the teacher, as when an art supervisor is asked to introduce a new medium of expression, or a music supervisor helps carry on two-part singing that had been introduced recently. Not only is the teacher ready for help, since he is the one who has requested the conference; the supervisor knows in advance what is wanted from him, and he can therefore marshall his resources effectively.

MATERIALS AS BRIDGES. Bringing instructional materials to the classroom or conference can often serve as a bridge which is appreciated by an instructional leader and teacher alike. The material constitutes something objective and impersonal to talk about; it is relevant to some phase of the instruction but is not, yet at least, the source of defensive feelings on the part of the teacher. It has promise of helpfulness and therefore has a positive quality. It also offers finiteness for concluding the conference or visit: that is, when the material has been delivered and commented upon, there is sufficient reason for either party to terminate the conference in a natural manner. Yet if conditions of time and interest warrant continuing the conversation, one relevant idea can lead to another until profound insights are reached. Hence materials often become the springboard for broadening, constructive discussions.

DISCRIMINATING PRAISE. It is usually in the individual conference that the supervisor has his best opportunity to express his awareness of and admiration for excellence of work on the part of the teacher. Human beings vary widely in their reactions to praise, with some individuals being almost instantly embarrassed, suspicious of hidden motives, or fearful of flattery, especially if the praise is offered in front of other people where personal or professional jealousy might ensue. Supervisors need to be sensitive to the recipient's response to praise, and control future statements accordingly.

Instructional leaders, being human too, vary in their ways of expressing approval, and have a right to individuality on their part. However, effusiveness even from a highly spontaneous and articulate person is scarcely defensible. Usually a simple statement which recognizes the genuine worth of a piece of work, or the skill and judgment involved in accomplishing it, conveys approval with greatest sincerity.

Perhaps two phases of the significance of expressing discriminating praise need to be mentioned. One relates to the fact that expressions of approval by his peers and status leaders enter into an individual's self-expectations and become one factor in his continuously evolving self-concept. To know that others found his judgments sound in past ventures gives the individual courage and confidence to keep on trying and to risk himself in new ventures. The second relates to the fact that the pace of modern living tends to crowd out not only moments of graciousness in human relations, but even the moment it takes to attest that the worth of an accomplishment is recognized and valued. Professional life should not be lived at such a rate that there is no time to give expression to awareness of worth.

System-wide supervisors and building principals are typically in the best position to express approval of excellent professional work. Parents, children, and superintendents may indeed express their satisfaction with the outcomes of a teacher's efforts, and this expression is highly important. But usually only the principal and supervisor have both the background of professional understanding and the knowledge of immediate factors which enable them to be sensitive to the nuances and delicate decisions which distinguish between excellent and mediocre choices on the part of teachers in a given situation. Discriminating praise thus provided by instructional leaders can be a vital and sustaining force.

Too great dependence on approval of others can, of course, become an enervating factor. Neither teachers, nor any other kind of professional worker, should expect approval of every move made. Persons who are well prepared professionally have to develop a considerable degree of sturdy confidence in their own judgments and their ability to accept consequences of actions. On the whole, however, probably too few rather than too many, words of approval and recognition are spoken in professional circles. One wonders whether this lack of expressed approval and confidence in one another may not contribute to the ease with which petty jealousies and hurt feelings occur. People who have a backlog of confidence in themselves and in one another are less likely to resist change, to perceive suggestions as threatening, or to feel defensive. Furthermore, society is the ultimate loser when individuals underestimate themselves and hesitate to trust themselves in new ventures.

SCHEDULING THE CONFERENCE. The individual conference is perhaps most often scheduled at the request of the teacher. It is also, however, frequently scheduled at the request of the instructional leader, as when a system-wide supervisor plans to confer with each new teacher, or when a principal systematically confers periodically with each teacher in the building. Some conferences might be called partially scheduled, in that a time of availability for the purpose is stated, and those persons come who have specific problems to discuss. Some supervisors and principals publicize the fact that they are reserving certain hours for individual conferences, and invite teachers to take the initiative in coming at that time.

Many short but effective individual conferences are unscheduled. If instructional leaders can move about their work in a relatively unhurried and unstrained manner, they themselves will notice many golden opportunities for brief conferring, and teachers will feel free to raise questions without thinking they are encroaching upon other responsibilities. Principals especially often find themselves going into a classroom or seeking out a teacher for one specific purpose or bit of information, and then staying for several minutes of highly productive conversation on related or entirely new topics.

RECORDS OF INDIVIDUAL CONFERENCES. Ideally some kind of record should be kept of all but the most informal conferences. Such a procedure is time-consuming, and hence is often neglected. At a minimum, however, some record should be made of:

a) the date and place of the conference
b) the general topics of discussion
c) any agreements reached for action

d) any specific commitments made by supervisor, principal, or teacher to send materials or to make arrangements of some kind by telephone or letter.

Without such a record, even persons with vivid memories can lose track of sincere promises, in the kaleidoscope of activity of a school day. The record can usually be made while the conference is in progress; in fact, the recording of pertinent information is often a convenient way of concluding a conference. Perhaps it should be added that supervisors and principals should not make notes in the presence of a teacher in the classroom or conference when the teacher cannot see what is being written. A negative feeling of suspicion and fear is almost sure to arise, even when the notation being made is complimentary.

A record is also important sometimes for the history it preserves. This is especially true where individuals are carrying on experimental work or planning changes. Over a period of time it is easy to forget the exact steps taken or materials used. The record of conferences can provide the needed information.

A record of conferences is essential when a teacher is having serious difficulty in his work, and supervisors and principals are trying to help the individual improve. For one thing, the record keeps account of the variety, sequence, and effectiveness of efforts made. But the record may become important in still another way, as proof that instructional leaders have offered help. In those rare cases when a teacher has to be dismissed for incompetency, the individual may try to defend himself by saying (what he may earnestly believe) that no one helped him. Without a record of some kind, the superintendent, principal and supervisors may find themselves without proof for the individual or a court that many efforts had been made to assist him.

Types of Individual Conferences

The individual conference takes several forms, each with its own advantages and limitations. Four types are discussed here:

CLASSROOM CONFERENCES. The classroom, while the pupils are not present, offers several advantages as a setting for the individual conference. Many of the instructional materials which may be under discussion are present, and incidents involving responses of pupils can be recalled or reconstructed readily. The work of pupils is available, and records for individual students which need to be consulted are accessible. The teacher feels at his best since he is on home ground and gains some sense of support, if he were prone to be ill-at-ease, from his familiar surroundings. In turn, the person who is trying to extend help through the conference may be at his best too, since the specifics of the classroom environment offer many points for a natural beginning and progression of the discussion, which lead ultimately to deeper insights regarding the problem under consideration. In most classrooms, too, there will be evidence of some strong points of work which give the consultant an opportunity to underscore positive elements.

Sometimes it is important for the students to be present, in order for the consultant to see for himself the students' responses in certain situations. He then is in a position subsequently to be of more help in analysis of the teaching-learning problems which are involved. Sometimes the students need to be present, because the teacher and consultant are engagd in trying *together* to initiate and conduct ventures or evaluate outcomes. In either event, while brief comments might be exchanged as needed while the students are present, extended discussions would have to await their departure. Once again, the fact that the conference occurs in the classroom means that naturalness is enhanced and strain and formality minimized. It is easier to "keep the eye on the ball" during a conference if the real playing field offers the setting.

OFFICE CONFERENCES. For some purposes an office or specifically designated conference room may be preferred. One advantage lies in having professional materials available which can be consulted immediately, such as pamphlets, facts from research findings, exact descriptions of procedures and pictures of arrangements. Conference rooms are usually the most private or quiet place for a conference, and are therefore conducive to sustained thinking and to matters of a confidential nature. Some offices are appropriate for quiet conferences, but others offer only a jangle of telephone ringing, typewriter noise, and unwillingly overheard conversations.

CASUAL CONFERENCES.   One type of individual conference which can be highly productive may be identified as casual, in the sense that it is undesigned, although not in the sense that it is unexpected or haphazard. Many a teacher and consultant learns to anticipate, help create, and seize upon chance opportunities for a few minutes of discussion on a specific problem. Lunchrooms, hallways, lounges, and parking lots witness some of the most productive individual conferences ever held. The informality of the situation, the known brevity of it, seem to make it possible for some persons to make inquiries, offer comments easily, and come to the point quickly where, under other circumstances, they would have hesitated to involve themselves seriously or at length.

OBSERVATIONAL VISITS.   At first glance it may seem strange to discuss observational visits as a type of individual conference; yet there is considerable justification for doing so. The full-scale observational visit, long regarded in education as a necessary technique, was subject to a grave limitation, namely, the artificiality of the situation for teacher, children, and observer. However, the technique was continued in use in spite of its limitations because it served, theoretically at least, the fundamental need of acquainting the observer sufficiently with first-hand situations (albeit distorted) to enable him to be of assistance in analyzing problems later and in extending help. This fundamental need for knowing the situation well is now often met through illustrations given in small committee and child-study groups, through working shoulder-to-shoulder on projects, and especially through individual conferences. Furthermore, the concept of supervision today as service, problem analysis and the evolving of solutions together means that there is little need for observer and observed, but there is instead need for persons engaged in provisional tries as they attempt to solve persistent problems.

Hence the observational visit as such is decreasing in importance, while the individual conference increases.

For the occasions when the observational visit is appropriate, Wiles offers a number of helpful suggestions as to procedures and purposes:

> The supervisor should sit where he can observe pupil reactions, because he will want to focus his attention on the interaction of children with their teacher, their fellows, and the materials of instruction that are used. He is not concerned with special mannerisms or techniques of the teacher except as they affect the children in the group. He will want to ask himself such questions as the following:
>
> Is the classroom one in which children feel secure in their relationships with each other and with the teacher?
>
> Do the children see purpose in what they are doing?
>
> Are children seeking ways of carrying out their purposes or are they seeking to discover what the teacher wants done?
>
> Is there opportunity for creative thinking and activity in the classroom?
>
> Is cooperation encouraged?
>
> Are children stimulated to evaluate their ways of working and to plan revision of procedures that will make their work more effective?
>
> Are the classroom equipment and materials organized to increase the efficiency with which the group achieves its purposes? [7]

Observational visits that focus attention upon such questions as the above can be extremely helpful to consultants and teachers alike as they try to ferret out cause and effect relationships in classroom situations. The focusing of attention upon significant questions helps the participants involved in the daily effort of a situation dis-

[7] Kimball Wiles, *Supervision for Better Schools*. 2nd Ed. (Englewood Cliffs, N. J.: Prentice-Hall, Inc., 1955), p. 307.

tinguish between the truly relevant elements and the transitory or tangential factors which may be obscuring the scene.

The three activities described in this chapter—large group meetings, small group meetings, and individual conferences—are in supervision somewhat like daily bread in nutrition. They are almost constantly in use, and they provide much of the nourishment for the improvement of learning opportunities. If this nourishment is well provided, then all persons concerned can live with increased vigor and satisfaction, through the tasks accomplished and the enthusiasm engendered.

AIDS TO STUDY AND DISCUSSION

1. With some of your classmates as collaborators, try to show through simple dramatizations what you consider to be a constructive individual conference (and, by way of contrast, a destructive one) or an effective small group meeting contrasted with an ineffective session.

2. State a belief you hold strongly. If you were to make a change to bring action into line with the belief, what would it be? If you were a supervisor, what could you do to help a teacher focus on stating a strong belief and finding a beginning?

3. What can you do to "release" (free or challenge) one person a day through an intentional expression of concern? For a week, keep a record of the opportunities you found and utilized.

SUGGESTIONS FOR FURTHER READING

Anderson, W. A., *The Workshop Handbook* (New York: Bureau of Publications, Teachers College, Columbia University, 1954).

Association for Supervision and Curriculum Development, *Extending the School Year* (Washington, D.C.: National Education Association, 1961).

"Improving Large Meetings," *Adult Leadership*, Vol. 1, No. 7, Edited by Richard Beckhard (December, 1952).

The Elementary School Principalship—A Research Study, Yearbook, National Elementary Principal, 1958 (Washington, D.C.: National Education Association, 1958).

Farley, G. J., and J. J. Santosuosso, "The Supervisor and Classroom Visitation," *Educational Administration and Supervision*, Vol. 43, No. 5 (May, 1957).

Festinger, Leon, "Informal Communication in Small Groups," *Groups, Leadership, and Men*, Edited by Harold Guetzkow (Pittsburgh: Carnegie Press, 1951).

Fromm, Eric, *The Sane Society* (New York: Holt, Rinehart & Winston, Inc., 1955).

Kelley, Earl, *The Workshop Way of Learning* (New York: Harper & Brothers, 1951).

Murphy, Gardner, *Human Potentialities* (New York: Basic Books, Inc., 1958).

Treanor, John H., "To Help a Teacher," *The National Elementary Principal*, Vol. 32, No. 5 (April, 1953).

Vergason, A. L., "Supervisory Conferences," *National Association of Secondary School Principals*, Vol. 34, No. 174 (December, 1950).

Wiles, Kimball, *Supervision for Better Schools*, 2nd Ed. (Englewood Cliffs, N. J.: Prentice-Hall, Inc., 1955).

CHAPTER 7

SUPERVISORY ACTIVITIES: PROFESSIONAL DEVELOPMENT

As indicated in the exploration of the bases of supervision, the evolving nature of our society makes continuous curriculum development a necessity. Likewise, the proliferation of knowledge and the very nature of a profession make in-service education, or professional growth, for all school personnel an equal necessity. To plan consistently and cooperatively for the induction of new teachers, for curriculum development and the continuing professional growth of the staff, and for working with professional organizations is one of the major responsibilities of supervision.

INDUCTION OF NEW TEACHERS

The induction of new teachers is one of the large responsibilities of supervision, and one of the most rewarding to instructional leaders. Whether a teacher is launching upon his first teaching experience or is transferred from another school, he needs help in making the most of himself in the new situation. The goal is not merely to navigate the first year without serious mishap; it is, rather, to make use of the individual's talents and enthusiasm in such a way as to further a career of unstunted professional development.

Specific Purposes Served

The successful induction of new teachers challenges supervision to exercise most of its major functions simultaneously. Teachers will need help immediately in analyzing teaching-learning situations, in integrating goals into a coherent working philosophy of education, and in extending experiences. The demand for facilitating efforts is almost continuous, and the opportunity to encourage creativity arises frequently among those who are in the act of seeking solutions to dilemmas. The new teachers expect leadership from those in supervisory roles.

Working Principles

LENGTH OF INDUCTION. The induction of teachers should be an extended process. Beginning teachers today who enter the classroom with professional preparation are not complete novices, thanks to effective student teaching and internship programs, but there is still much to learn, as almost anyone finishing an internship period would be glad to testify. Teachers need help over a period of several years, if they are to achieve the flexibility in use of principles, the resourcefulness, and the swiftness and sureness of judgments that mark the skilled professional person. Probably the induction period should be thought of as extending over two or three years; certainly a few days of pre-school orientation, plus initial visits from the principal and system-wide supervisor, cannot be regarded as adequate, even though helpful.

SYSTEMATIC PLAN. There should be a systematic plan for the induction of new teachers. Obviously the plan needs to provide the newcomers with opportunity to become acquainted with system-wide policies, materials, and personnel, and with the individual school policies, resources, and faculty. The plan also needs to include opportunities for individual analysis of teaching-learning situations, for organized group study, and for sharing of experiences among beginning teachers. The means for carrying out the plan are usually to be found in the procedures discussed earlier, in Chapter 6, such as in the individual conference and large or small group meetings. A well-developed plan for induction of teachers involves close teamwork on the part of superintendents, supervisors, consultants, principals, experienced teachers, and beginning teachers if the work is to be both practical in the sense of dealing with immediate pressures, and yet productive of long-range professional growth. On a day-to-day basis the principal undoubtedly carries a major role in implementing the plan.

SUPPORT FOR LEARNING. Those responsible for induction should aim to provide support for new teachers while they learn, and to prevent loss of energy and aspiration from undue discouragement. New teachers are learners of the first order, and since learning usually goes better where there is emotional support and concern for the learner, supervision can assist by bringing the material aid and expressing the emotional support needed. Carrying the responsibility for a full day of teaching takes more strength and stamina (physical, intellectual, and emotional) than many a person would suppose, including one who has interned. When the awkwardness, extra effort, and uncertainty naturally accompanying a new venture are added, it is small wonder that the beginning teacher becomes weary and is prone to enervating discouragement. If the teaching conditions are unusually difficult, it is possible for the new teacher to become so disheartened that he rejects teaching entirely, withdrawing from the field without discovering that better situations exist; or, perhaps still worse from the standpoint of persons he meets later, he continues in teaching, but with a cynical outlook and negative approach to new events.

The induction of new teachers should aim to go beyond the mere preserving of the good qualities the newcomers bring, and expect to stimulate further the development of creativity and aspiration. Not all the conditions conducive to creativity are known, but a problem-solving approach, flexibility in procedures, keen sensitivity to the existence of problems, and an atmosphere of confidence and respect would seem to be important. Supervision can help develop these conditions.

A point of caution is to be noted. Occasionally beginning teachers are so eager to do things in the approved way, or to find immediate solutions to problems, that they adopt suggestions too thoroughly, settling quickly into a kind of orthodoxy which blinds them to new needs or better solutions. If the new teacher becomes a stereotype, then his further development is stultified, and supervision has failed him in his induction period. On the other hand, if his aspiration and insight increase, supervision has served him well.

Types of Induction Activities

Many kinds of activities are appropriate to purposes of induction. Only a few are elaborated here.

ORIENTATION HANDBOOKS. A number of school systems prepare handbooks for new teachers, and sometimes send them to the person before he arrives in the community. Such handbooks usually include sections on the history of the community, resources, school policies, professional organizations, and information on living arrangements. The handbook is a means of answering many questions, but school personnel can expect to repeat much of the information as questions become pertinent for each individual.

ORIENTATION DAYS. In the pre-school period certain days are frequently set aside for beginning teachers from the entire system. At this time policies are explained, supervisory staff presented, and trips into various aspects of the community arranged. Similar days are needed in the individual school, where the new teachers can become acquainted with local adaptations of policies, the immediate neighborhood, the instructional materials of the school, and most of all, their own co-workers. Much of what is said in these opening days will have to be said again in the following weeks, partly because so much is presented in concentrated form that it cannot be wholly assimilated, and partly because some of the information will not take on much meaning until a problem situation makes it pertinent.

PERSONAL NEEDS, SOCIAL EVENTS. Principals, supervisors, and experienced teachers can expedite the induction of new teachers by helping them make satisfactory living arrangements, locate churches, and attend to the routines of moving into a new community. It is now a fairly common practice for community groups to entertain new teachers at one or more social events, in order to help them become acquainted with people outside the school.

VISITATION. When beginning teachers have made enough initial efforts of their own to discover what some of their problems are, they often want the opportunity to see experienced teachers at work. Here supervision can render service by knowing where some of the appropriate situations are, making arrangements for the visit and for the new teacher to be away from his own class, and seeing that there is opportunity for analysis of what was noted. Without adequate analysis with the visited teacher or principal or consultant, stereotyping could result. It would also be easy for the observer to ascribe the success of some of the procedures to the wrong reasons.

PROFESSIONAL GROWTH AND CURRICULUM

DEVELOPMENT

Most of the activities discussed so far are avenues for curriculum development and for the professional growth of the staff. Four aspects of the matter are discussed at this point: (1) relationships among curriculum development, professional growth, and personal development; (2) identification of needs for in-service education; (3) continuity of planning; and (4) nurturing change.

Curriculum Development, Professional Growth and Personal Development

When some of the curriculum revision programs of the 1930's yielded a surprising paucity of outcomes, an analysis of the efforts led to the realization that too few people had been involved in the decision-making and goal-setting. Energy had been applied *to* the curriculum *from* the outside when in reality the change, if it was to be sustained and genuine, had to come within the people who were daily living the experiences. It became apparent that the curriculum change was primarily social in nature, involving changes in human beings. Workshops, curriculum councils, and other procedures providing for wide participation of persons affected, led to more successful efforts toward curriculum changes. Sharp, in his insightful and helpful small volume with the significant title, *Curriculum Development as Re-education of the Teacher*, gave especially clear expression to the basic concept that curriculum develops fundamentally as a result of development in teachers' personalities.[1]

In-service education became a term heard on many occasions; indeed, in the eyes of some persons, it appeared almost a panacea. Yet it was also clear that some individuals achieved a great deal of professional growth from in-service education activities, while others did not. Why was an experience productive for some persons but not for others? One answer, of course, was in the direction of meeting felt needs. If the individual perceived the experience as offering something he was aware of needing personally or professionally, the experience could make a difference. But more than this seemed involved. Or at least, why were some people aware of needs and relatively open to new experience, while others were unaware and resistant?

Work in perceptual psychology and other areas began to supply

[1] George Sharp, *Curriculum Development as Re-education of the Teacher* (New York: Bureau of Publications, Teachers College, Columbia, 1951).

clues. Apparently persons can easily be so pre-occupied with personal problems and with fears (both real and imagined), that there is neither attention nor time for ideas that involve change. Also, persons who are defensive, through lack of normal self-confidence or other reasons, often feel threatened by proposed changes, and hence cling all the more rigidly to familiar routines.

Jersild, in *When Teachers Face Themselves*, presents many examples of personal problems in teachers engendering hostilities toward children, fellow teachers, and suggested change. Regarding the impact of anxiety he observes:

> "The ghosts of old hurts, the souls of agonies of an earlier day, live on in many of our children at school—and in the colleagues with whom we work, and in ourselves. And it is to the extent that each of us has the courage to look into the haunted house within himself where these ghosts reside that he can gain some insight into the way the lives of others are ravaged by anxiety." [2]

Persons responsible for supervision must become sensitive to the interrelationships among curriculum improvement, professional growth, and personal development, and they must recognize that helping teachers take the next step in personal growth is often the most significant thing they can do.

Identifying Needs

Finding out what problems teachers are concerned about is naturally important if supervision is to arrange for productive professional growth activities. Instructional leaders can often ascertain needs when they *analyze a learning situation* with a teacher, when they help committees *search for appropriate materials*, when they *listen* while teachers talk, when they *ask* directly, when they *search records* of school board hearings and P.T.A. meetings for evidence of concern, when they *work with professional organizations* on vital questions, when they *engage in action research* with whole faculties

---

[2] Arthur T. Jersild, *When Teachers Face Themselves* (New York: Bureau of Publications, Teachers College, Columbia, 1955), p. 55.

or small teams, and join with faculties to *evaluate* programs. In short, each day's work is a microcosm for revealing the next steps needed for professional growth. Persons responsible for planning the means of in-service education must, in turn, devise ways of recording and grouping their findings into available information.

Continuity and Cooperation in Planning

It goes almost without saying that since many persons are involved, the planning must be cooperative if it is to be effective. While many suggestions will reach instructional leaders or a planning committee informally, there should be clearly defined channels through which identified needs and proposals can be transmitted. Some council or designated individual should be in a continuing position to receive suggestions and have them available for planning sessions.

If major activities for professional growth can be planned in relation to one another, there is an opportunity for continuity and follow-through. For instance, a system where teachers wanted to learn more about a discriminating use of television planned its preschool conference, several extension classes, a program of visitation, and some action research around this theme.

It is true, of course, that the basic continuity is within the individual. It is also true that when a person enters a profession, he accepts the commitment to keep on learning. Hence it is each individual who extends his own experience; no one else can do it for him. But if opportunities are present in a coherent way, the individual's efforts can be greatly enhanced. Thus, making learning opportunities available is an important task of supervision.

Facilitating Change and Nurturing Creativity

Even when individuals have felt a need, sought solutions, and found an improved approach, actually making changes is not easy. Old habits and ways of perceiving are strong; venturing into the untried takes extra effort and sometimes considerable courage. Instructional leaders can facilitate the effort to change: (1) by making their own friendliness and concern manifest, so that the individual *knows* he is surrounded by a supportive atmosphere; (2) by assisting with initial steps when the individual feels uncertain or awkward; (3) by supplying essential materials; and (4) perhaps most of all, by themselves being adaptive, growing persons who daily demonstrate the effectiveness and joy of a creative approach to problems.

It is through professional growth activities that creativity is often evoked. Supervision becomes a vitalizing force when it helps school personnel anticipate and relish the free play of intelligence upon problems, and the upsurge of energy accompanying creative solutions. Zirbes, writing about the characteristics of a creative conception of in-service education, suggests the following criteria for evaluating whatever is proposed or projected:

It should be practical, but not didactic.
It should be refreshing in a new sense, i.e., challenging and engaging.
It should *not* purvey "hows," methods, or devices.
It should *not* train teachers.
It should *not* tell teachers what to do, or stereotype their practices.
It should *not* be prescriptive or directive.
It should *not* be tied to particular texts or manuals.
It should be a resource for adaptive use in any situation.
It should cultivate insight.
It should respect individuality.
It should begin with "self."
It should raise morale and lift aspiration.
It should improve the quality of living and learning.
It should develop concern for the development of children's creative potentialities.
It should develop and mature teachers' value judgments.
It should give supervisory leadership a satisfying creative role.
It should give teachers a sense of increasing professional adequacy.[3]

[3] Laura Zirbes, *Spurs to Creative Teaching* (New York: G. P. Putnam's Sons, 1959), p. 287.

Types of Professional Growth Activities

The kinds of activities that lead to professional growth are un-limited. Indeed, almost every effort toward curriculum development and general improvement of materials and facilities holds a potential for the professional growth of each person who participates. Three broad types of activities are described here: large group efforts, small group efforts, and transition steps.

LARGE GROUP EFFORTS. The efforts of large groups are essential in curriculum development and in the professional growth of staff. Special considerations regarding the work of pre-school conferences, workshops, and councils were discussed in the preceding chapter (pp. 112–118). Another type of group effort for which supervision often carries responsibility is the university class, on campus or by extension service. If the planning for classes is well-coordinated, teachers can have an opportunity to deepen and extend their knowledge in chosen areas, and at the same time the whole school system can feel the benefit from concerted effort. In large school centers this coordinating of offerings through university classes is no small achievement, for the diversity of need is great, and the range of possible offerings is correspondingly wide. Instructional leaders usually need to spend much time in ascertaining local needs, planning with the system-wide staff, and corresponding with university representatives, all on a long-range basis, if systematic, optimum help is to be obtained from the classes.

One kind of university class, the field seminar, warrants special mention, partly because of its increasing frequency of appearance, but largely because of its degree of impact on the schools that make use of it. A field seminar is usually organized around specific problems identified by a faculty or representatives from several faculties in the same system; or it may be centered in the evaluation of the total program of a given school, with the entire faculty taking part. In either event there is a deep probing of problems, practices, and purposes; and action usually stems from the united study.

SMALL GROUP EFFORTS.   Many types of small group efforts were also discussed earlier (pp. 118–122). Special purpose committees, grade group meetings, and faculty meetings in small and medium-sized schools are typical of efforts to achieve curriculum development and professional growth through small group work. The relaxed atmosphere and more informal procedures usually possible in small groups form an advantage, since these qualities are often conducive to clear thinking and undefensive, constructive attitudes. However, a word of caution is appropriate with regard to the potential for growth in some situations. For instance, a grade group or subject area committee of five or six members whose concerns are already sharply focused on one age level or subject area may find itself suffering from an inbreeding of ideas, or thinking in too tight circles. The use of "outside" resource persons might prove especially helpful to such committees. Here instructional leaders can often assist in person, or suggest resource personnel from other schools, community agencies, lay persons, or university staffs.

TRANSITION ACTIVITIES.   School personnel sometimes engage eagerly in activities intended to stimulate curriculum development and professional growth, and are pleased, even enthusiastic, about the working sessions; yet ultimately very little seems to happen, or at least what happens is small compared to the individual and corporate effort expended. Something, some vital ingredient, is missing. For many persons that "something" may be primarily a matter of self-confidence, a modification in self-concept, or a picture-in-the-head of themselves doing the new proposal. A transition or intermediate step seems needed, to make the movement from intellectual commitment to new behaviors less abrupt or formidable. Sometimes the transition is hindered by lack of confidence in self or in the idea, but more often, perhaps, it is hampered by lack of a clear-cut picture of what a person or classroom looks like when the desired change is in actual progress. For instance, what does a teacher do, what does the classroom look like, when a person is trying to nurture creativity or promote reflective thinking? Here instructional leaders who are trying to be helpful face a real dilemma. Pat answers are out of the question, since a great variety of situations might be productive of creativity, and since the dynamic, complex nature of any episode precludes predicting with nicety which combination of factors will be successful the next time. Any listing of desiderata is likely to prove to be a static affair, easily subect to distortion. Yet teachers deserve help in putting sound ideas into practice.

Several procedures hold promise as transition media, apparently because they enable a person to try something in a small way first, to try it in a non-threatening situation, or to explore verbally to a degree that brings clarification of concept and identification of a beginning point. One such procedure is role-playing or simple dramatization. For many people, trying out a new desired behavior in a non-threatening, good-natured, even humorous, situation gives enough confidence in themselves and in the idea to enable them to try it again soon in a small way in a real situation. From subsequent trials increased understanding and skills emerge. Some persons who are themselves uncomfortable in role-playing gain from seeing other people in action, either in dramatizations or through visitations and films.

A second procedure which may facilitate action revolves around the use of slides, filmstrips, tapes and other aids. If the slides portraying the desired action have been locally produced or made in the home state, they may be especially effective, since there is some tendency to feel that "if the other fellow can do it, so can we." The significant point, however, is that there be full, exploring discussion with every person joining in the questioning. The visual material serves as a means for elaborating and refining concepts as the discussion brings out qualifying conditions, limiting factors, and unexpected dividends. In the course of the discussion, participants often begin to see several ways in which they themselves might start, or adapt ideas. In a similar manner, a common study and discussion of specific case histories might lead to a refinement of concepts and a feeling of familiarity with a new idea, to the point that individuals would feel able to take action.

Brain-storming or a free flow of ideas on how a desired goal might be achieved offers still another approach. When persons give their imaginations full reign and do not make instant or hasty judgments about the worth of ideas produced, they often provide a variety of ideas which eventually prove workable. What is equally important, they gain confidence in themselves as persons who have ideas, who can be adaptive, and who, therefore, can afford to risk themselves to make a start even though the path ahead is not completely clear.

In most of the approaches just described, it will take the help of instructional leaders to make opportunities possible for teachers to be together, for appropriate materials to be assembled, and the effort to be launched. Hence, again, the expediting role of supervision is evident.

WORKING WITH PROFESSIONAL
ORGANIZATIONS

Professional organizations, like supervision, are concerned with the ultimate improvement of education. Again, as in supervision, cooperative effort, coordination, provision of leadership, contributions to knowledge, integration of goals, and continuous growth are key concepts. It is not surprising, therefore, that supervision and professional organizations often complement and supplement one another's efforts.

In a country such as the United States, where a largely decentralized school system has developed, professional organizations at the national, regional, and state level hold a unique place in the wide dissemination of ideas, the production of professional materials, and the encouragement of some commonality of approach to educational problems of organization, curriculum, and instruction. The organizations also constitute media for concerted efforts by individuals and small groups. Since professional organizations are voluntary in nature, the success of their work depends, in large part, upon the breadth of participation and quality of work of the members. Instructional leaders are concerned with professional organizations in at least three ways: as active participants, as expediters, and as coordinators.

Direct Participation

Instructional leaders have much to gain from and much to contribute to professional organizations. Attendance at annual meetings of the organizations is usually a refreshing and enriching experience for members, as well as a source of new information; the journals and yearbooks of the societies are a continuing source of information throughout the year; and attempts to reach goals through cooperative efforts often lead to the refinement of goals and an increase in aspiration of the individual. In turn, members contribute through their ideas, their time, their writings and reports of work, and through their implementing of plans developed by the organizations. The best possible planning at the national, regional, or state level would remain largely fruitless, were it not for the professionally-minded persons at the local level.

Facilitating the Participation of Others

A second way in which instructional leaders can help is in facilitating the participation of teachers and other personnel in professional activities. A leader's own willing acceptance of organizational responsibility is one means of helping others anticipate similar effort and satisfaction for themselves. He becomes a subliminal model. A second means is to inform teachers of opportunities, and to suggest and discuss with them the possibilities of participation. Apparently it does not occur to some people to take an active part unless someone else initiates the idea or expresses confidence in the individual's ability to make a contribution. Third, instructional leaders can facilitate participation by making it possible for teachers to have some time free for organizational activities. The teacher's daily involvement with the students, in a schedule that has little flexibility, makes it impossible for him to attend meetings without securing help. Instructional leaders can help by arranging for substitutes, expense funds, and transportation, and also by building with the school board and community an awareness of why some organizational work is necessary and valuable in education as a profession.

Coordination of Efforts of Professional Organizations

Each professional organization has some area upon which it focuses effort, but since all the areas are within the general field of education, there are naturally many occasions when two or more groups may have converging interests. This condition can result in overlapping and duplication of effort, or it can lead to constructive collaboration and hastening of accomplishment. Instructional leaders are persons of broad interest, by virtue of their positions as well as by experience, and hence usually hold membership in several organizations. They can do much, at the local level especially, to keep organizations well enough informed regarding emerging interests and plans to prevent overlapping and to encourage collaborating. Frequent communication among professional organizations is a necessity if true teamwork is to be achieved. Often the instructional leader can serve in a liaison capacity in furthering communications among organizations.

Also by virtue of their positions, persons in a supervisory role, especially on a system-wide basis, become cognizant of needs as problems begin to emerge. Therefore, they can make helpful suggestions to appropriate organizations as to work needed. For instance, a supervisor may frequently hear elementary principals and teachers express dismay over the amount of energy expended in preparing student records compared to the use made of the records. When he hears a similar concern expressed by secondary principals and teachers, the supervisor is in a strategic position for perceiving the common need and for drawing the attention of appropriate organizations to it as an area of productive work.

The activities discussed in this chapter—induction of new teachers, professional growth and curriculum development, and working with professional organizations—are especially rich in opportunities for instructional leaders to help all school personnel (including themselves) turn into reality a greater proportion of their human potential for learning and for cooperative effort than is now being commonly achieved. If supervision can help lessen the dissipation of human energy in needless fears and inhibitions and can, instead, convert that energy to constructive, coordinated efforts, it will be performing a great service in the improvement of education.

AIDS TO STUDY AND DISCUSSION

1. What human beings say to one another and their manner of speaking have great impact upon the desire to keep on developing. For a period of two weeks or more keep a journal of statements made by colleagues to one another in meetings, lounges, lunchrooms, or halls. Which are:
   a) killer statements?
   b) supportive statements?
   c) curiosity-arousing statements?
   If possible, note the facial expression of the person to whom the remark is made.

   Keep a similar record of such statements from teacher to pupil, and from pupil to pupil. Analyze your journal from the standpoint of content of the words, tone and manner of speaking, frequency, and apparent impact upon the listener.

2. For a number of years *Childhood Education*, publication of the Association for Childhood Education, has carried the masthead statement, "To Stimulate Thinking Rather Than Advocate Fixed Practice." What significance do you see in this statement, in light of the goals of continued professional development?

3. Consult at least three handbooks or programs for the orientation of new teachers, in search of excellent features in each. If you were helping with the preparation or revision of a program for your individual school (or city), what would you include or delete? Why?

SUGGESTIONS FOR FURTHER READING

Anderson, Vernon E., "Professional Organizations Aid In-Service Growth," *Educational Leadership*, Vol. 9, No. 1 (October, 1951).

Clark, L. M., "Supervision as Leadership In Curriculum Development," *Education*, Vol. 78, No. 4 (December, 1957).

Ferguson, M. E., and H. R. Rouse, "Principal and Supervisor Help the New Teacher," *Educational Leadership*, Vol. 13, No. 1 (October, 1955).

Jantzen, J. M., and J. C. Stone, "More Effective Supervision of Beginning Teachers," *Journal of Teacher Education*, Vol. 10, No. 2 (June, 1959).

Jersild, Arthur T., *When Teachers Face Themselves* (New York: Bureau of Publications, Teachers College, Columbia University, 1955).

Sharp, George, *Curriculum Development as Re-education of the Teacher* (New York: Bureau of Publications, Teachers College, Columbia University, 1951).

Spears, Harold, *The Teacher and Curriculum Planning* (Englewood Cliffs, N.J.: Prentice-Hall, Inc., 1951).

Wilkinson, R. D., "Adjustment of Beginning Teachers," *Educational Forum*, Vol. 21, No. 1 (November, 1956).

Zirbes, Laura, *Spurs to Creative Teaching* (New York: G. P. Putnam's Sons, 1959).

CHAPTER 8

SUPERVISORY ACTIVITIES: RECURRING PROCEDURES

CERTAIN activities which are vital to the daily life of the school are used so often that they may be regarded as recurring procedures in supervision. They occupy a large portion of supervisory time and attention, and could seldom be carried to fruition without the sustained effort of instructional leaders who are in a position to comprehend the educational program broadly. Four such procedures discussed in this chapter are: research; selection, production, and utilization of materials; evaluation, accreditation, and testing programs; and interpreting the program to the public.

RESEARCH

The importance of research is widely recognized and acclaimed in our society, and the outcomes of research in many fields, such as medicine and engineering, are eagerly anticipated and appreciated.

Research in the social sciences, including education, has a relatively short history, and the effort to utilize findings frequently encounters the extra burden of changing deeply-rooted habits of perceiving and behaving. Yet what has been accomplished in the relatively short period since learning process, human development, and social aims and institutions have been the subject of study, has been remarkable, and the need for intensified effort is enormous. Because supervision has its reason-for-being in the improvement of learning, and because persons charged with responsibility for supervision are in leadership positions, supervision and research are strategically related.

All of the purposes of research which are relevant to education cannot be elaborated here, but a few which are closely related to supervision must be mentioned.

Specific Purposes

EVALUATION OF CHANGE.   An interdependent society, which is constantly undergoing change from rapid invention and discovery in both the natural and social sciences, feels not only a direct impact intended by the change, but also a host of chain-reaction impacts that were not an intentional part of the original change. A change in foreign policy, for instance, regarding the importing of sugar, has repercussions upon the domestic sugar industry—a fact which influences migrant labor which, in turn, influences the nature of the school population in a community, and hence the specific learning problems confronting a faculty. Or the invention of television opens up a new teaching medium, and educators have to find what purposes, persons, and conditions are involved in its optimum use. Without a research approach, educators could easily remain insensitive to the effects of change, and also act upon unwarranted assumptions regarding the worth of certain changes. Research is a necessity, then, in order to evaluate change.

SAVING OF TIME.   Research helps educators save time in developing effective procedures. To seek evidence systematically usually produces in a short time what would take generations to distill as folk wisdom. In addition, repetition of mistakes, costly in time and effort, can be largely avoided through research, if careful records are made and findings kept accessible. Wasteful blundering with human lives can also be avoided. An individual adolescent goes through his junior high school years but once. When those valuable years are gone, they cannot be re-lived by *him* although a succession of other pupils will occupy his chair. Hence random "experimenting" is too costly, for too many students remain unbenefited and unprotected.

THE SEARCH FOR ECONOMY OF EFFORT IN LEARNING. To do well just what has been attempted in the past is not enough today. Findings from several studies indicate, for instance, that middle-grade children today read better than did those of their parents' and grandparents' generations.[1] But that achievement, while commendable on the part of both children and educators, is not enough, for the demands for reading have soared in the past generation. Professional people such as doctors, lawyers, and editors must read with swiftness and deep comprehension in order to acquaint themselves with new developments; citizens and consumers must read with increasing discrimination; everyone must read and read well for economic survival and personal safety.

The variety and complexity of what a person must learn in the course of his school years, and in his adult living, demand that psychologists and educators concentrate attention upon research into ways of learning that are more economical of teacher-learner effort. For instance, the effort made by most children and youth to learn parts of speech in the attempt to improve writing and speaking is enormous. Can the best use of our present knowledge of maturational levels, understandings, and needs improve the situation and save some of the time and effort for other valuable learnings? Can a break-through in our knowledge of learning processes throw open new doors? Supervision can help find answers.

[1] Emmett A. Betts, "Reading: Now and Then," *Education*, Vol. 78, No. 2 (October, 1957), pp. 85–86.

UTILIZATION OF LEARNING POTENTIAL. Human beings may be entirely equal to the learning task before them if they are free to use themselves to full advantage. Sensitive teachers have noted for a long time that individuals who were tense and fear-bound could rarely learn well. In recent years psychologists and psychiatrists have documented the fact that intense anxiety usually inhibits or limits learning. Kubie presents a provocative point of view and challenge in regard to the greater use of human mentation:

> Eventually, education must accept the full implications of the fact that the free creative velocity of our thinking apparatus is continually being braked and driven off course by the play of unconscious forces. As long as educational procedures refuse to recognize this, they will continue to increase this interference from masked and unrecognized neurotogenic processes. This happens in school today from the first grade through the highest echelons of postgraduate study.[2]

Chapter 12, *Frontiers of Supervision*, contains a further discussion of anxiety and learning. If supervision can participate in research which identifies the conditions and forces which distort mentation, then it will indeed be improving instruction.

Working Principles

EXPECTATION OF RESEARCH. All persons connected with schools should hold an expectation of research: the public, school boards, superintendents, principals, teachers, students, and special service personnel. Research should be regarded as a normal part of the year's work. Many of the research activities will involve a team approach.

There should also be the expectation of financial support for research, with the full conviction on the part of the public that tax money spent on carefully designed research is well invested. The understanding and technical skill needed for many phases of worth-

---

[2] Lawrence S. Kubie, "Are We Educating for Maturity?", *Journal of the National Education Association*, Vol. 48, No. 1 (January, 1959), p. 58.

while research, together with the urgency for sustained time to be given to research, mean that school systems should anticipate employing one or more persons as research consultants.

PREPARATION FOR RESEARCH RESPONSIBILITY. Students preparing for positions of instructional leadership need to concentrate part of their work in the fields of measurement, evaluation, and research. While an introduction to this field might come in pre-service preparation, the major part of it would probably fall in the in-service years, either in graduate programs of work toward advanced degrees, or in in-service study programs within the school system. The important point is that whatever his first preparation is, the instructional leader has to become a life-long student of research.

EXCHANGE OF FINDINGS IN EDUCATIONAL RESEARCH. School personnel are not the only people interested in educational research. Industry, the military services, many community agencies, and adult educators are concerned with human learning, and in many instances are conducting large-scale research in learning procedures. Schools and other agencies need to profit from one another's efforts, and it is here that instructional leadership can be of service in an exchange of information, and sometimes, perhaps, in collaborating on projects.

IDENTIFYING PROBLEMS FOR INVESTIGATION. Findings from research in education and related fields, such as psychology, human development, and sociology, usually are in a "bare bones" state when they reach the educator. The full significance of the findings for educational procedures has yet to be established. It is often the task of instructional leaders and teachers to glimpse a possible relationship and formulate a hypothesis to be tested. For instance, from work in child development it is learned that hearing acuity does not reach its peak until a child is about ten.[3] The educator, in turn, has to ask many specific questions which are turned into hypotheses to be

[3] John P. Zubek and Patricia Anne Solberg, *Human Development* (New York: McGraw-Hill Book Co., Inc., 1954), pp. 193–194.

tested, in order to find the relation of this fact to such matters as the effectiveness of phonics instruction for some primary children, or the best age for the inclusion of certain phases in music instruction. It is the asking of these pertinent questions, the constant seeking of possible relationships, that is one of the important aspects of the role of supervision in research. As teachers and persons responsible for supervision seek improvement of instruction, they live in the expectation that the "I wonder" moments are to be caught and turned into research problems.

Once a problem area has been identified, there is the important step of planning the experimental procedures appropriate to the specific questions. Without great care at this point, schools may find themselves "trying out" or "experimenting" with an idea which they subsequently continue or abandon on the basis of "liking" or "not liking," having to use casual observation in making judgments, since the need for and means of obtaining data as to the effectiveness of the idea had not been anticipated far enough in advance.

INTERPRETING RESEARCH FINDINGS. Of great significance to faculties planning for improvement of instruction through experimental work is awareness of the Hawthorne effect: i.e., the accelerating effect brought dramatically to attention in the Western Electric Company studies at its Hawthorne plant (Chicago), of knowing that one is engaged in an experimental project and is teamed with others in a common undertaking.[4] Faculties may well rejoice in the increased enthusiasm that may come to teachers and learners alike in an experiment in educational procedures, but they will have to plan in some manner to disentangle the possible effect of enthusiasm from the merits of the procedure.

Another aspect of interpreting findings which involves supervision is that of helping one faculty use what another has learned. Sometimes the primary role of supervision here is that of transmitting information and making developments known from one part of the system to another, especially since many helpful studies are

---

[4] Henry A. Landsberger, *Hawthorne Revisited* (Ithaca, N. Y.: Cornell University, 1958).

not published in any accessible form. More often, however, there is the added need for providing more detailed information regarding the exact purposes, procedures, findings, and limiting conditions of a study or project. It is fairly easy for a concluding generalization to be picked up from a report at a professional meeting, in a journal, or from a telecast; but the use of the general idea may then be attempted without keen enough discrimination as to its central purpose or the modifications needed in a new setting.

Types of Research

Types of research can be classified in several ways, but for the purposes of discussion here as to supervision and research three broad types are identified: fact-finding investigations, action research, and basic research. Lines of demarcation among them are not always clear, and the three are not assumed to be completely independent categories. Furthermore, a study initially involving one type could easily lead into one or both of the others before it is finished.

FACT-FINDING INVESTIGATIONS. In planning for improvement of instruction many specific questions arise. Firm answers are needed before wise policies can be formulated. The finding of answers involves careful inquiry and persistent ferreting out of data. The pursuit of answers constitutes research in the sense of its being a systematic inquiry, a careful searching out of relevant facts.

Typical of simple questions which turn into fact-finding investigations are: What is the expected range of reading accomplishment in ninth grade classes in a school system? What per cent of the students in the senior high school elect a course in world history? What proportion of children entering school before their sixth birthday make normal progress in the primary years, and is this proportion the same as or less than for children who are fully six before entering school?

An interesting aspect of fact-finding for instructional improvement purposes is that the data are often already available, but are to be found in records kept for other reasons. Hence such investigations often call for ingenuity in using what is already present in individual permanent record folders and in the school's monthly and annual summaries. Some questions, of course, lead to the gathering of new information before answers can be supplied.

As teachers, principals, supervisors and other consultants work together, they often can raise more questions than there are time and manpower to answer. Here the concept of an educational secretary is especially helpful. A secretary prepared for his specialty, just as a medical or legal secretary is, could carry to conclusion many of the fact-finding investigations needed by the individual teacher or faculty.

ACTION RESEARCH. When an inquiry is of a nature that a hypothesis is being tested, when it is expected that immediate action in the local situation is going to stem from use of the findings, and when several persons are collaborating in the study, the term *action research* is widely used to designate the style of research. Sound action research is clean-cut in design, rigorous in its procedures, and aware of the extent to which local conditions limit the generalizations drawn from the findings.

A whole faculty may engage in action research, several teachers may pursue a project together, or an individual teacher may plan an inquiry. The undertakings may be short or long. The hypothesis formulated may be relatively simple or it may be complex. Some representative questions which might be pursued through action research are: What are the effects of teacher-pupil planning upon student interests and motivations in the upper elementary grades at Lakeshore School? Do pupils and teachers make similar evaluations of the school's junior high activity program at Eastside? How near a mutual understanding are the parents and teachers of Riverdale in their perception of the essential responsibilities of the school? How can a school organize its program to make a definite contribution in helping youth achieve positive concepts of self?

The role of supervision in action research is obviously a large one. The coordinating of efforts, the stimulating of creativity, the exercise of leadership in such a way as to release energies of people, the analysis of problems, the contributing to knowledge, the nurturing of professional development, and the increasing of satisfaction in teaching are all functions of supervision which are especially well served when action research is pursued. Meanwhile action research is expedited when supervision:

(1) provides opportunity for interested persons to work together in study groups or faculty meetings, and thus give expression to felt problems needing research;

(2) helps formulate hypotheses for testing and suggests appropriate procedures;

(3) is sensitive to the moment when expert help is needed and secures that specialized assistance;

(4) provides technical and clerical help in processing complex or voluminous data;

(5) helps in planning for and securing materials needed for the investigation and putting into effect changed policies stemming from the findings;

(6) helps in surveying relevant previous research.

Some persons feel that classroom research or classroom investigation is a more descriptive term than action research for the type of activity described above. Other persons feel that to try to distinguish action research from other types is superfluous. In any event, supervision has a great responsibility and opportunity for aiding educational advance through that kind of systematic inquiry which is characterized by a high degree of cooperative action and by the immediacy of use of the results of the study.

BASIC RESEARCH. Basic research attempts to establish generalizations which are universally true under the stated conditions. The long-range nature of much basic research, the complexity of design and treatment of data, the technical knowledge needed and the sustained attention upon the problem go beyond what supervision can provide in many systems, and mean that supervision usually has a less direct involvement with fundamental research than with action research. However, a number of systems now employ full-time research specialists who have the knowledge, access to resources, and allocated time to conduct extensive research. Education may expect large contributions from the addition of their efforts to the process of school improvement.

Yet, supervision is related to basic research in at least four important ways: (1) helping identify problem areas, (2) collaborating in the collecting of data, (3) helping detect distorting factors, and (4) putting implications drawn from laboratory findings to the empirical test in the classroom.

SELECTION, UTILIZATION, AND PRODUCTION
OF MATERIALS

The selection, utilization, and production of materials is an activity which occupies an important amount of time and attention in supervision, and which holds high potential for helpfulness. Work with materials gives school personnel, and sometimes lay persons too, an opportunity to pursue common interests together, to uncover shared concerns, and to explore new ideas or procedures in an atmosphere free enough from ego-involvement to permit a sustained focus of attention upon ideas rather than feelings.

Specific Purposes Served

In addition to the impersonal quality, or objectivity, just mentioned, there is a tangibility about working with materials that is extremely welcome to most people. Word symbols are, of course, a marvelous invention for conveying ideas in educational developments as well as in most other transactions of life; but words carry multiple meanings and the possibility of partial or erroneous understanding is always present, especially when novel ideas are under discussion. Therefore the sturdy, "show-me-some" quality of materials helps people know what they are talking about.

There is also an immediacy about the help to be had from materials that is highly welcome. The impact from well-chosen materials which are put to discriminating use can be immediate, whereas many other valuable helps in education are so long-range in nature or so indirect in approach that their full effect is not clearly visible at any one time. Many materials have *enabling* quality: that is, they are the means for carrying out significant ideas, ideas which would otherwise languish. Materials, either those for use with students or those designed for use by teachers, frequently enable teachers and consultants to follow through on planning done in individual and group conferences.

With regard to the major functions of supervision, the selection, utilization, and production of materials is a valuable resource. Change is facilitated, not only because of the tangibility and immediacy of the help just mentioned, but also because of the depth of understanding and keener insight that grow out of the careful study of the nature of the materials and the purposes they are designed to serve. Working with materials serves another major function of supervision when it becomes a vehicle for the coordination of effort. Personnel who work together over a period of time in the study of materials offered for use, in planning for full utilization of materials, or in the production of locally needed guides often learn to trust themselves in cooperative projects, developing greater skill as they go, and finding increased satisfaction in joint efforts of many degrees of complexity.

The stimulation of creativity is another function of supervision served through work with materials. Creativity is obviously called for in the writing and publication phases of the preparation of such materials as curriculum guides, but it is also called for in the imaginative adaptation of materials to local situations. The best instructional materials in existence still have to be put to work in a specific situation, and with a fine sensitivity on the part of the teacher to the nuances of responding by learners. Contributions to knowledge often grow out of efforts to use, adapt, or devise appropriate materials. The continuous effort to apply new knowledge, which is characteristic of a profession, and to seek further improvement of the theory and practice of the discipline, is also apparent in the utilization and production of materials.

Working Principles

INVOLVEMENT.   High in importance as a principle in the selection, utilization, and production of materials is the involvement of the persons who are to use the materials. This involvement is significant not only because a principle of democratic decision-making is at stake, but also because the full understanding of the nature of a new material, which is so necessary to its discriminating use, can be attained while the material is being studied for possible selection. Many a principal or materials chairman has had the experience of ordering a promising looking instructional aid, announcing with pleasure its arrival, and then finding that the aid remains largely unused, collecting dust. Unless the persons who are to use the materials have felt some need for them, and have had an opportunity to explore the field in search of appropriate means, it is difficult for them to realize the maximum help from the chosen items.

Obviously, not all members of a faculty can review all materials and still have time for other important activities. Some kind of representative system has to be devised, often in the form of a reviewing or materials advisory committee. If the membership of this committee is on a rotating basis, each member of a faculty eventually has an opportunity to experience the enlightenment and the trials relevant to the careful weighing of values expressed in materials.

It is important for all persons in a system to know how materials are selected for the schools, and that involvement of teacher judgment has been part of the process. It builds confidence in the materials chosen, and confidence in the operation of the system as a cooperative venture. When people do not know the care and widespread judgments that have gone into the selection of materials, it is easy for them to assume that choices were made by one or a few leaders in an arbitrary or pre-emptory fashion. Hence morale may suffer needlessly, and the materials themselves may be carelessly used.

CRITERIA FOR SELECTION AND USE. When persons are selecting materials, it is essential for them to have criteria to guide them. Sometimes these criteria, which should include as clear as possible a statement of the purposes the materials are to serve, are given to the selection committe by another group, such as a curriculum or courses of study committee, which has responsibility for detecting and giving expression to instructional needs. Sometimes the selection committee has to draw up its own statement of criteria. In either event, time spent in the study or formulation of criteria is well invested, even though a newcomer may at first think, "We aren't getting anywhere." Without such analysis, members of the committee may find themselves working from different value bases, but not quite detecting the fact. Or they may assume erroneously that they all have the same meaning for a common educational term, realizing too late that riled tempers and wasted hours have been a needless by-product of their efforts.

KNOWING ABOUT NEW MATERIALS. Knowing about new materials is one of the big responsibilities and, at the same time, one of the rich opportunities of supervision. The great proliferation of materials today, both classroom instructional aids, and professional materials for the teacher, makes it important for consultants, supervisors, principals, and materials specialists to read widely and seek other avenues of learning about new materials. Instructional leaders sometimes feel a little guilty if they reserve any time for reading while other demands for service surround them; yet the very help they are seeking to render can often be vastly expedited if they are cognizant of materials that have become available. A round-table discussion of new materials can be an important part of faculty or central staff meetings, with each participant giving a short synopsis of the help to be found in the item he presents.

An especially valuable resource for instructional leaders is the wealth of pamphlet and booklet material issued in recent years, primarily by professional organizations. These small documents, usually totaling less than 100 pages, typically are concise, practical, well-founded in defensible theory, and limited enough in their scope to enable a person to select the pamphlet he needs. Many of them contain research findings and current bibliographies which help the reader pursue a problem still further if he desires. Generalists in instructional work can often supplement their own knowledge in special areas from such sources, and greatly help the teacher by placing the pamphlet in his hands. Since the pamphlet material is inexpensive compared to tomes on a broad subject, several copies can often be put into immediate use at one time. Librarians, materials specialists, and faculty chairmen for materials, can collaborate effectively in making new materials known to one another and to teachers.

ACCESSIBILITY.   It goes almost without saying that materials should be easily accessible, for the best materials in the educational world profit no one if they are miles away or under lock and key at the time they are needed. Yet developing and maintaining a satisfactory system for distribution of materials is a complex matter, especially in a large school system. School board members and citizens, as well as school personnel, need to be aware of this complexity in order to appreciate the man-hours of work needed to accomplish the task efficiently.

Instructional leaders have several responsibilities in helping to make materials accessible. One is in helping to devise a workable system. Another is in acquainting teachers, especially those new to the school, with what is available and how to ask for it. Instructions for ordering from a materials center are often mimeographed and placed in the hands of new teachers, but it seems to take far more than the written word to make the procedures operative. A kind of personal induction seems necessary as the individual begins to need specific materials.

Instructional leaders can also help to make materials available by actually bringing items to the classroom. System-wide supervisors often joke about the quantity of material to be shifted around in their automobiles if passengers are to accompany them, and principals sometimes appear to be operating a dray service between the school and a central office; yet help in obtaining materials at the opportune time is a service deeply appreciated by teachers, and is productive of much good work.

EVALUATION OF THE EFFECTIVENESS OF MATERIALS. The use of materials must be evaluated constantly if improvements are to be made either in the material itself or in the manner of its use. Here supervision plays a large part by helping devise means of ascertaining effectiveness, and by coordinating the efforts of individual teachers and schools in testing materials. The effectiveness of materials is hard to judge objectively for several reasons. Enthusiasm for the novel, extravagant claims of promoters, eagerness to find some short cut or Royal Road to learning, a desperate desire to try almost anything in an effort to help children with learning difficulties, all create an atmosphere of such high expectation that perception of the effects of the use of the material is easily distorted, and either unwarranted sanction or undue disappointment can follow. In addition, whenever the effectiveness of materials is being sought, a whole syndrome of other factors is also present for the learner, including such important factors as previous experience and degree of motivation. Hence it is difficult to assess just what outcomes are traceable to the material. Instructional leaders have an important job to do in helping design the fact-finding investigations and action-research studies needed to determine the usability of materials, and the adaptations that may be necessary in a local situation.

Types of Materials Committees

The selection, evaluation of use, and production of materials is usually carried on by committees. Supervision is concerned with these committees in several ways: (1) consultants, principals, supervisors, and superintendents often serve on the committees themselves, and are called upon to exercise their professional judgment;

(2) they are asked to suggest teachers and other co-workers for membership on the committees; (3) where a needed committee does not already exist, they are often responsible for becoming sensitive to the need and initiating the organization of the group. The committees commonly needed are of two broad types: selection and production.

SELECTION OF MATERIALS.   Committees for the selection of materials may be rather small, as when three teachers from a faculty assume the responsibility for choosing new professional books for the shelf in the conference room: or they may be large, as when a system (local, county, or state) appoints a textbook selection committee with representatives from many geographic areas and teaching fields. The committee may be temporary and discharged when its specific task is finished, or it may be a standing committee with overlapping three- or four-year terms for its members, and a regular schedule of meetings. Instructional leaders have a large part to play in such matters as helping the committee members find a suitable place to work, arranging for released time and travel expense in some cases, clarifying purposes for which the materials are to be used, securing information and obtaining resource persons to aid in making technical judgments, serving as a pro tem leader while a new committee is organizing, and providing information regarding the realities of budget regulations and business policies of the school board. Here the facilitating, coordinating functions of supervision are quickly apparent.

Instructional leaders also have a responsibility to see that the opportunity for participation on selection committees is widely spread, and to help a committee disseminate the reasons back of its choices. Serving on a selection committee is a highly educative experience in at least two important ways, and therefore many persons should share in the privilege. First, intensive study and discussion during the experience broaden and deepen understanding of worthy educational goals, and the variety of possible procedures for reaching them. Second, awareness develops, often for the first time, of the vast care and effort that go into the production of good educational materials, and into the selecting of specific materials to match purposes. Persons who have served on selection committees often become more discriminating in their own use of materials, more appreciative of the efforts of their co-workers in choosing materials, and less given to superficial criticism.

Building principals especially have an additional responsibility to help members of a selection committee be truly representative: i.e., to communicate with the groups they represent. Members often need help from the principal in arranging opportunities for the two-way flow of information, where the committee member can bring ideas and sample materials to the faculty, and the faculty can study the materials and offer thoughtful judgments regarding them.

PRODUCTION OF MATERIALS.   In the sustained effort for the improvement of instruction, the production of materials frequently plays a vital role. Here the supervisory functions of coordination, integration, and stimulation of creativity are highly significant. Several types of materials are usually needed. Curriculum guides at the local, county, and state levels, guides to local resources for instruction, handbooks and instructional policy statements, newsletters and leaflets, and orientation booklets for new teachers are among the materials for which supervision has a responsibility. For at least the past thirty years, a number of schools have engaged in the production of materials, and several generalizations can be drawn from accumulated experiences:

1. Wide involvement of persons is essential. If a curriculum guide, for instance, or a resource handbook, is to prove beneficial, many people must feel a need for it, understand its formulation, take part in producing it, and anticipate its appearance. Not all persons need to make equal contributions of time and energy, and only a few can do the final writing, but the more who know about it, the wider will be its impact.
2. Time to study or to gather information is important before the production of materials. A committee needs time to establish (and often enlarge) the social and psychological base from which it is operating and to locate information pertinent to the problems at hand; otherwise the material produced may prove superficial or even unsound. The provision for study time should be included in a realistic production schedule for a committee.

3. A trial run or tentative edition is usually desirable. A try-out period with opportunity for reactions is helpful. Many ambiguities can be cleared up and helpful suggestions incorporated before a wide circulation of the material is made, and of course the wide participation possible during an exploratory period is beneficial.
4. Frequency of revision is important. One of the reasons for having locally produced materials is that they may be kept up-to-date. The revision of a curriculum guide or resource book should be a part of the original planning for its production.
5. Conciseness is helpful. Thick volumes tend to have their information so imbedded that the user cannot find what he wants when he wants it. Careful attention to format, headings, and margin guides can make locally produced materials more useful than they have sometimes been in the past.
6. Safeguarding against rigidities of interpretation is important. The tendency to regard printed material as final or absolute, and to see suggestions as dicta, is strong in many human beings, including school personnel. Hence it is important for production committees to be sensitive to the way ideas are phrased.

Representative of schools which have published curriculum materials extensively for a number of years are Austin, San Diego, Denver, Minneapolis, Cincinnati, and St. Louis, to name but a few. The wide variety of materials prepared is obvious from an analysis of publication lists available from such systems as the above. A careful look at the preface or foreword pages of a sampling of bulletins also reveals the cooperative planning and effort that went into the production of the materials.

EVALUATION, ACCREDITATION, AND
TESTING PROGRAMS

Supervision has a large part to play in the successful use of evaluation, accreditation, and testing programs which schools often undertake in their efforts to improve learning. Practically all of the major functions of supervision identified earlier—coordination of efforts, provision of leadership, extension of experience, stimulation of creative effort, facilitating and evaluating change, analysis of learning situations, contributing to a body of knowledge, and integration of goals—are discernible in the carrying out of evaluation, accreditation, and testing work.

Evaluation, whether of the individual student's progress or of the total school program, is usually regarded as having three aspects: stating purposes or values which the school deems important, securing evidence regarding the extent to which the values or purposes are realized in practice, and planning ways in which the purposes or values might be better achieved or more fully realized and related. Faculties make use of criteria to help themselves state purposes, seek evidence, and plan for improvement. Accreditation programs make use of criteria, stated as standards, by which a school's achievements are stimulated and given official recognition by an appropriate association or a state department of education. Testing involves the careful measurement of status and growth.

Thoughtful examining of a school's program, to ascertain the degree to which stated purposes and goals are being achieved, and to identify next steps for improvement, calls for sustained cooperative effort and the best of instructional leadership. From the effort usually come not only an improved program, but also a greater zest for work, derived from the clearer integration of goals and from the mutual respect engendered by good teamwork.

Working Principles

Supervision has a wide range of responsibilities in connection with evaluation, accreditation, and testing efforts. Three important duties are mentioned here.

OBTAINING INFORMATION. One of the first responsibilities for instructional leaders is that of obtaining information. Some studies are a part of the regular school reports, such as state accreditation programs, or are locally organized for specific purposes. Here the building principal especially has a large part to play in making purposes known to the faculty, in providing time for thoughtful work, and in focusing upon the opportunity for instructional improvement, rather than routine checking of items or supplying of facts.

Many evaluation, accreditation, and testing studies are sponsored by professional organizations, regional and national associations and councils, or foundations. Here the superintendent and system-wide supervisors or consultants are the first people approached with regard to a school system's participation. Most such programs are voluntary: i.e., schools are invited to participate. Before faculties can know whether they wish to commit themselves to participation, there will be many questions to answer regarding purposes and scope of the study, the kind of work involved, and the benefits to be expected. Instructional leaders need to obtain accurate information to transmit to faculties, in order that the decision to accept or reject can be well-founded. Evaluation and accreditation studies typically involve hard work, and without genuine conviction regarding the worth of the study the hard work turns to mere drudgery, instead of yielding the satisfaction of a difficult task well done. Professional people relish purposeful work, and take joy in its accomplishment. Instructional leaders need to be able to make vivid the purposes served by evaluation, accreditation, and testing studies.

WIDE INVOLVEMENT. Instructional leaders also need to see that participation is widespread. Maximum understanding cannot be attained and benefits felt if only a few persons engage in the work, even if the efforts of the few are intensive and productive. Within a full-scale evaluation of program, there is much opportunity for real teamwork in the faculty or system, and the use of individual talents and interests. In the work of numerous small groups and sub-committees needed, there is also ample opportunity for shared leadership, and for the detection and cultivation of leadership potential among members of the faculty. In order to make wide involvement possible, instructional leaders often have to use ingenuity in finding ways to provide time, clerical help, substitute teachers, and temporary release from some routine tasks, in order for energy to be given to the evaluation, accreditation, and testing studies.

USE OF FINDINGS. Instructional leaders need to marshall all resources for following through as quickly as possible on some of the short-range recommendations based on findings from evaluation and accreditation studies. Few things can quicken the spirit for further work as much as seeing the fruits of early efforts begin to be harvested. Many of the changes recommended may involve school board policies, community interests, or budget considerations, and these will take months or several years to achieve fully; but there are usually some changes indicated that can be achieved within a matter of a few weeks. Building principals especially have a large responsibility for the immediate and long-range following through of recommendations.

Instructional leaders also play a big part in the interpretation of findings, especially of testing programs. Many persons, among them some teachers, are prone to attach great and long-lasting significance to something as apparently objective as a score. The true nature of a median score, the range of deviation, the limits of the scope of work tested, and the conditions inherent in the tests are easily overlooked. Hence, there is often a job at hand to prevent misunderstanding from information as to test scores achieved by students.

Types of Studies

Most states provide accreditation service through the state department of education. Six regional accrediting associations—the Southern Association of Colleges and Secondary Schools, the Middle States Association of Colleges and Secondary Schools, the New England Association of Colleges and Secondary Schools, the North Central Association of Colleges and Secondary Schools, the Northwest Association of Secondary and Higher Education, and the Western College Association—provide an additional accrediting service with standards similar enough in the regions to permit mutual recognition of programs throughout the nation. Standards are kept under continuous revision. The emphasis today is upon the stimulation and recognition of continuous growth and achievement, rather than just the initial meeting of standards. Instructional leaders have great responsibility for helping make the "continuous growth" a reality, and for help in the frequent revising of standards.

Evaluation studies are usually undertaken by an individual school or a whole system. State and regional groups also sponsor evaluation studies, and have been helpful in formulating criteria for adaptive use that would have consumed a vast amount of time if each faculty prepared its own criteria separately. Foundations, councils or associations, such as the Metropolitan School Study Council, the Southern Association's Cooperative Study in Elementary Education, or the Associated Public School Systems, sponsor evaluation programs of many kinds, some of a brief and highly specialized nature, and some of a long-range nature. Once again, in all types of programs for school improvement, instructional leaders occupy a crucial spot. If they are ill-informed or indifferent to the many possibilities, teachers will have little opportunity to function at their best. On the other hand, if they are well-informed and enthusiastic, educational advance will be hastened.

INTERPRETING THE SCHOOL PROGRAM
TO THE PUBLIC

Interpreting the school program to the public is another responsibility of supervision which requires time and judgment to discharge successfully. In a democracy a system of public education, along with other social institutions making efforts toward improvement of society, is highly dependent upon the level of understanding attained by the citizens. It is, of course, a fundamental assumption of a democracy that its citizens are capable of reasoning clearly, and coming to sound conclusions when they are well-informed regarding issues. Hence instructional leaders have great need to bring pertinent information to the public in varied but systematic ways.

From its discharge of other major functions, especially the stimulation of creative efforts, the facilitating and evaluating of change, and the contributing to a body of knowledge and techniques, supervision has many findings to bring to public attention. A problem often exists, however, in getting citizens who are already busy with vocational and civic pursuits to pause long enough to notice the significance of new needs and developments in education. Ingenuity and imagination are needed in bringing pertinent information to the public.

Basic Considerations

Several basic considerations can facilitate the work of supervision in keeping the public informed.

TIMING AND COORDINATION.   The presentation of information needs to come naturally, almost steadily, primarily reflecting the work going on in the schools. It should not be sporadic and bunched, like a high-pressure campaign followed by a void. The planning for a program of interpretation to the public needs to be long-range in nature, so that balance can be achieved, and a complete picture of school concerns presented over a period of time. The cooperative planning needed within the school and among schools, in order to present to the public a complete picture of activities, can vitalize a whole series of faculty meetings or committee sessions. With proper long-range planning, the need for saving certain classroom materials for future use can be foreseen, and school events can be utilized for interpretation purposes when they are most timely.

VARIETY OF MEDIA.   A variety of media for interpretation is usually helpful. The constant use of one form alone limits unnecessarily the richness of ideas obtained, and also tends to become routinized. But whatever forms are used, inferences need to be drawn clearly and interpretations made. For instance, if children's work is exhibited in store windows, or photographs of children at work are used in the newspaper, captions of some kind are needed to point out the educational significance of the product or event; otherwise,

much of the meaning escapes the casual beholder, and the effort
made to bring him some new ideas is largely wasted.

AWARENESS OF MULTIPLE REFERENTS. Along with every other profession and every area of specialization in the modern world, education has a problem of communication arising from the use of
technical terms. Since many of the words in the technical terms
have other ordinary meanings, it is exceedingly easy for a speaker to
use a word in one sense and for a listener to hear it in quite another
sense, without either person realizing the difference at first. Professional terms used by teachers to communicate with one another
are not always understood in the same way by lay persons. For
example, teachers may speak of "letting a child work at his own
rate," meaning that they are trying to stimulate him to work at his
optimum; but a lay person may visualize the teacher standing idly
by with folded hands, while the child dawdles and gradually slows
to a halt. Or a primary teacher may speak of urging the child to
"guess" a word in reading, meaning that he is to use swiftly every
clue at his command—phonetic, structural, configural, contextual,
or pictorial—to estimate carefully the probable meaning of the word;
but a lay person may easily visualize the child making a random, haphazard, anything-will-do stab at the word. Such terms as "real life
experience," "immature," "free play," are readily subject to misunderstanding or only partial understanding, and can easily become
the subject of harmful caricature and ridicule. Specialists in any
area owe the non-specialists the courtesy of clear explanations. Great
foresight, sensitivity, and good-humored patience are needed on
both sides.

When news items and other material are being prepared for
public release, it is often well to have one or more lay persons read
them for needed clarification or amplification. Multiple referents
and ambiguities can then be detected in advance, and confusion
prevented.

SIMPLICITY AND ACCURACY. Most printed efforts to interpret the
school program to the public need to have as their goal simplicity,

conciseness, readability, sharp focus, and accuracy. Many of the materials prepared by educators tend to encompass too much at one time, or tell more than the reader cares to know. It is indeed ironic that some of the qualities which make a person a competent educator, such as his sensitivity to subtle relationships and tangential factors, may interfere with his skill in direct, brief expression.

ANTICIPATION OF CHANGE.   When change is imminent, interpreting the program to the public gives instructional leaders an opportunity to explore and set forth the conditions which have given rise to the need for change, and to show how the proposed change is expected to meet new needs. If explanation can precede a change in board policy or long-standing school procedure, as in the modification of a system of reporting to parents, then the actual change can usually occur without misunderstanding and disgruntled surprise.

UNINTENTIONAL INTERPRETATION.   School personnel occasionally interpret the program to the public unintentionally and unfavorably through belittling remarks and small talk in dress shops, in barber shops, at the grocery store, or at the post office. Often it is no more than the small complaining and petty grumbling through which human beings release minor frustration and normal weariness, but it creates a non-professional atmosphere and leaves an unfavorable picture in the minds of listeners. The subtle impact of derogatory comments previously heard can sometimes be felt as supervisors and principals talk with lay persons. Supervision has need to help all concerned reach a higher level of professional responsibility and awareness.

NOTICING SIGNIFICANT ACHIEVEMENTS.   Supervision has a large role to play in locating significant accomplishments and events which need to be brought to the attention of the public. When principals and supervisors find especially good work going on, they can often arrange for a photographer to catch appropriate pictures, or prepare a press release, or ask for a record to be made for future use. System-wide supervisors especially need to serve as educational scouts, seeking significant scenes to share with the public and with other parts of the school system. The individual teacher is often so close to the scene that he does not grasp its salient quality. In addition, he may lack ready access to the equipment and channels necessary for informing the public.

Media for Interpreting the Program

The means for interpreting the program are numerous. Recent developments in technology make the variety even greater than in former years, and the accessibility and ease of use, such as in color photography, far greater than formerly. Imaginative use and time now become large factors in benefiting from technological advances. Brief comments on several media follow.

CHILD HIMSELF. No matter how elaborate programs of interpretation become, the child himself returning to his home each day is an inevitable interpreter of the school program. Instructional leaders can assist teachers in helping children and youth become aware of purposes behind daily experiences, and articulate in response to the oft-repeated question, "What did you do in school today?"

REPORTING TO PARENTS. A school's system for reporting pupil progress should also be recognized as an inevitable means of interpreting the school program in some measure. In former years the report card, with its shorthand number or letter grade assigned to each subject field, did little more than show the scope of subjects offered. Whatever richness of experience existed was not revealed. But in today's efforts to communicate with parents through elaborate folders, letters, and individual conferences, there is better opportunity to describe the purposes behind activities and procedures.

PHOTOGRAPHIC RECORDS. Photographs of important activities in a school, or of a sequence of stages in a program, are sometimes made in an evaluation study, or as a part of a school history. Sets of slides and filmstrips of a school's activities can be arranged for P.T.A. meetings or other sessions in the individual school, and then used subsequently in other parts of the system. Once again supervision can be of assistance by offering leadership, coordination in planning, and facilitation of the many steps between saying and doing.

EXHIBITS. Exhibits in public buildings, stores, and fairs offer another means of explaining the school program to the public. Relatively new devices like the overhead projector, tape recordings of children's work, and flannel board materials can also be used to tell the school's story. Supervisory personnel are needed in the cooperative planning involved in the effective use of these materials, in the assembling, and in the preparation of necessary captions and other explanations.

NEWSPAPER AND TELEVISION. Because of their large audiences and impelling manner of presentation, newspaper and television are important means of interpreting the school program to the public. The tendency to distort school events in the interest of vividness and newsworthiness is a hazard, but one with which school people must cope. If real rapport can be established between instructional leaders and certain editors and reporters, it is often possible for a background of understanding to be developed which forestalls most of the unintentional distortion. Also, if a school system designates certain persons to serve as a clearinghouse for press releases, reporters have someone specific to whom to turn when they are in doubt or are seeking further information.

BROCHURES AND LEAFLETS. When curriculum guides are prepared and new programs or materials introduced, it is sometimes practical to prepare a relatively inexpensive folder or small brochure describing the new project or material, and addressed primarily to parents. The purposes and anticipated outcomes of undertakings can often be made clear in this manner. A single-page illustrated newsletter can sometimes serve the same purpose. Such leaflets or newsletters are sometimes effective when mailed; other times they may be carried home by children; on still other occasions they are incorporated in parent-teacher conferences. It is often a supervisory role to prepare the leaflets and newsletters.

REPORTS FROM SCHOOL BOARDS. Some school boards have found it profitable, in terms of public understanding, to distribute widely an annual report to the public, usually in the form of an illustrated booklet. When pictures are well chosen, and explanatory paragraphs complete enough to point out the significance implicit in the scene, these booklets can be of great help in interpreting new developments, and in showing the scope of the total program.

The four major activities described in this chapter—(1) research, (2) selection, utilization, and production of materials, (3) evaluation, accreditation, and testing programs, and (4) interpreting the program to the public—are not the only ones which recur frequently in supervision. But they are of a sustained nature, they occupy a large portion of the time of instructional leaders, and the needs they serve are basic ones continuing into the foreseeable future. Hence persons now engaged in supervision, or those preparing to serve as instructional leaders, will want to examine the competencies involved in discharging these responsibilities well, and plan their own experiences for growth accordingly.

AIDS TO STUDY AND DISCUSSION

1. From your own experience, class discussion, and conferring with colleagues, list a number of questions for which you wish you had answers, in order to carry your work forward more successfully. Are there any of the questions for which information is probably available in the local system if someone had the time and skill to secure it?

2. Divide the class into small teams of three or four members each. Project a piece of research that could be carried out locally, with

each team choosing a different area of needed research, based upon some of your above questions. Or have several teams use the same area, projecting plans independently, and then seeing the variety of ways a problem might be approached.

3. In broad outline prepare a year's plan for interpreting to the public the program of your school. Be sure to indicate how you would achieve variety and balance in such factors as:
    a) involvement of personnel
    b) scope of presentations
    c) media used

SUGGESTIONS FOR FURTHER READING

Adams, Harold P., and Frank G. Dickey, *Basic Principles of Supervision* (New York: American Book Company, 1953), Especially Ch. 10, "Supervision Through Instructional Materials."

Association for Supervision and Curriculum Development, *Research for Curriculum Improvement*, 1957 Yearbook (Washington, D.C.: National Education Association, 1957).

Best, John W., *Research in Education* (Englewood Cliffs, N.J.: Prentice-Hall, Inc., 1959).

Betts, Emmett Albert, "Reading: Now and Then," *Education*, Vol. 78, No. 2 (October, 1957).

Burton, William H., and Leo J. Brueckner, *Supervision: A Social Process*, 3rd Ed. (New York: Appleton-Century-Crofts, Inc., (1955). Especially Chs. 13 and 17, relating to evaluation of materials and improvement of resources.

Comparative Achievement of Pupils Today and Yesterday (Washington, D.C.: Research Division, National Education Association, February, 1952).

Cox, Johnnye V., "Supervisors Gain Skills of Action Research," *Educational Leadership*, Vol. 12, No. 8 (May, 1955).

Hymes, James L., *Effective Home-School Relations* (Englewood Cliffs, N.J.: Prentice-Hall, Inc., 1953).

Jacobson, Paul B., William C. Reavis, and James D. Logsdon, *The Effective School Principal* (Englewood Cliffs, N.J.: Prentice-Hall, Inc., 1954), Especially Ch. 8, "The Use of Tests in Instruction."

Kubie, Lawrence S., "Are We Educating for Maturity?" *Journal of the National Education Association*, Vol. 48, No. 1 (January, 1959).

Landsberger, Henry A., *Hawthorne Revisited: Management and the Worker, Its Critics and Developments in Human Relations in Industry* (Ithaca: Cornell University, 1958).

McCloskey, Gordon E., *Education and Public Understanding* (New York: Harper & Brothers, 1959).

Melby, E. O., "Role of Evaluation in Improving Teaching," *Educational Leadership*, Vol. 15, No. 4 (January, 1958).

Yaeger, William A., *School Community Relations* (New York: The Dryden Press, 1951).

Zubek, John P., and Patricia Anne Solberg, *Human Development* (New York: McGraw-Hill Book Co., Inc., 1954).

CHAPTER 9

EXPERIENCES THAT PREPARE FOR SUPERVISION

SINCE the responsibilities of supervision are broad and the potentialities for constructive service almost unlimited, it becomes important to consider what experiences might be educative for those persons engaged in or preparing for instructional leadership. It is not assumed that the education of supervisors can be reduced to formulae or that undergoing a set of selected experiences guarantees the desired learnings by an individual. Yet to whatever extent there is reason to believe that human beings learn from their experiences, so that they derive meaning in such a way as to control future actions, to that same extent there is reason to believe that what an instructional leader experiences and what opportunity there is to generalize from that experience have significance.

Before attempting to describe some of the experiences with high potential value for the education of supervisors, perhaps it is well to examine some of the competencies and qualities especially needed by instructional leaders.

QUALITIES ESPECIALLY NEEDED BY
INSTRUCTIONAL LEADERS

Throughout the preceding chapters dealing with the functions and activities of supervision, the qualities and competencies needed by persons in the field have frequently been stated or implied. Both the variety of abilities needed and the degree of proficiency expected are impressive. Within the span of a few hours, for instance, a supervisor might be making such judgments as these calling for specialized knowledge: (1) in reading development of ten-year-old slow learners as he analyzes instructional problems with a group of intermediate grade teachers; (2) in printing and format as he helps decide on size of type and page arrangements for a curriculum guide in junior high mathematics; (3) in community concerns and in basic educational philosophy as he prepares to participate in a televised panel discussion; (4) in research techniques as he plans with principals regarding a proposed investigation; and (5) in group process and human relations as he confers with the superintendent about the agenda for a board meeting centered on policies affecting instruction.

Lay persons and school personnel alike rightly expect instructional leaders to exhibit a broad, liberal education, depth of knowledge and scholarship in chosen areas, and competency in the transactions of daily work. In addition, leaders must show a high degree of foresight, confidence, balance in judgments, persistence, hospitality to new ideas, and skill in helping people work together with optimum productivity.

Any listing of qualities needed in supervision tends to make it appear that only paragons of personal and professional virtues could be considered for appointment to supervisory positions. However, at least three factors make it possible for mortals to be considered. First, no one individual is expected to possess in equal measure all the qualities which are counted as desirable. Minor, or even distinct, deficiency in one area may be more than compensated for by strength in others.

Second, not all supervisory roles call for the same array or distribution of talents. For instance, a helping teacher with special responsibility for the induction of new teachers would have extensive need for ability to analyze teaching-learning situations, for friendliness and easy rapport with children as well as adults, and for first-hand familiarity with classroom materials. A director of instruction, however, would have less need for these qualities but great need for a comprehensive grasp of the whole school program and facility in summarizing ideas from group discussion.

Third, some of the qualities and competencies needed are acquired or brought to a higher level of accomplishment *after* the individual begins his supervisory work. The daily demands of his work, the frequent evolvement of new programs and techniques, and the effort to relate the old and new, thrust a supervisor forcibly into the role of learner. Sometimes the situation is almost ideal for learning since there is urgency in the demand, eagerness on the part of the learner, and opportunity to pursue the new knowledge or skill. Indeed, the situation often forces the individual to make a beginning try and then learn from self-analysis and tutelage of co-workers.

In writing of the personal attributes of supervisors Hicks describes the following as contributing to achievement: sincerity, empathy, openmindedness, intellectuality, objectivity, creativity, inspiration, proportion and balance, and respect for people.[1]

Crobsy points out that because supervision is an adventure in cooperative action, the qualities needed for participation are mutual characteristics of the good teacher, principal, and supervisor. She states three essential qualities:

> accepting every child, professional colleague, and parent because of their innate worth as human beings and bringing to that acceptance real support and understanding;

[1] Hanne J. Hicks, *Educational Supervision in Principle and Practice* (New York: The Ronald Press Company, 1960), pp. 58–64.

creating an environment of warmth which reflects the philosophy of a person who is a happy, outgoing, optimistic leader having rich resources of knowledge and know-how which others draw upon freely and frequently;

having the insight to read in behavior of children and adults alike the purposes and goals toward which each is struggling and the skill to help them learn for themselves that which is needed.[2]

Out of the many qualities that are significant five are elaborated here. To a large extent they are personal qualities and are the product of an individual's entire life experience and life style; but because they can be to some extent nurtured intentionally, they become lodestars for the planning, seeking, and selection of experiences appropriate to the education of instructional leaders.

Approachability

A person who is approachable is typically a friendly person, although not necessarily talkative. Pertinent here is the old observation that to be friendly a person does not have to go more than halfway in friendliness; he just needs to go his half of the way first. But in addition to being friendly, a person in supervision who is approachable has to be able to move naturally and freely from amenities and pleasant small talk to a deeper level of communication. He has to be hospitable to a consideration of new ideas. He needs to be an especially good listener, able to grasp quickly the essence of an idea or description and see its implications. Sometimes he needs to help the other person bcome articulate about an almost-sensed observation, and welcome opportunities to explore partially formed ideas.

Two cautions are worth stating. Instructional leaders are often in a hurry, for the duties to be discharged are numerous. But if haste becomes a habit for the principal or consultant, teachers may soon begin to feel that the matters they wish to discuss are perhaps

[2] Muriel Crosby, *Supervision As Cooperative Action* (New York: Appleton-Century-Crofts, Inc., 1957), p. 31.

trivial after all and scarcely worthy of the attention of such a busy person. A person who is bustling and panting with business is rarely approachable. Second, in somewhat like manner, persons who are preoccupied with pending events and decisions may *appear* aloof or indifferent without realizing it and hence seem unapproachable.

Perceptiveness

Perceptiveness is another quality needed daily in supervision. A high degree of awareness enables a person to notice the significant elements in situations, in materials, in the behavior of others, and even in his own actions. The observation has been made that man is the only creature that laughs or weeps, because he is the only animal that notices the difference between what *is* and what *ought* to be. Without keen awareness both of what is and what ought to be, instructional leaders can scarcely expect to help individuals work productively together toward goals.

Sensitivity to other people, their needs and purposes, enables supervisors to respect others, to find something worthy in their work, to anticipate responses, and to have foresight of how events and actions may look to others. Sensitivity helps supervisors identify with teachers who may have at first been rejected for one reason or another and to be truly concerned in helping them. Sensitivity to the intentions of others and to the way the situation looks to them also keeps a supervisor from any tendency to belittle the efforts or purposes of others.

Aspiration and Faith

Aspiration, vision, and faith should characterize instructional leaders. Furthermore, persons in supervisory roles need to be able to be articulate about their aspirations and faith. They need to know well the social, philosophical, and psychological underpinnings of their faith in order that they need not panic in the face of unexpected challenge and in order that they can accommodate new knowledge and developments in the immediate situation without losing their sense of direction toward ultimate goals. It is not easy for educators to maintain perspective and proportion, for they are subject to the same primary forces of social and scientific change affecting the local community, state, nation and world. In addition, they are subject to a secondary or rebound force, as individuals and agencies react to the primary forces in their own ways and press forward with their proposed solutions relevant to schools. Unless instructional leaders know why they believe what they believe to the point of saying it clearly for themselves and others, they may find themselves pushed and buffeted by partly plausible but conflicting suggestions, until their own initiative and vigor as leaders are impaired or lost.

Young teachers are often prone to discouragement because their high ideals and aspirations are necessarily difficult to attain and must be long in the achieving. Beginning teachers are sometimes strengthened and saved from debilitating attitudes if they hear instructional leaders speak out clearly, in time of crisis or simply in working sessions of faculty projects, to state concisely the rationale behind beliefs and the source of their faith.

Fromm speaks of rational faith as "a conviction which is rooted in one's own experience of thought or feeling . . . the quality of certainty and firmness which our own convictions have." [3] Perhaps it is this firmness or depth of conviction on the part of instructional leaders which, when expressed, is heartening to others.

A "Becoming" Person

The concept of continued growth is important to the theory and practice of supervision. Teachers, supervisors, consultants, principals, and superintendents are all in the process of "becoming," to use Allport's term. They are constantly seeking and striving.

Instructional leaders must be growing individuals, not only to carry their own role in professional life but also to serve as living examples of the becoming process. As they exhibit adaptability in

[3] Eric Fromm, *The Art of Loving* (New York: Harper & Brothers, 1956), p. 121.

their mature years and take joy in a flexible approach to problem solving, they silently testify to the satisfaction human beings find in the growth process. They also tend to become trusting of new experiences and relish the opportunities for further growth.

Imagination and Resourcefulness

Imagination and resourcefulness are required in supervision. Vision and aspiration can be left stranded, and almost superhuman effort made ineffective, if imagination and resourcefulness are missing. Instructional leaders may often feel that ability to fall back and regroup is their most frequently used talent. Fresh perceptions, seeing new uses for familiar materials and procedures, noticing previously undetected elements in a situation, willingness to take a calculated risk are all characteristic of good leadership. Persistence, resilience, and willingness to try with good cheer another way when a first way is blocked should be a part of the standard equipment for supervision.

EXPERIENCES THAT PREPARE FOR SUPERVISION

What experiences are likely to nurture in people the ways of responding just described, either prior to, or after, an individual's entering the field of supervision?

Teaching

Obviously the experience of classroom teaching is needed by those who become instructional leaders. From teaching come essential understandings of children as learners, of their interests and individual differences, of curriculum content and of materials of instruction. Insight is also gained as to the detailed nature of the teacher's job, and the satisfactions and problems of teaching. Teaching at more than one grade level or in more than one subject field greatly enlarges the knowledge of curriculum and of the reactions of children and youth of different ages and interests. Teaching in more than one school or community also enlarges understandings of the individual, for he is better able to see the universal quality of some problems and conditions, and on the other hand, the uniqueness of some problems pertaining to individual students, classrooms, or schools.

Serving in different types of teaching positions is also helpful in enlarging and deepening understanding. For instance, a person who serves as the directing teacher for an intern or one who teaches in a demonstration or laboratory school situation usually becomes supersensitive to what he himself is doing and becomes more insightful as to *why* he does what he does. He also gains experience in helping others plan, in giving encouragement, and in arranging opportunities for others to learn—all of which are helpful in supervision.

It is from teaching, too, that a person learns much about developing rapport with others, both students and colleagues, and about the increasing of perceptiveness. It becomes "second nature" for a teacher to be watchful of such factors as a child's facial expression, body posture, mode of movement or tone of voice as indices of his understanding and needs, and the degree to which learner and teacher are communicating. This same watchfulness is part of the alertness or sensitivity needed by supervisors.

Leadership and Service Activities

PRINCIPAL OR ADMINISTRATIVE HEAD. Serving as a principal, assistant principal, department head, or some other administrative head of a school unit yields certain insights in supervision. Grasping the scope of the total school program, seeing the individual school as a part of the larger local and state system, knowing firsthand the problems of public relations and community pressures, and experiencing the decision-making crises of administration make a person sensitive to many facets of the school day which are usually only dimly perceived as long as he is occupied full time with classroom teaching. To carry administrative responsibility enlarges the area and the depth of his understandings.

A principal also has excellent opportunity to see the significance of pupil-teacher relationships and teacher-teacher relationships. He comes to appreciate the variety of successful procedures used in classrooms, as well as know the variety of problems arising there. He usually develops respect for the individuality of teachers, the uniqueness of situations, and the numerous ways there are of working together in faculties. These same understandings, of course, are needed in the supervisory role.

FACULTY CHAIRMAN.   Serving as a faculty chairman for either a temporary or a standing committee is another experience which helps prepare for supervision. The experience aids a person in using committee procedures to a point of being at ease with them, in participating in group thinking, in genuinely wanting group participation, in understanding adults' reactions, and in enlarging his own knowledge.

Serving as a committee chairman is sometimes the beginning step which takes a capable individual up a long ramp of responsibilities of increasing importance. The gradual building of competence and confidence enables him to function later without crippling fears and self-distrust.

PARTICIPATION IN PREPARATION AND EVALUATION OF MATERIALS. Participation in the preparation and evaluation of materials provides the opportunity for developing several abilities and understandings needed in supervision. Becoming acquainted with the variety of materials available in a given situation, finding commonalities and differences among them, judging suitability of materials, matching materials to carefully analyzed student needs, and using techniques of group evaluation are among the values possible to obtain. Learning how to differ respectfully with co-workers and how to support a point of view with evidence are skills which can be developed in the process of preparing and evaluating materials and which are needed throughout supervisory work.

PARTICIPATION IN SURVEY AND EVALUATION STUDIES. Teachers and other school personnel often render service in other schools as well as their own by serving on survey teams and evaluation study committees. Such service is usually a means of a teacher's own enrichment too. Broadening the view of the total school program, developing a habit of thinking in terms of long-range objectives, seeing familiar things through the eyes of others, developing awareness of the importance of equal educational opportunities, discovering the variability among schools with regard to student personnel, resources, and procedures and seeing the effectiveness of planning systematic steps toward goals, are among the values to be gained from survey and evaluation work. Again, these understandings are needed throughout supervision.

PARTICIPATION IN CURRICULUM AND STEERING COMMITTEES. Another helpful activity is serving on curriculum and steering committees, including the preparation of curriculum guides. The nature of the helpfulness seems to be in the experience of coming to grips with basic issues, in working with persons and groups having somewhat differing points of view, in seeing the problems of the county or state as a whole, in analyzing needs and organizing ideas, and in organizing plans through democratic procedures.

PARTICIPATION IN CONFERENCES. Attendance at local, state, and regional conferences is another experience which prepares for supervision. The gaining of perspective and an increase in aspiration are often the outcomes for those who participate in well-designed conferences, and these are two of the qualities needed in supervision. Those who benefit from conferences usually ascribe the helpfulness to the over-all view of the program, the exchange of ideas, an increase in vision, the learning about materials and services, the creating of a feeling of unity of effort in the state or other unit, and the stimulating of ideas.

VISITING OTHER SCHOOLS. Visiting another school as part of his in-service education is sometimes the beginning step for a classroom teacher along a road to broader vision and a desire to serve. Among the possible values are the recognition of the commonality of many problems, the realization of new possibilities, the affirmation of some former ideas and the questioning of others, the stimulation to thinking, and the recognition of the importance of adjusting to changing needs and conditions found in different communities.

Non-Professional Experiences

A number of experiences, primarily non-professional in nature, yield a considerable residue of value for those persons entering supervisory work. For instance, participating in civic and church work leads a thoughtful person to a greater understanding of human relations, awareness of community problems, and appreciation of spiritual values. Engaging in domestic and foreign travel can contribute to new perspectives, understanding of people, and an increase in social conscience. Working in industry and business has potential for enlarging understanding of people and learning what the business world expects of schools. Engaging in personnel work and counseling in summer camps can be helpful through the opportunities presented for working with people and seeing personality evolvement in children and adults.

An Appraisal of Preparatory Experiences

How do instructional leaders themselves evaluate their experiences? A group of 107 general supervisors on the job and 23 state department of education members and professors of education identified with supervision were asked to appraise the helpfulness of their experiences, and to indicate where possible the nature of the helpfulness of the experience. The types of experience judged most helpful, arranged in descending order, were:

Serving as a classroom teacher
Participating in state and regional supervisors' conferences
Participating in leadership conference (summer)

Taking college courses in supervision
Serving as a principal
Visiting schools in other counties or states
Participating in school surveys and evaluative studies
Participating in the preparation of state, county, and local curriculum guides
Serving on county-wide curriculum or steering committees
Participating in campus and county workshops.

An analysis of the appraisal of the nature of the helpfulness indicated that benefit was derived from the opportunities these experiences gave for:

1. Understanding children, perceiving their needs, achieving skill in dealing with children, and selecting materials and activities for meeting their needs.
2. Understanding adults, working with teachers as individuals, perceiving their needs, developing skills and acquiring information for helping teachers with their problems.
3. Working with adults in groups, developing skill in the use of democratic procedures, participating in group efforts, discharging leadership responsibilities, and understanding the dynamics of human relationships.
4. Recognizing changing conditions and needs, and seeing education in relation to the local community and specific situations.
5. Seeing the total school program, recognizing the interrelationships among kinds of activities and levels of work, and helping teachers integrate their efforts toward long-range goals.
6. Stimulating thinking, increasing background from which to make varied approaches to problems, and raising doubts as to routinized ways of work.
7. Developing state-wide interests and commonality of concern, and drawing inspiration from concerted efforts.
8. Developing perspective, broadening the view of potentialities in education, seeing relationships among conditions and principles, and increasing breadth of vision.
9. Developing new aspirations and widening the horizon of educational advance.

Respondents were also asked what experiences they wished they might have had or could have in the near future. Ten areas received frequent mention in the following descending order:

1. Individual counseling and group guidance
2. How to study children
3. Community-school relationships
4. Human growth and development
5. Education of exceptional children
6. Resource-use education
7. Interpreting test data
8. Public speaking
9. Mental health
10. Group dynamics.

A resumé of the experiences instructional leaders prized and of their estimate of the nature of the helpfulness leads to several implications for education and supervision. Pre-service and in-service education for instructional leaders should provide for growth in the following areas:

1. Understanding children and youth

Instructional leaders are removed from direct contact with children and youth in the classroom, yet supervisors must have opportunity to continue the study of human growth and development, of children's reactions to the problems of daily living, and of the learning process.

2. Understanding cultural and socio-economic trends of the times

Recognition of the impact of cultural and socio-economic factors upon personality and upon motivation for action is essential to understanding children in relation to their daily living. Supervisors frequently need to help teachers recognize the process of acculturation at work, since teachers are so close to the child and his problems as to lose perspective.

3. Understanding human relations

Instructional leaders need to be able to understand child-teacher relationships and relationships among adults. Helping adults organize for the coordination of their efforts is a significant activity of leaders. Therefore, understanding of peer relationships, of committee work, of group procedures, of democratic leadership, and of group dynamics is essential.

4. Understanding teaching problems

Instructional leaders need opportunities to study the immediate problems of teaching, such as curriculum problems relating to experiences suitable for children and the attainment of goals, and problems of materials and organization.

5. Gaining perspective

Helping teachers and other school personnel achieve perspective with regard to their work is one of the greatest services of supervision. Therefore, supervisors need opportunities to see relationships among activities, to see the individual teacher's part in relationship to the whole school program, to see the school program in relation to the other factors in a child's life, to see the school's relationship to the community and to the improved quality of living. Instructional leaders need experiences that will enable them to exert an integrating force in education.

6. Increasing vision

In similar vein, instructional leaders need experiences that increase their vision and aspiration. Sharing ideas on a local, county, state, regional, and national level is one way of increasing vision and preventing concepts from becomnig place-bound and crystallized. Instructional leaders need opportunities at intervals to intellectualize the rich educative experience they frequently undergo, to deepen understanding currently held, and to systematize their thinking with regard to supervision, to the point that they grasp the full scope of supervision and achieve a sense of direction and integration in their own work. From their broad experiences they need to attain overarching purposes to guide themselves and to share with others.[4]

[4] Mildred Swearingen, *Developing Bases for the Education of Supervisors in Florida* (Unpublished doctoral dissertation), Ohio State University, 1950.

FORMAL PROFESSIONAL PREPARATION

It goes without saying that those who carry supervisory responsibility will want more than a legal minimum of formal preparation through college work at the undergraduate and graduate levels. Qualifications for many supervisory positions already stipulate more than a master's degree program by way of preparation.

University Preparation

BREADTH.   Preparation for an instructional leader should be both broad and liberal, i.e., liberating from ignorance and provincialism, for a leader will be dealing in the community with individuals and groups of diverse interests and concerns. His general education would, ideally, include considerable work in such areas as history, economics, anthropology, sociology, and social psychology.

DEPTH.   The preparation for an instructional leader should also provide depth in one or more areas of knowledge. He needs depth not only for the command of knowledge and relationships it gives him, but also because through scholarship he attains a systematic way of continuing learning.

SPECIALIZATION.   Several areas must be included in an instructional leader's specialization. Need for work in supervision, curriculum development, administration, human development and learning, group dynamics, and community relations is self-evident. Then, depending upon the nature of his responsibilities, his specialization should include the attaining of a high degree of competence in several general aspects of educational work such as evaluation, guidance, testing and measurement, and research techniques.

The instructional leader also needs unusual competence in speaking and writing. If other experiences have not yet led him to proficiency in these areas, his formal preparation might well include work in speech and journalism.

INTERNSHIP.   The concept of internship as the gradual assuming of the responsibilities of an active position while under the guidance of an experienced person is important for those in supervisory roles. For an individual to begin the process of translating understandings into actions appropriate to specific situations, while he has ready access to consultation service, usually means that he utilizes and refines his knowledge with little loss of time or energy.

Leadership Conferences and Workshops

Leadership conferences and workshops specifically designed to serve beginning and experienced supervisors and sponsored by universities or state departments of education have been an important part of the systematic preparation of instructional leaders. Such conferences vary in length from a few days to several weeks. Some have a relatively limited scope, such as acquainting new supervisors with the services of state agencies; others are elaborately organized and offer participants an opportunity to extend their knowledge in several fields such as child development, the use of language laboratories, or development of research design. The significant contribution of leadership conferences and workshops to the preparation for supervision may well stem from two facts: that irrelevant considerations are stripped away, and that each participant knows he is going to have immediate use for the knowledge obtained.

Cooperative Programs of Preparation

Also among the formally organized efforts are found cooperative programs of preparation. Several states, usually through a cooperative plan sponsored by universities, state departments of education, public school systems, and appropriate professional organizations, have evolved systematically delineated programs for the preparation of supervisors. These programs usually give emphasis to:

Careful selection of candidates
Interspersing of university courses and experience on the job
Internship under direction of the university or a follow-up responsibility on the part of the university

Flexibility in planning the candidate's program of work so that individual needs can be met and personal development stimulated
Emphasis upon human relations and learning processes.

CONTINUED PROFESSIONAL GROWTH

Whatever the nature and extent of their preparation may have
been, instructional leaders must continue their professional growth,
often at an accelerated pace, after they assume supervisory responsibility. The impact of socio-economic changes, findings from research, and the assigning of new tasks to education make such
growth necessary and almost inevitable. Fortunately, the process of
professional growth is usually a rewarding and satisfying experience.
The means of its accomplishment are numerous.

Daily Work

The daily work of an instructional leader is educative. There is
little sheer repetition of activities to lead him into thought-discour-
aging routines. At the same time the new demands in a situation
are usually so imperious as to push him into additional experiences.
The great variety of undertakings falling within a normal work-week
is in itself a means of growth. The opportunity of seeing the work
of many classrooms and schools is also a means of enlarging experience. It is not uncommon to hear supervisors speak with gratitude
of the privilege of being in schools where they can witness so much
professional skill and insight.

Instructional leaders, however, need time to analyze their experiences, to discern the principles involved in good practices, and to
formulate generalizations which can serve them in the future. Some
of this analysis of experience can be accomplished in collaboration
with co-workers through staff meetings and office conversation. Co-
workers are in themselves an educative medium, for usually each

one has several areas of competency from which his fellows can learn.

Participation in Work Projects

Participation in state, regional and national projects is a valuable means of education for persons in supervision, for it brings them into a close working relationship with individuals beyond the confines of their own school system. Sharing ideas while in pursuit of common goals is usually a vivid way of benefiting from one another's experience. For instance, the projects of the Southern States Work Conference, such as the one culminating in the publication of *Guidance Services in the Public Schools*, or the projects in educational administration supported by the W. K. Kellog Foundation and school groups leading to the bulletin, *Experimentation in Preparing School Leaders*, brought enlargement of understanding to all who participated, as well as building confidence in one another through working together.

National Conventions

Well-planned conventions of professional groups bring together keenly interested and highly informed persons. In addition to being a major medium for disseminating research findings and pertinent knowledge and for taking corporate action, conventions of professional organizations have, in recent years, often become a veritable practicum of creative attempts to serve and improve leadership. Participants in the convention have an opportunity to experience first-hand some of the leadership and group processes that, up to that point, they have only read or heard about. They also have an opportunity to help refine the use of new processes.

Persons who benefit from conventions point out that the experience widens horizons for them through the association with other people and contact with new materials and plans. Perspective is restored and enlarged by the individual being free from the hourly demands and the minutia of his job long enough to think coherently about why he is doing what he does, and aspiration increases as new goals and means of reaching them are glimpsed.

Workshops and Conferences

Workshops, seminars, and short conferences specifically designed around matters of deep concern to supervision are a chief means for the continued education of instructional leaders. Some such sessions are sponsored by state departments of education, universities, or professional organizations, and others may be sponsored locally. Some take the form of a series of afternoon meetings, while others are concentrated into one or more days of sustained effort. The co-operative planning involved is discussed in a later section of this chapter. The significant point here is that workshops, seminars, and conferences can each have a sharp focus of scope and purpose, and the people who attend know what they are seeking. Hence, learning can be efficient and the impact of the learning upon action can be forceful.

Time for Learning

Another facet of continued professional growth in supervision is the need for time for learning. It is true that many of the experiences which are educative are bound up in the daily work of instructional leaders, but it is necessary to take some time for noticing, interpreting, generalizing, and systematizing. In other words, instructional leaders need some opportunity for contemplation and re-orientation of thinking. Very often, however, they feel vaguely guilty if they sit quietly in thought or even pursue reading in professional literature in a speculative mood, instead of on a harried hunt for specific help for a teacher. It should be respectable to sit still and think.

Many instructional leaders work under a twelve-month contract and consequently need the help of the employing board or agency in obtaining leave to attend conferences and especially to do advanced study.

COOPERATIVE PLANNING FOR
THE EDUCATION OF SUPERVISORS

Since the successful education of instructional leaders is far-reaching in its impact and potentially can benefit the work of the entire school system, it is essential to consider how leaders can come by the experiences which help qualify them to discharge the unique functions of supervision. While the individual has great responsibility for his own continued growth, the range of experiences needed is so great that his single-handed efforts can seldom be sufficient.

Continuous and Cooperative Planning Needed

The very nature of supervision demands an education for supervisors which, in the first place, is continuously *being* planned, and, in the second place, is cooperatively planned. Supervision takes the present as a point of departure and projects a program for the future. Therefore, the education of those who work in such a program must be on-going and continuously replanned. It necessitates constant evaluation of the supervisory situations (persons, local setting, and program for action) to determine what the situation is in relation to what it has been, and the direction in which it needs to move.

Education for supervision must be cooperatively planned, since it involves several groups with closely related but unique functions: supervisors themselves, as individuals and professional workers; local county and state officials who have a legal as well as a professional responsibility for education; universities as centers of higher education and research; and professional organizations such as state education associations and the Association for Supervision and Curriculum Development.

Education for supervision also needs to be planned continuously and cooperatively in order to achieve *consistent* growth. Long-range purposes should be present and discernible if there is to be relatedness and continuity in the individual's professional development. Formal courses are usually insufficient, although they have a contribution to make. Conferences are helpful but sometimes unconnected with one another. Individual experiences are often too limited and their values only partially intellectualized. Planning for education for supervision should make use of varied learning situations. It should avoid the extreme, on the one hand, of stereotyping and perseveration and, on the other hand, of haphazard or sporadic experiences.

Some Characteristics of Cooperative Planning

In cooperative planning, certain understandings and attitudes toward the development of a common frame of values must prevail if members of a group hope to reach agreements that will foster planning for action.

ATTITUDE TOWARD A PLAN. First is the attitude toward a plan itself. Members of the group need to see the plan not as a blueprint but as a statement of agreements as to goals, commitments, functions and responsibilities to be recognized. Plans themselves are emergent and cannot be allowed to crystallize permanently. A plan has to be kept responsive to changes in conditions.

ATTITUDE TOWARD CRITICAL THINKING. Second is the attitude toward critical thinking. Critical thinking is essential to attaining the just stated attitude toward planning. Members of the group must be willing to hold decisions tentatively, to keep channels of communication open, to hold no ideas to be above examination, and to respect the integrity of those with whom they differ in opinion.

ATTITUDE TOWARD A GOAL. Third is the attitude toward a goal. A goal is recognized as giving direction to activity but not always dictating each act performed in the process. Means for reaching goals must be adaptable to situational needs, including differences in human as well as environmental factors. While means for reaching the same or similar goals may be quite diverse, care must be exercised that they do not contradict or negate some other value that the group prizes.

ATTITUDE TOWARD AGREEMENT. Fourth is the attitude toward agreement. Development of a common frame of values often necessitates the acceptance of similar, rather than identical, goals and ideals. Cooperation at the level of action and agreement at the level of generalization are often possible when agreement as to ultimate reasons or philosophic justification would be difficult and perhaps undesirable, or when entire agreement as to specific application would be long-delayed. The particular pitfalls of semantic problems should be recognized as a hazard to agreements.

COMMITMENT TO COORDINATION. Fifth is commitment to the principle of coordination of roles and functions of cooperating agencies. The groups concerned must have confidence in cooperative effort as an effective way of work. They should have willingness not only to use democratic procedures skillfully but also to work creatively and experimentally for the further improvement of democratic procedures. They should have a particular concern for the role of the specialist or special group interest in a complex society and a concern for the dynamics of group effort.

Roles in Cooperative Planning for Education for Supervision

Several groups or agencies are concerned with education for supervision. Each one has some common and some unique functions to perform. A consideration of the functions of four important groups follows.

STATE DEPARTMENTS. State departments of education have a legal responsibility for the improvement of the school system, and the professional growth of instructional leaders is a part of that responsibility. State departments are in a favorable position for making some unique contributions to education for supervision. They can collect information that reveals school needs. They can transmit information readily since they have access to all schools, and legal responsibility to call conferences. State department representatives, through their correspondence, travel, and first-hand contact with school situations, are in a position to detect needs that are often not expressed formally and to detect trends as they first appear. This continuous analysis and estimate of current needs is a significant contribution to planning realistic in-service education for supervision. Also state departments can, in some situations, make certification and appointment contingent on suitable conditions or qualifications. They can foster, support, and put into action concerns or provisions agreed upon through cooperative planning.

UNIVERSITIES AND FOUNDATIONS. In addition to having some functions in common with other agencies, universities and foundations have the specific function of carrying on research, of noting social trends leading to the improvement of living, and of encouraging the development of philosophies as to what constitutes the good life. Universities have a pioneer function to perform in setting forth scientific and social findings in pertinent special fields, and showing their probable relationship to educational procedure. Universities and foundations need to take initiative in conducting research in both laboratory and field situations, cull findings from research here and abroad, systematize relevant outcomes, and make the information accessible to educational leaders. There is an especially large role for universities and foundations in designing and supporting the applied research necessary to establishing relationships from findings in such areas as group dynamics, mental health, learning aids, and cultural integration, to proposed changes in educational practices.

PROFESSIONAL ORGANIZATIONS. Professional organizations have a contribution to make in providing for free mutual association and stimulation among members, and in providing channels for the release and productive flow of the creative energy of individuals and small groups. State-wide, regional, and national professional organizations and councils also have the function of increasing vision through new ideas and experiences. Concepts and procedures in advance of present practice are often first glimpsed through attendance at conferences of such organizations and association with persons of like interest but varied experiences.

LOCAL AND COUNTY GROUPS. Local and county groups, including the administrative officials, have a function to perform. Theirs is the responsibility for taking into account situational differences and needs, and for seeing how theory and values guide practice in specific situations. Local and county groups have the responsibility for giving expression to the needs they feel, and helping plan for solutions to problems in light of the immediate situation. Administrative officials, especially, have to plan in terms of financial resources and facilities as these factors influence education of school personnel.

State Programs of Education for Supervision

As indicated earlier in this chapter, a number of states have developed clearly-defined programs of education for supervision. Georgia, for several years, has had a program which gives emphasis to: (1) the careful selection of those who enter the program; (2) the interspacing of university courses and workshops with experience on the job; and (3) an internship period of two years, during which university and state department of education personnel visit the new supervisor in his first position.[5] West Virginia has also used a somewhat similar plan for some years.[6]

[5] Jane Franseth, "Georgia's Program of Education for Prospective Supervisors," *School Life*, Vol. 30, No. 6 (March, 1958), pp. 2–3.
[6] Maud Broyles, "An Emerging Program of Supervision," *Educational Leadership*, Vol. 6, No. 3 (December, 1946), pp. 169–171.

In Kentucky, the university, the state department of education, and a foundation have sponsored a plan which again intersperses university study through courses and workshops with guidance on the job. The center of emphasis here has been upon supervision as personal development, and many of the efforts have been focused on the supervisor's own growth as a person and his development of skill and insight in stimulating growth in others.[7]

Several significant generalizations regarding state programs can be drawn from the work so far:

1. Cooperation between state departments of education and colleges is widespread. Cooperation among teacher-education institutions within a state is also extensive, and planning in one part of the state is communicated to other parts.

2. The rise of cooperative planning has accelerated, especially since the creation of teacher-education advisory councils which have become almost universally used in the states since the 1940's.

3. Coordinated programs have come about in an evolutionary rather than revolutionary manner, with many persons participating in the delineating of a program.

4. Voluntary professional groups, such as state units of the A.S.C.D. in New York and Michigan, and the Southern States Work Conference, have encouraged individual and group initiative and have made contributions through their studies in leadership and instruction.

5. There are at least some pioneer efforts to locate and select prospective instructional leaders.

6. Field experience is recognized as important for prospective or beginning supervisors.

7. A democratic framework for planning has been achieved in many states which encourages, but does not automatically result in, long-range planning. Committees must take time to weigh values and shape policies according to desired goals, rather than according to immediate pressures and matters of expediency.

[7] James R. Ogletree, *Person-Centered In-Service Education, Why Not?* (Lexington: University of Kentucky, September, 1957).

Implications for Further Coordination of Efforts

The progress already made in cooperative planning for the education of instructional leaders and precedents already established are extensive. Several implications can be drawn for the guidance of continuing efforts.

First, there needs to be a representative committee for planning, so that channels of communication among groups are open and known by all members.

Second, meetings of the committee should be of sufficient length to enable participants to consider issues and problems carefully, rather than superficially, and to arrive at mature judgments. Freedom of inquiry and experiment should be fostered and freedom of communication should give creative experimentation a hearing.

Third, evaluation and adjustment of the program in action should be continuous. There should be planned, periodic, evaluative studies on which decisions may be based. There should be records of commitments and projected action so that an interim of exploration can be followed by further evaluation, and then further projected action.

Fourth, there should be deliberate effort on the part of persons doing cooperative planning for the education of instructional leaders to vary their own experiences sufficiently to obtain clear vision which they can share in developing wider horizons and recognizing the significance of education in the total scope of living.

AIDS TO STUDY AND DISCUSSION

1. After a review of your own experiences and of what you think should prevail, list eight to ten personal-professional qualities you think an instructional leader should possess and continue to cultivate.

2. Interview five or six teachers to ascertain what characteristics of instructional leaders are most appreciated by colleagues. How do your findings compare with those of other members of the class or with studies reported in the literature?

3. Make a simple outline of the types of experiences suggested in the chapter as helpful in the preparation for supervision and add other activities you consider relevant. Mark those experiences you have already encountered and be ready to share an example with the class. What additional opportunities do you anticipate in the next year?

SUGGESTIONS FOR FURTHER READING

Allport, Gordon W., *Becoming* (New Haven: Yale University Press, 1955).

Broyles, Maud, "An Emerging Program of Supervision," *Educational Leadership*, Vol. 6, No. 3 (December, 1946).

Cox, Johnnye V., "Educating Supervisors in Changing Concepts," *Educational Leadership*, Vol. 16, No. 8 (May, 1959).

Crosby, Muriel, *Supervision as Cooperative Action* (New York: Appleton-Century-Crofts, Inc., 1957).

Farley, Genevieve J., and John J. Santosuosso, "The Effect of Training in Leadership on a Supervisor," *Education*, Vol. 78, No. 6 (February, 1958). Topics consider leadership patterns, supervisory personnel, qualifications of supervisors (concerning their experience), and leadership training.

Franseth, Jane, "Georgia's Program of Education for Prospective Supervisors," *School Life*, Vol. 30, No. 6 (March, 1948).

Fromm, Eric, *The Art of Loving* (New York: Harper & Brothers, 1956).

Hicks, Hanna J., *Educational Supervision in Principle and Practice* (New York: The Ronald Press Company, 1960).

Mosier, Earl E., "In-Service Education of the Superintendent," *Educational Leadership*, Vol. 9, No. 1 (October, 1951).

Ogletree, James R., *Person-Centered In-Service Education, Why Not?* (Lexington: University of Kentucky, September, 1957).

Swearingen, Mildred, *Developing Bases for the Education of Supervisors in Florida*, unpublished doctoral dissertation (Ohio State University, 1950).

CHAPTER 10

PROBLEMS OF BEGINNING SUPERVISION

A SUCCESSFUL beginning is naturally desired by any person entering a position; but the cost of a poor start in a supervisory position is extraordinarily high. Instructional leaders who make wrong judgments not only fail to move the work forward, but actually lose ground. The loss of confidence, probable frictions, and chain-reaction outcomes created by erroneous choices persist long after the immediate incidents and confusions have been resolved. It is important, therefore, to give careful thought to what steps persons with supervisory responsibility might take to assure a productive and satisfying start.

WHO IS A BEGINNER IN SUPERVISION?

It may prove helpful to raise the question as to who is a beginner in supervision. In a considerable sense, of course, everyone in supervision is a beginner each year, in that no matter how many years he has been in a position, the situation changes and the individual grows enough in the course of a year so that each September finds the situation and individual full of new potentials for interaction.

In general, however, a beginner is one who is serving as an instructional leader for the first time or one who has some previous supervisory experience but is entering a new position. The position in turn may be simply in a new location, or it may be a newly-created position with or without a clear definition of scope of work. Each kind of beginner has some unique problems but each has much in common with the others.

Persons Without Prior Supervisory Experience

A person assuming the responsibility of supervisory work for the first time may find a problem in his own lack of confidence in himself, and in his awareness that the people he is to serve have no basis as yet for confidence in him. If he remembers two things, however, this lack of confidence need not prove to be a paralyzing or detrimental factor; it may indeed merely supply him with a healthy caution. First, the persons who employed him must have noticed something about him and his qualifications to make them think he was capable of doing the job. Whatever they noticed would also be at least partly visible to others and hence a basis for confidence, even when the reasons are not entirely clear to himself.

Second, he is not really as inexperienced as he seems. The title of his work may be entirely new for him, but the nature of what he is going to do holds much that is familiar. His classroom teaching and the professional responsibilities already discharged successfully have given him insights and skills that equip him for new activities. If he were to peruse any listing of experiences that prepare for supervision, he would discover that he has actually encountered many of them and benefited from them.

Persons With Prior Supervisory Experience

A person who enters a supervisory position from a former position is not entirely free from the uncertainties which plague the complete beginner. However, his larger problem is likely to be that of overcoming expectations, often unconsciously held, which were derived from his previous work but are not realistic in the present setting. His assumptions have to be rudely shaken sometimes before he discovers that he is operating within one framework of habits but his co-workers within another. For instance, the protocol for arranging an intervisitation schedule might be quite different in two communities. If the new leader acts on the basis of former expectations, he may unintentionally offend his new colleagues. If prior experiences slant new perceptions too far, a person may be several months in a new position before overcoming the resultant distortions.

Persons going from one established position to another are rushed so rapidly from one set of demanding engagements to another that they have little opportunity to obtain a new orientation. Indeed, the situation is analogous to a person jumping off one moving merry-go-round and onto another without either vehicle slowing its momentum to discharge or pick up passengers.

Persons in Newly-Created Positions

Individuals entering newly-created positions have certain advantages, especially in being free from hampering commitments or routines. However, in many cases, the lack of a clear definition of what is expected from the new position constitutes an obstacle. Even where desired outcomes are clearly stated, the impact of the new position, in terms of personal relationships and the incorporating of a new member of the team, may not be fully anticipated.

Commonality of Problems

For the most part, however, persons beginning supervisory work find themselves facing quite similar problems, in spite of variations in situations and in their own preparatory experiences. Gilbert found, for instance, in a study of the problems of beginning supervisors, that 60% of the problems encountered were concentrated in the three areas of curriculum, supervision of learning, and professional growth. Problems in five other areas were encountered in the following descending order of frequency: instructional materials, establishing the supervisory program, evaluation, human relations, and public relations. Within the areas, nine specific problems were encountered by 50% or more of the supervisors:

1. Budgeting own time
2. Helping teachers evaluate their programs
3. Inspiring creative thinking
4. Encouraging instruction leading to critical thinking
5. Helping teachers in transition from subject mastery planning to development of children planning
6. Teachers not well prepared for creative art
7. Individual differences in heterogeneous classes
8. School time for teacher meeting
9. Out-of-school demands upon your time.

When data were analyzed from the standpoint of certain factors in the background of the beginning supervisors, it was found that: (1) persons with the greatest amount of education encountered problems with somewhat greater frequency than others, (2) that men identified more problems per person than women, (3) that individuals with prior experience as principals or as supervisors encountered problems with greater frequency than complete novices. But in all cases the types of problems encountered showed high similarity.[1]

Even persons who have been continuing in the same position for several years find themselves concerned with many of the same problems faced by beginning instructional leaders. It may well be that instructional leaders of all kinds are actually dealing with some persistent problems of supervision rather than encountering something reserved for or germane to beginners; but the fact of beginning does sharpen awareness and heighten the urgency to learn. Five areas of common concern are discernible.

---

[1] Robert G. Gilbert, *The Problems of Beginning Supervisors in Florida Schools,* unpublished doctoral dissertation (Tallahassee: Florida State University, 1961).

LEARNING ABOUT THE COMMUNITY

Many customs and ways of operating in a school system are plausible only when the school is seen in relation to its community. Many of the choices regarding curriculum content and appropriate procedures for instruction have to be made in the light of community conditions and aspirations. Hence instructional leaders need to give time and attention to learning about the community. The specialization of labor is so great today and the organization of a community so complex that learning about a community is by no means a simple matter.

Aspects

SOCIO-ECONOMIC SETTING. The newcomer will want to take note of the economic base of the community, whether it has primarily a single economy or a diversity of agricultural and industrial pursuits, whether young people are absorbed into the work life of the community or have to plan to move away, and whether families are frequently on the move. He will note the range of socio-economic classes, the concentration of persons in those classes, and the ease with which persons might change status. He will notice the quality of housing throughout the community and estimate whether the school population will be similar in each school or quite diverse in nature.

SOCIAL AGENCIES. The newcomer would also try to find out about the social agencies already at work in the community, especially those concerned directly with children and youth. Not only does the total amount of social agency help for children differ markedly from one community to another but the range is also great as to what agency provides what help. For instance, in one community an effective summer recreation program might be sponsored by the city recreation department, in another by the school system, and in still another by the Y.M.C.A. Or, a child in need of dental care might be aided in one community by the P.T.A., in another by the County Health Unit, and in another by a local civic club. The beginner must expect to take time to inquire about the means and patterns of organization among social agencies, both public and private. To rush in with inappropriate requests can cause unnecessary irritation and delay.

CIVIC ACTION. Instructional leaders new in a community would want to note the evidences of former civic action and learn what specific matters are currently of concern. The presence or absence, for instance, of a public library, park system, and recreational facilities would indicate something of a community's expectation of taking cooperative action to achieve desired goals. The presence or absence of current plans for civic improvement would also indicate something of the enthusiasm or lethargy with which a community approaches civic action.

HISTORY. The newcomer needs to examine the history of the community, including the reasons for its early beginnings and for the attraction of inhabitants in more recent years. Links with events in state and national history should be noted, and also family names that have been prominent in the community's development. Anything of special pride (or shame) in the community's past needs to be known to an instructional leader. Not to know things of significance recognized by others causes him to appear naive and sometimes leads to blundering and clumsy handling of situations.

CHURCHES. The beginning supervisor will want to observe the churches represented in the community, the proportion of the population identified with churches, and the evidence of the seriousness with which the members take their church life. The extent of youth programs identified with the churches and the degree to which churches cooperate with one another in the improvement of community life are also important. Often it is significant for an instructional leader to learn quickly of traditional divisiveness among the church groups in a given community if he is to avoid irritating people.

SUB-CULTURAL GROUPS. Communities differ widely in their degree of cultural similarity and solidarity of interest. The beginning instructional leader needs to note the ethnic groupings, the range of socio-economic classes, the range of educational levels among parents, the concentration in age groups, the distribution of groups in different parts of the city, the ease with which individuals can cross group lines, and the variation in groups as to aspirations for their children through the school and other community offerings.

EDUCATIONAL AGENCIES. The presence of other educational agencies is of concern to the newcomer. Private schools, adult education opportunities sponsored by industry and by federal, state and local agencies, forums and lecture series, programs of public or private libraries, museums, and galleries are to be found in some communities but not in others. It is somewhat easier for a person to become acquainted with these opportunities when he first arrives in a community and is making inquiry about many facets of life, than it is after he is in the habit-forming routines of full responsibility in his new job.

Persistent Questions

Running through the analysis of aspects of a community made by a new instructional leader are several persistent questions, questions for which he will continue to seek answers as he becomes a veteran in the position.

1. How much solidarity of interest is there in the community? Is there essentially one community or are there many? Is there primarily one voice speaking for community interest in the school or are there many?
2. Is there a habit of cooperative action in the community? Do members expect to give voice to ideas for community improvement, to take initiative, to formulate and revise plans for co-

operative achievement of goals? Have they taken action together in the past or do they typically expect someone else to provide initiative and means of accomplishment?

3. What is the community outlook toward change? Is the community past-oriented to the degree that present needs and future possibilities are unnoticed? Is there complete satisfaction with the status quo? Is there expectation of change?

4. What agencies and families are admired and respected? Who are the gate-keepers of ideas? Who and what help give voice to and influence public opinion?

5. Is the community friction-prone? Does it have a habit of factionalism, of bitterness and retaliation, in issues over civic matters? Do members tend to choose sides even before examining an issue?

6. Are there groups with intense convictions for whom exceptions must be made in general policies regarding school, health, or other civic concerns?

Means for Studying the Community

Several media for learning about the community are available. One is to read extensively, especially factual information. Census data provide a surprising amount of information about the socio-economic life of a community. A quick glance at the yellow pages of the telephone directory tells much about the range of economic activity to be expected. Publications of the Chamber of Commerce and pamphlets from historical societies yield considerable information. Novels about the community or general area often supply some insight as to local values and outlooks. A few hours spent perusing old newspapers can help create a feeling for past events and concerns.

A second medium is that of observing. For example, what is in store windows, especially hardware stores, tells something of the economic life of a community. The cleanliness of the streets, the status of the parks, and the efforts toward beautification reflect something of what the community expects from civic cooperation. Following a school bus along its route, or actually riding on it where he can hear children's conversation and informal language usage, shows the new instructional leader much about the economic aspects of the community, sub-cultural groupings and their attitudes toward one another, variations in housing conditions, and types of civic problems.

A third source of information is found in asking questions, providing the newcomer asks his questions of several people. Blind spots in any one person's information and his bias of perception mean that the responses from one individual should be received gratefully but not regarded as verified fact nor a complete picture of the situation. Asking questions is, of course, one of the quickest ways of obtaining information relevant to the new leader's needs.

A fourth way of learning about the community is through participating in church, civic, and other non-school activities. Actually taking part in such activities gives the newcomer a natural and direct way of knowing persons outside of school circles and of sharing their concerns. A new instructional leader often needs to use some foresight or caution about the extent of his involvement, however, for he can become over-committed before he is aware of the many responsibilities he is expected to discharge in his school role.

LEARNING TO KNOW NEW CO-WORKERS

Learning to know new co-workers is a problem of beginning supervision of which a new instructional leader is keenly aware. Indeed, in large school systems, the matter at first seems almost overwhelming. The beginner needs to be realistic enough to recognize that becoming genuinely acquainted with his colleagues will take considerable time. There are system-wide staff members, principals, and teachers to know, as well as parents and community representatives. A few he will see almost every day, but others only once in a few weeks or months; yet he is expected to know all of them well enough to coordinate his efforts with theirs in a productive, friction-free manner. Hence he needs to learn as rapidly as possible their professional aspirations and procedures, something of their personal values and commitments, and something of the individuality of behavior that each person has developed through his endowments and life experiences.

Avenues for Becoming Acquainted

SOCIAL EVENTS.   In terms of order of occurrence, social events often come early among the opportunities for becoming acquainted with colleagues. The new principal, for instance, is often entertained by the faculty, by the P.T.A., and by many individuals. Social events are not the most significant way for becoming acquainted and they sometimes consume time and energy out of proportion to their worth, but they do have several distinct values. (1) The relaxed, friendly atmosphere encourages people to be approachable, lowering the barriers of restraint and concentration present in a work-day situation. (2) There is opportunity for discovery of personal interests, common experiences in the past, and perhaps special compatibility of outlook and tastes. (3) The specific social event begins the building of a common experience background. The new leader and his colleagues have now shared something and have a starting point for mutual concerns. (4) In addition, at least some few people possess a talent, and perhaps more could cultivate it, for moving from the casual, superficial conversation of most social occasions to a deeper, more significant level of communication. For them, the gambits of social conversation really become thresholds for greater understanding of their fellow-workers and themselves.

DIRECTORIES AND RECORDS.   A new instructional leader can profitably spend some time in studying directories and personnel records, especially just before meeting with a specific faculty, committee, or individual. He can acquire some familiarity with names, note the locale of prior educational experience and preparation, and become aware of some of the special interests and potential contributions of members. For instance, it might be helpful to know that certain secondary teachers had had elementary school experience, that some elementary teachers had certification in some secondary areas, that some teachers had lived abroad for several years, or that some had conducted travel groups in the summer. Both personal and professional interests can be found in the study of records.

INTERVIEWS.   A deliberate attempt to meet each colleague and talk with him uninterruptedly for a time is usually well worth the effort. The interview can be scheduled or unscheduled, formal or informal. If the conversation can revolve primarily around the newcomer's efforts to understand the current program in the individual school and system, then attention is focused in such a way that the two persons can be mutually helpful. At the same time they are revealing to each other their professional, and probably some personal, concerns.

WORKING TOGETHER.   It is, of course, primarily through working together on common undertakings that people really come to know one another. The new instructional leader needs to remember that becoming acquainted with colleagues is not to be accomplished as a task apart, in some kind of vacuum; it is part and parcel of pursuing common concerns in daily work. It is in full-scale doing that individuals, including the new leader, reveal their understandings, their idiosyncrasies, and the growing edge of their professional and personal lives. It is from close working together, too, that people develop a real basis for mutual respect and confidence.

OUT-OF-SCHOOL CONTACTS.   The community, neighborhood, and church all offer opportunities for some out-of-school associations with co-workers. These occasions should be recognized as the means of increasing knowledge about the other person's interests and talents and the development of common experiences.

Expectation of Variation and Individuality

As the new instructional leader works with colleagues he will be noting the variations and expressions of individuality expected among human beings. He will be noticing especially which persons have enthusiasm for new ideas, who find challenge in conditions that need improving, and who sparkle with suggestions for innovations and undertakings. He will be watching for those who are articulate about ideas and can give expression to values held by themselves and others. He will usually find fairly soon those who are excellent thinkers but who cannot verbalize their ideas readily and those, too, who are capable in a performance situation but largely unable to express the principles underlying their sound practices.

The new leader will be watchful of varying types of resistance to change, noting those persons: (1) who are cautious but who can consider evidence freely and then support a proposed change; (2) who chronically resist change as though they had some compulsion to say, "No," but who, having said it, then seem to relax and consider possibilities; and (3) who are merely habit-bound through lack of stimulation and fresh perception rather than through conscious devotion to the status quo or through fear of change. He will also be noting those who appear to resist change because of timidity or lack of self-confidence, where supervisory assistance might be the very help needed to outgrow the too small, limiting concept of self. He may also find examples of a fear of change that has reached neurotic proportions and is an expression of serious maladjustment needing psychiatric treatment.

LEARNING ABOUT THE ON-GOING PROGRAM

There are few quicker ways of alienating new colleagues than for the beginning instructional leader to assume that nothing has been going on in an educational situation prior to his arrival. Therefore, it is imperative for him to take time to observe and inquire regarding previous and current efforts toward school improvement. While he is making this inquiry, he also has opportunity to learn about two other areas to be discussed in the remaining portions of the chapter, namely, current educational needs in the situation and role expectations with respect to supervision.

Need for Inquiry

The newcomer who assumes, or appears to assume, that little of importance has been going on in the way of instructional improvement prior to his own appearance not only damages his first attempts by offending his new co-workers; he also blinds himself to many realities in the situation which offer excellent points for harnessing his own energy to the efforts already under way. He insults his co-workers in several fundamental ways: their intelligence in recognizing and dealing with problems, their professional knowledge, and their aspirations for children. Small wonder, then, if they cannot respect the suggestions and judgments of the new leader as he begins his work! But if he takes time to learn what problems have prevailed in the past, what efforts (often enormous) made to solve the problems, and where he as a newcomer can begin to help, then his co-workers have a basis for confidence and respect.

Since the pitfall just pointed out is fairly obvious, it is worth considering why it is rather common for persons new in any leadership position, not just in education, to find themselves trapped therein. Perhaps the explanation is to be found largely in the normal hazards of any beginning. An individual usually feels a press of time or sense of haste. He needs to prove himself. He may fear that people will think he isn't doing anything, or that the position isn't worthwhile, unless he can point almost immediately to a list of tangible accomplishments or a big program in the making.

Second, any beginner makes some diffuse efforts, whether it is in learning to bowl, to use a voting machine, or to become an instructional leader. It is a normal phase of early learning, as the individual tries to differentiate among the relevant and irrelevant factors in a situation. But the diffuse action has consequences, and for a person in a leadership position the impact is not just upon himself but upon other people too.

Third, many individuals have a fear of appearing naive or dependent if they have to ask questions or inquire frequently for information. Certainly there is no intellectual osmosis by which a newcomer can get at the facts in the local situation without taking time to ask many questions and to seek clarification of partial understandings. Yet persons often feel slightly embarrassed when they do not know and hesitate to ask, as though it were somehow a reflection on their professional preparation or their intelligence. Hesitating, the beginner lets the moment for inquiry go by. Then, later, those around him assume he is informed, and they can interpret his failure to take the facts into account only as indifference or arbitrariness. It is in this manner, perhaps, that beginning leaders sometimes give the impression that they are ignorant of or don't care about all the efforts that have been made before they assumed the position.

Fourth, the unsureness and natural unease of any beginner make him thrash about a little: that is, he feels he has to do *something*, and so he moves out to act even if he is not quite sure of his direction. In its effect this is akin to his diffuse movements of beginning, but it has a second effect also. The individual can become preoccupied with his unease and tendency to thrash about to the point that he is unperceiving of what is really around him. He is somewhat insensitive to what the responses of people should be telling him.

If the new instructional leader will give consideration to the natural hazards present, but not insurmountable, in any beginning, if he will examine his own feelings and motivations carefully, and if he will give himself time to make inquiry, he can learn about the on-going program and team himself with it in a successful manner.

Scope of the Inquiry

In trying to ascertain what the on-going program for instructional improvement is like, he can usually gain the total picture more quickly if he seeks systematically within a framework of major questions. The questions constitute something of a grid through which to view the expanse of a school system with its complex of personnel, activities, and materials, while the newcomer seeks understanding of the relevant factors.

The major questions he will ask himself are basic to the appraisal of most educational enterprises. Are there agreed upon goals? Have they been or could they be clearly stated? What is the scope of the program offered for achieving these goals? Do teachers, parents, and children see the program as relatively adequate or inadequate? What are the facilities and resources for implementing the program? What are the means of appraising the progress of the learner and of diagnosing and helping meet his problems? What are the plans for research and the gathering of evidence? What are the extent and quality of relationships between school and community? What are the provisions for the professional development of school personnel? What are the already operative channels or media for cooperative efforts toward instructional improvement?

Procedures for Inquiring

The beginning instructional leader actually has many avenues of learning at his command. Several suggestions are offered here. He can:

Listen—really listen to what teachers, principals, central staff workers, the superintendent, children, and parents say when he asks questions similar to those itemized above. It takes time and effort to listen thoughtfully and a degree of self-control in repressing the next question until the response to a previous one has been assimilated.

Read—publications and reports from the central office or from individual schools. Curriculum guides, superintendent's reports, evaluation and research studies tell much about the aspirations in a system, as well as the status of affairs.

Skim—school board minutes in search of the problems that have been brought to board members' attention and with which they have struggled in the recent or remote past.

Examine—the professional materials available in central and individual school libraries and note the use, or lack of use, of magazines, yearbooks and other publications of professional societies.

Look—for evidence of activities of professional organizations and of councils and standing committees elected or appointed in previous years, and confer with representatives of such groups.

Note—any evidence of ideas and movements which are also prevalent in other parts of the state or nation.

Seek—evidence of in-service education activities, especially in such basic, continuing areas as child study.

Visit—in individual classrooms and schools as a friendly person eager to know about the good work already accomplished and currently being carried on.

ASCERTAINING PRIORITY OF EDUCATIONAL NEEDS

Another problem confronting new instructional leaders is that of determining priority among many possible activities related to the educational needs in the current scene. As the beginner has tried to become acquainted with the on-going program, he has learned much of what he needs to know to make wise choices among starting points. In addition, there are several other avenues for learning that should take priority in the efforts to meet needs.

Media for Ascertaining Priority of Needs

DIRECT INQUIRY. One approach is to ask teachers and other school personnel directly what they consider to be the most urgent needs in the system and what they see as next steps in meeting them. The inquiring can be in casual conversation, by partially structured interviews, by questionnaire, or occasionally by something as simple as a postcard survey to find out from teachers what they would choose as topics for newsletters, short bulletins or leaflets, or for a series of professional meetings.

PROFESSIONAL LITERATURE. A large number of studies have been made over a period of time in different parts of the country to find out what kind of help teachers want from supervision. Most of these studies show a high degree of similarity in the major categories of help desired. A beginner in supervision would anticipate that many needs would be shaped by the nature and history of the local school in its community, but he would also know from the professional literature that helping teachers study children, provide for individual differences among learners, secure varied materials, and interpret school procedures to parents would appear in almost any listing of problems, and hence would constitute worthwhile starting points for work.

SYSTEM-WIDE SURVEYS AND STUDIES. Sometimes extensive surveys or studies sponsored by curriculum councils, principal or teacher groups, professional organizations, or special committees can provide valuable information. The wide involvement of personnel in making the study leads to an unusual depth of understanding regarding any recommendations for action. Consequently, there is a favorable expectation regarding anything that supervision can do to help meet the revealed needs.

JOINING FACULTY EVALUATION STUDIES. An instructional leader who joins a faculty in a shoulder-to-shoulder working relationship as it tries to appraise its program usually is able to get a feeling for the relative urgency of some of the needs revealed. Having become alerted to the needs in one school, he may also become more acutely sensitive to similar needs in other schools, and hence reach some conclusion regarding starting points for his own efforts.

HELPING BEGINNING TEACHERS. As he helps beginning teachers become familiar with local resources in the school system and community, and as he helps them analyze their instructional dilemmas, the new leader is able to assess the frequency with which some problems are encountered. Hence he again gains clues as to where his own efforts can best be directed.

Cooperative Decision-Making

After a new instructional leader has become acquainted with the on-going program and is aware of current needs, he faces the hard decisions of how to use his time and energy to best advantage. His own judgment will usually be the dominant force for choice of specific activities, but the general direction or focus of effort is often chosen in conjunction with other members of a staff or faculty. The superintendent and all other instructional leaders bring their pooled judgments to bear upon the establishment of priorities as to the areas of concentrated effort. The new leader is not isolated as he assumes his responsibilities.

IDENTIFYING ROLE EXPECTATIONS
IN SUPERVISION

Still another problem encountered by beginning instructional leaders, and one for which they gain much understanding as they acquaint themselves with the on-going program, is that of identifying role expectations with regard to supervision. Situations are different enough, patterns of organization different enough, and the individual's prior experiences with supervision varied enough, that persons now in the same school system may find themselves holding quite contradictory expectations regarding the role of supervision. A fresh difficulty is introduced by the fact that the ideas are held at the level of assumption or expectation, and hence are not necessarily verbalized until some misunderstanding forces the discovery of differences. For example, a new supervisor may expect to make his time available on an on-call basis for school visiting; but the teachers may expect him to take the initiative in arranging some kind of schedule. Each waits for the other person to act and eventually becomes irritated or annoyed when nothing happens. Or in another situation, some teachers in a large system may expect a recently appointed elementary supervisor to spend most of his time in classroom assistance; but the supervisor may see himself primarily as working with committees and councils in initiating and carrying through long-range projects.

The major consideration is not that one set of expectations is wholly right and another wholly wrong in a specific situation, but that confusion is almost sure to arise and multiply when people act on the basis of conflicting assumptions which remain unexamined and of which they are largely unaware. To prevent this confusion it is necessary for the persons concerned to talk through the purposes of supervision in the local system, looking unhurriedly and unaccusingly for points that need clarification.

Meanwhile the new instructional leader's own actions will have much to do with the role that comes to be identified with him. The kinds of questions he asks, the manner of his response to requests for aid, and the types of assistance he volunteers will help shape what others expect of him in the future. His role is never static, but develops through the interactions of his daily work.

AIDS TO STUDY AND DISCUSSION

1. If you were being offered a supervisory position for next September, what are four or five specific questions you would want to ask about the school system? the community?

2. If you were a new principal in a school, what steps would you take before and during the first month of the term to learn what efforts had been made toward improvement of instruction during the last three years? To find out what dreams were still unfulfilled?

3. What should an instructional leader, new in a school system, listen and look for as clues to the role expectations his associates hold for him? How can he contribute to the development of expectations?

SUGGESTIONS FOR FURTHER READING

Boardman, Charles W., Harl R. Douglass, and Rudyard K. Bent, *Democratic Supervision in Secondary Schools*, 2nd Ed. (Boston: Houghton Mifflin Company, 1961). Especially Ch. 18, "Educational Leadership and the Individual Teacher."

Burnham, Reba M., and Martha I. King, *Supervision in Action*. Association for Supervision and Curriculum Development (Washington, D.C.: National Education Association, 1961).

Cottrell, Martha J., "Problems of Giving and Receiving Help," *Educational Leadership*, Vol. 16, No. 8 (May, 1959).

Educational Supervision—A Leadership Service. A Report of the Southern States Work Conference on Educational Problems (Tallahassee: Florida State Department of Education, 1955).

Gilbert, Robert G., *The Problems of Beginning Supervisors in Florida Schools*, unpublished doctoral dissertation (Tallahassee: Florida State University, 1961).

Gingerich, Wesley, "The Principal's Role in Instructional Leadership," *The National Elementary Principal*, Vol. 35, No. 2 (October, 1955).

Kearney, Milo E., "For Good Supervision—Facts and Follow-up," *The National Elementary Principal*, Vol. 37, No. 2 (October, 1957).

Wiles, Kimball, "Where Does Co-operation Start?" *Educational Leadership*, Vol. 11, No. 5 (February, 1954).

———, *Supervision for Better Schools*, 2nd Ed. (Englewood Cliffs, N.J.: Prentice-Hall, Inc., 1955). Especially Ch. 6, "How Much Faith Is Necessary?" and Ch. 7, "How Can Staff Harmony Be Promoted?"

CHAPTER 11

EVALUATION OF SUPERVISION

IN supervision, as in other phases of the educational enterprise, evaluation is the process of seeking out the values in a situation. It seeks evidence as to what activities are being carried on and for what purposes, how well the selected activities are serving in achieving the desired purposes, and what steps need to be taken next toward the improvement of learning. Evaluation is a sustained, systematic inquiry into the *why, what, how well,* and *what next* of supervision.

Values relate to the sense of worth or significance which influences choices. They are derived from man's own nature, his cultural heritage, and his ideals or aspirations. In general, *values, underlying purposes,* and *ultimate goals* are similar in meaning and express the need of man to give direction and coherence to his work. *Criteria,* frequently used in connection with evaluation, are agreed-upon statements of expectation by which excellence is to be judged. Evaluation, then, may be regarded as a process for ascertaining how well the consciously sought values are being attained and for gaining data for the intelligent re-setting of immediate goals and choosing of procedures.

Evaluation cannot be a simple process, swiftly accomplished, for it must be comprehensive enough to hold many factors in relationship if it is to be meaningful. Evaluation of supervision is further imbedded in the entire educational enterprise. When individuals or whole school systems attempt to appraise the effectiveness of supervision, they are usually in considerable doubt as to whether they are seeing the effect of supervisory help or a host of other influences as well. Nevertheless the effort to appraise is worthwhile. This chapter deals with the major purposes of evaluation, some working principles helpful in the process of evaluation, several types of evaluative study together with examples of criteria and instruments, and some of the benefits that accrue to those who engage in evaluation.

MAJOR PURPOSES OF EVALUATION
OF SUPERVISION

Recognizing Progress

Man is a striving creature. To set goals, achieve them, and set new goals is a satisfying rhythm to most people. The sense of fulfillment is basically gratifying. If school people, including instructional leaders, are to experience this rewarding feeling, they must perceive their goals so clearly that they can not only work toward them efficiently, but also recognize the satisfaction of knowing that they have arrived. Unless they take the opportunity provided through evaluation to state goals and to seek evidence, often objectively measurable evidence, of progress toward goals, instructional leaders may go for indefinite periods of time without any clear-cut sense of accomplishment. In that case they are also deprived of the renewed energy that flows from awareness of achievement.

Clarifying Values

Another purpose of evaluation is to help clarify values. A person's values may be somewhat unclear for several reasons, three of which are discussed here: inconsistency in values held, generality of statement, and lack of awareness.

INCONSISTENCY.   An individual evolves his value system over a long period of time and from many facets of his culture, a culture which is usually characterized by great diversity. Furthermore, an individual, in the course of a lifetime, carries many roles. The expectations and perceptions appropriate at one time in his life are not entirely in harmony with what is needed at another time. Consequently, many inconsistencies and even direct conflicts may exist in his value systems. For example, a person who in his adult years may be committed intellectually to the idea of democratic leadership, may in his childhood have been an extremely dependent member of a highly authoritarian (albeit benevolent) household. To a degree that he is not aware of, his present concept of leadership may still be based upon the image of a leader as an all-wise, security-giving person, whether he himself is serving as leader or someone else. He consequently harbors an undetected value conflict. In the course of evaluation study, where there is urgent need to think through and talk out with others the values being sought and the rationale behind choices, inconsistencies or conflicts often become evident to a person for the first time, and he is henceforth in a position to try to resolve the points of confusion.

GENERALITIES.   Values are sometimes easily held at a level of generality, without any keen awareness of what is implied for action. For instance, members of a faculty or of a central staff might be in complete agreement that respect for the individual is a great value. But it is not until they start seeking evidence for the achievement of that value, or perhaps earlier in their discussions try to formulate criteria regarding it, that they discover wide variation in the concepts held or uncertainty as to what really constitutes evidence. Evaluation, then, precipitates refinement or elaboration of thinking.

LACK OF AWARENESS OF VALUES.   Evaluation presupposes an awareness of the values being sought. Yet it is a common experience for those engaged in evaluation studies to discover that many of their controlling values are only vaguely felt or dimly perceived. Values are often held at the level of assumption where they may remain unanalyzed and unchallenged for years. It is one of the major contributions of evaluation study that the need for being articulate about values held becomes imperative. As persons engaged in evaluation try to assess the worth and efficacy of an activity or procedure, they are obliged to bring to the level of consciousness the basic question as to what the ultimate aim or value is.

At least three beneficial things typically occur when values are held consciously and can be expressed clearly: (1) the pulling or motivating power of the value is enlarged, since the ultimate goal is sharply perceived; (2) greater flexibility in approach is possible, since the goal is recognizable from any direction; (3) conflicts in values become noticeable, whether within the individual or among individuals, and the process of resolving the conflicts can be undertaken.

Seeking Evidence

A third major purpose of evaluation is to seek evidence, highly specific evidence, as to what is being done in the name of supervision and how well the service is being rendered. Neither question is easily answered. For instance, one of the basic functions of supervision is to coordinate efforts of personnel toward improvement of learning. The coordinating work may take a dozen important forms, but if one of them is the organizing of a system-wide curriculum council, then the second question remains of how well the council is functioning. What evidence is there for believing that the council is serving its purpose? It would be easy for wishful thinking to distort the perception of those who are hard at work in the numerous activities of the council. Their observations from within need to be supplemented by other efforts to appraise ways of work and outcomes.

The aims of supervision, whether stated formally as culled from professional literature or informally by an individual on the job, are usually worthy ones. But the aims may remain in the realm of good intentions or exist merely as pious hopes unless systematic, persistent efforts are made to find evidence of progress in achieving the aims. Evaluation attempts to meet this need.

Identifying Needs

As evaluation of supervision proceeds, it is possible to formulate plans for improvement of the teaching-learning situation. Some needs take priority over others. A basis can usually be found for organizing into long-range and immediate activities. The whole effort to appraise is undertaken in order to obtain information essential to planning the next steps intelligently. Hence the information derived from appraisal should not be left in notebooks and summary reports, but rather put to use in identifying areas for work.

Incorporating Research Findings

A fifth purpose served by evaluation is to bring research findings out of the academic realm and into vital use. When value-conscious instructional leaders are in pursuit of means of judging the worthwhileness of specific efforts, they find themselves seeking findings from relevant research reported in the literature. Often, too, they find it imperative to engage in local research over a period of time to arrive at needed information. In either event, the research findings are put to significant use.

BASIC PRINCIPLES IN EVALUATION
OF SUPERVISION

As individuals, whole faculties, and system-wide personnel have engaged in evaluation, several operational principles have emerged. The generalizations thus derived can help guide future work.

Evaluation Is Three-Dimensional in Time

Evaluation is three-dimensional in time, involving the past, the present, and the future. It is an effort to appraise the present situation, with full awareness of the past, in order to plan for the future. It is important to understand the past conditions in order to grasp both the direction and rate of change represented by the present circumstances. For instance, in a system which incorporates only six days in the teaching year for professional growth activities, instructional leaders might tend to be discouraged. But if, in the previous year, only five days had been included, and ten years ago only one day, then a different picture is present and there is reason for encouragement.

Of course, as pointed out just above, if the future is not benefited by the appraisal of the present, then the whole effort of evaluation has been in vain. It is to obtain a more precise and differentiated basis for planning the future that the painstaking effort to evaluate the present is undertaken.

Situations Have Multiple Values

Fortunately, each value does not always have to be pursued in a separate venture. Any one activity is multi-potential with regard to values, and a host of values can be obtained from the same event. The curriculum council, just referred to above, is an avenue for coordination of effort. But at the same time it provides for the realization of other long-range goals or values such as stimulation of creativity, opportunity for leadership, extension of experience, integration of goals, professional growth, and contributions to professional competence and knowledge.

It is significant to note, however, that values must be held at the conscious level if the cluster that is potentially present is to be realized. Unless individuals are aware of the potentialities and expecting to utilize them, the moments for realization may be so fleeting that the opportunity passes before they are recognized. Thus, if a curriculum director meeting with a system-wide council holds the expectation of using every occasion to nurture nascent leadership in new members, he recognizes an opportunity instantly when he is asked for suggestion for membership on a sub-committee. If, on the other hand, he is not conscious of the value held, the opportunity to nurture leadership may slip by unused.

In a somewhat similar manner, if a person does not have his values clearly in mind, he may not perceive the full worth of the experiences he undergoes. For instance, a regular member of the council may have had several half-day sessions in which he exchanged ideas with other members on effective procedures in social studies instruction. Yet, unless he sees this discussion as an extension of his own experiences, as well as a means of coordinating work in the system, he may go about feeling slightly abused, saying that he has not been given the chance to spend a day in another school, as a co-worker on his faculty had been invited to do, in order to gain fresh experience.

Values do come in clusters, but they must be sought in order to be realized.

Values Are Influenced by Changing Circumstances

What is good in one situation may not be equally good in another; what is desirable in one amount may not be helpful in another amount. There can be too much, even of a good thing. For example, individual conferences with teachers are an important aspect of work, but if they occupy practically all of an instructional leader's time, even more valuable experiences may be inadvertently excluded. Or a leader may devote himself so enthusiastically to action research that it usurps all of his attention and energy, with a consequent loss in other worthwhile activities.

Instructional leaders only rarely find themselves in a position of having to choose between good and bad activities. However, almost daily they have to distinguish the more subtle relationship between good and better, or between better and best. Judging when an activity is yielding the optimum achievement is indeed difficult. The process of evaluation helps provide both the large picture in which relationships are discernible and, at the same time, detailed appraisal of progress which is essential to the decision-making.

As further evidence of the degree of goodness being dependent on the circumstances as well as the amount, it is usually difficult for one school to use in detail evaluative criteria developed in another, or for one supervisory program to be evaluated by criteria written elsewhere. Criteria prepared for regional or national use are often, of necessity, so broad or general in their statements as to be almost exasperatingly vague when applied locally. A symbol is usually suggested in such criteria for items which "Do Not Apply," and the symbol has to be used frequently.

Values Must Be Sought through Suitable Media

Objective measures are lacking for many of the values which are at the core of supervision. Attitude scales, Q-sorts, journals, inventories, and other devices developed in recent years are helpful, but much ingenuity and imagination are still needed in formulating means for detecting and recording evidences of growth.

One would not make the mistake of trying to measure the illumination of a room with a yardstick, nor its length with a light meter, for the instrument chosen would obviously not be applicable to the quality about which information is desired. Yet, in appraising supervision, sometimes evidence of progress has been sought only in increased knowledge of subject matter on the part of children, as reflected in achievment test scores. Evidence of increased achievement would be significant, of course, but such important aspects of supervisory effort as stimulation of creativity and coordination of efforts would remain largely unreflected and perhaps undetected. The progress in creativity and in coordination of efforts might have been extensive, but the measuring instruments chosen simply had no way of registering the growth.

To note progress in achieving values in supervision calls for varied evidence, some of it gathered and recorded formally, but much of it collected informally, although systematically. For instance, examples of changed practices stemming from a series of afternoon workshops in science could be noted on cards and placed with the participants' evaluation made earlier at the time of the close of the workshop. Indeed, once a faculty or supervisory staff has felt the challenge to ingenuity in locating evidence and devising measures of progress toward complex goals, evaluation takes on the zest of intellectual venturing and discovery.

Evaluation Has Continuity

It is a truism in education to say that evaluation should be continuous. Measures taken individually, without reference to past or future attainment, could be quite misleading. Furthermore, if the planning ahead for evaluation is not continuous, the opportunities for collecting evidence often slip by unutilized. In evaluation of supervision, several aspects of continuity are important.

HORIZONTAL CONTINUITY. What might be called horizontal continuity takes on special significance since, in any one situation, supervision will have many facets at any one time. Without the use of foresight as to the varied phases of work, much evidence might be collected, for instance, on the success of committee work in preparing curriculum guides, but no record made of the efforts to extend the experiences of beginning teachers, as a phase of supervisory work.

VERTICAL CONTINUITY. Most of the aims of supervision are long-range in nature. Efforts may have to be followed through several years before progress becomes apparent. Without benchmarks along the way, persons in the thick of the work might have the impression that no progress at all is occurring. The recognition that way-stations are being attained also brings encouragement of further effort. Without continuity in planning for evaluation, the awareness of progress toward long-range goals would be largely lost.

PERSISTENCE. Gathering of evidence is seldom easy. Plans for measurement often encounter unexpected difficulties, and new plans have to be devised. The preparing of usable reports, once the data are in, takes time and effort. Persistence of a high order, which often involves adaptive flexibility in reaching intermediate goals, is needed to keep the evaluation process going. Without continuity in planning, it would be easy to become confused, even though tenacious, and lose sight of the real objectives.

Evaluation Involves Both Cooperative Effort and Individual Appraisal

In the evaluation of anything as complex as a program of supervision, the well-coordinated efforts of many people are needed. As the people work together in pursuit of first-hand knowledge of purposes, status, progress, and steps for improvement, they not only build a base of common information and understanding; they also find themselves engaged in genuine teamwork with a high sense of mutual involvement and concern which is rewarding and energizing. The success of evaluation of supervision plainly hinges upon cooperative efforts, from the initial planning through the numerous fact-finding investigations to the ultimate utilization of findings in planning for improvement.

At the same time, evaluation involves much individual and self-appraisal. As he looks at supervision in the whole school or system, the individual instructional leader has to ask himself a central question: In view of my particular responsibilities and goals, considering the situation I started from and the resources available to me, how far have I progressed? Often the answers are not found until there has been much self-appraisal, as well as drawing of inferences from the cooperative study phases of evaluation.

A person engaged in self-appraisal needs to muster all his maturity of perception and judgment. Simple self-accusations, reproaches, or belittlement are not helpful; neither are unrealistic expectations of self, nor illusions of constant success. But a candid effort to analyze situations to see where one's own approaches might be modified to achieve greater outcomes is worthwhile. In the process of analysis the individual gains in self-direction. The goals he glimpses for his own next phases of development are *his* goals and he therefore can feel complete commitment to them.

Evaluation Is a Creative Process

As indicated at several points in the paragraphs above, creativity is often needed in evaluation, especially with regard to providing means for appraising progress toward the more subtle values. In addition, there is a uniqueness about each effort to evaluate that demands creativity. Each situation has an indigenous quality, something native to that set of circumstances at that time, which necessitates a fresh approach. The means and procedures for evaluating supervision should reflect the values dominant in a system, the nature and needs of the children, teachers, and instructional leaders involved, the resources of the school, and expectations of the community. While much guidance is to be gained from previous evaluative efforts in the system or elsewhere, any tendency to fall into a tight pattern of procedure or to rely exclusively on nationally standardized measures would contradict the spirit of evaluation.

To seek evidence of growth uncreatively within the close confines of a few fixed instruments, quantitatively oriented, can lead persons to experience evaluation as a stultifying, dead-end affair, with findings stored in the archives. But to seek evidence creatively, starting from known instruments and criteria appropriate to the occasion, and freely trying to devise means for appraising the whole range of important values, leads persons to experience evaluation as an invigorating affair through which they gain a sense of direction, a refined perception of goals, and a basis for conviction and confidence as they move into the next steps of their work.

TYPES OF EVALUATION IN SUPERVISION

There are many types of evaluation in supervision, and numerous approaches, criteria, and instruments have been devised. In the following paragraphs five types of evaluation study are described briefly and some specific examples of each cited.

Clarifying the Nature of the Supervisory Task

Sometimes the major purpose of an evaluation study is to establish what is being done in the name of supervision. The ascertaining of just what is being attempted through supervisory service is often quite difficult to accomplish. The diversity of goals and activities is enormous, and in a large school system where there is great specialization of labor to carry out tasks, there is the added diversity arising from the background of many talents and experiences. To know what supervisory services are being rendered and how supervisors, individually and collectively, use their time takes definite planning and study.

An analysis of time logs or journals has been used to learn the scope of activities and use of time. In Chapter 1 reference was made to a study, *Louisiana Supervisors Examine Their Practices*, in which a sampling of supervisors kept a time record of what they did on specified half days over a period of a school year, and then analyzed the material to ascertain how they spent their time and what techniques were used frequently to improve instruction. They also examined professional literature to see if the things they were doing were considered good practice. Thus there was an effort to learn not only what was being done, but also whether, from a theoretical viewpoint, it was worth doing.[1]

In a somewhat similar manner a group of Chicago supervisors

[1] *Op. cit.*

engaged in a study of the nature and effectiveness of their services. The study was two-fold. One part involved the keeping of time logs of activities by sixty supervisors covering a selected week each month for six months. The logs were then turned over to a committee, and a classification was made of the descriptions of service. Five categories, each with several sub-categories, were found to provide a classification system. The five major categories, with the computation of time spent on each, were as follows:

Supervisory Functions and Activities	Percentage of Time Used
Teaching, Training, and Guidance	30.3
Curriculum and Materials of Instruction	23.2
Administrative Functions	20.8
School and Community Relations	13.9
Research and Evaluation of Learning Program	10.9

A second phase of the study attempted to appraise through organized interviews the effectiveness with which functions of supervision were discharged. A questionnaire was devised which listed ten functions of supervision, with a rating device using a four point scale, and space for comments and suggestions by those interviewed. Some 454 principals and teachers were asked to appraise the effectiveness of each of the ten items. Fifty-eight per cent of the principals and teachers interviewed rated supervisory services as 1 (high), 15 per cent as 2, 7 per cent as 3, and 8 per cent as 4. Twelve per cent of the items were not rated, indicating a reaction of no opinion rather than adverse opinion.[2]

An attempt to describe supervision through a categorizing of activities is, of course, at best an approximation of the supervisory service rendered. Categories, no matter how carefully developed, tend to overlap and also to leave gaps, making exact classification difficult. Also, in supervision, one activity often fulfills several functions. Therefore, estimating amounts of time devoted to kinds of functions cannot be entirely precise. Nevertheless, in spite of the

---

2 *Supervisors Study Their Services.* A Cooperative Research Enterprise, Department of Instruction and Guidance (Chicago: Chicago Public Schools, 1955).

limitations inherent in any measurement effort, the Louisiana and Chicago supervisors had much more than sheer guesswork on which to base their replies when responding subsequently to the familiar question, "Just what does a supervisor do?" Furthermore, they had valuable information for planning future work with greater insight and assurance.

Appraising the Effects of Supervision

If the ultimate aim of supervision is the improvement of the teaching-learning conditions, then it seems as though it should be possible to detect the impact of supervision by looking at the learning outcomes for children. This process is fraught with difficulty, however, since the learning outcomes are products, not of supervision alone, but of the whole educational complex composed of the child himself, his home and community, as well as the services of the entire school system.

Attempts have been made, however, in spite of the difficulty, to appraise the effects of supervision upon the learning of children and upon teaching procedures which presumably enhance learning. In one study, Franseth compared the achievement of children in supervised and unsupervised schools in Georgia. The equated group method was used, with the two groups being similar on such factors as: size of staff and classes, characteristics of teachers (education, experience, and salary), education of adults, economic status of adults, children's capabilities for learning, and qualifications of administrators. The children in supervised schools achieved more, according to the Iowa Every Pupil tests, than children in unsupervised schools in reading, work-study skills, arithmetic, and language. The children in supervised schools also developed more skill in democratic citizenship as appraised by the McCall's School Practices Questionnaire. In these schools there was a conscious effort to use principles of good supervision.[3]

If supervision has a desirable impact upon teaching, the learning

[3] Jane Franseth, *Learning to Supervise Schools* (Washington, D.C.: Superintendent of Documents, Government Printing Office, 1951), 50 pp.

opportunities for children should be improved in some way. Supervisors often arrange in-service education activities, especially child study programs, to help teachers understand children better and hence plan more effectively for learning. Greene analyzed anecdotal records to ascertain whether teachers who were enrolled in a child study group actually changed their practices in working with children. He found that during the three-year period studied, there was a statistically significant increase in the more positive ways teachers worked with children. Based on pupil response to these positive ways of handling, it appears that reasoning or guiding, motivating intrinsically, and being supportive were effective methods which teachers use in teacher-pupil relationships. There was a highly significant decrease in the more negative ways teachers handled children, such as using shame, sarcasm, or threat. The hypothesis was supported that the child study program was effective with high school and elementary teachers in improving teacher-pupil relationships.[4]

Self-Appraisal by Supervisors

Just as self-appraisal is important for children, teachers, athletes, business men, and indeed for anyone who is assuming responsibility for giving some direction to his own development, so it is important for instructional leaders to appraise themselves. They especially need to be sensitive as to whether or not their actions are in line with their intentions, and how those actions appear to others. Instructional leaders also need to learn to look for appropriate evidence: that is, to consider what might constitute evidence that some of the goals, especially the less tangible ones, are being approached.

Adams and Dickey suggest the following questions as indicative of the factors to which a supervisor should give attention in evaluating himself: [5]

----

[4] John Greene, A *Study of Some Curriculum Changes of Teachers Who Participated in the Child Study Program* (Unpublished doctoral dissertation), Institute for Child Study, University of Maryland, 1952.

[5] Harold P. Adams and Frank G. Dickey, *Basic Principles of Supervision* (New York: American Book Company, 1953), pp. 259–260.

1. Do I give the teachers a share in deciding what to do?
2. How general is the participation of teachers in the formulation of policies which affect them?
3. Does participation of group members result in desirable action?
4. Am I giving enough attention to growth in the techniques of cooperative planning and action?
5. Do I let teachers know in advance about changes which affect them?
6. How has the "our" attitude been developed?
7. Have I been successful in convincing teachers of the importance of their jobs?
8. Have I used praise discriminatingly?
9. In what ways have I attempted to discover and to capitalize upon the strengths of teachers?
10. Do I know of special work the teachers are doing?
11. Are credit and publicity given teachers who deserve them?
12. Do I let teachers know how they are getting along?
13. Have teachers been made to feel financially and professionally secure?
14. Do teachers desire to improve enough to try new methods?
15. How have I helped teachers to become self-directive?
16. Am I more likely to begin working with teachers on their problems or on my own?
17. Do I recognize and provide for differences among teachers and their needs?
18. Are teachers given a chance to save face?
19. Do I recognize the uniqueness of teachers' personalities?
20. Do I recognize that there is no universally successful teaching technique?
21. Do I maintain self-control in the face of tactless remarks?
22. Do I admit mistakes when I am shown to be wrong?
23. Do I get the facts concerning an error, and weigh and decide them before taking action?
24. Is the assistance of teachers sought in the selection of new staff members?
25. Are new staff members properly oriented to the community, the school, and the job to which they are assigned?
26. Do all concerned share in the evaluation of the program?

27. Which of my stated objectives have I failed adequately to achieve?
28. How can I help teachers to do better those things they already do well?

Appraising One Phase of the Program

A fourth type of evaluation focuses attention upon one phase of the program. Persons involved in the evaluation, and especially those who will base future actions upon the findings, would have to keep clearly in mind that they are looking at just one side of a many-faceted program. It is often helpful, however, to be able to concentrate attention upon one area, to put it under a kind of magnifying glass, in order to see more clearly its strengths and weaknesses, and to find the relationships that need improving. Sometimes situations that go along month after month on a generally acceptable basis reveal many points and means for improvement, when the persons involved stop to ask themselves some orderly questions.

Adams and Dickey describe an evaluation of ways of working in supervision, which constitutes a good example of focusing attention primarily on one phase of a program. Two supervisors in the Kenwick Elementary School (Fayette County, Kentucky) wanted to obtain the teachers' appraisal of the ways of working during the first year of supervision in the system. They used a combination of interviews and written questionnaires in seeking answers to fifteen questions. Seven of the questions, indicated by asterisks, were repeated on the questionnaire, which teachers could return if they wished, when they had an opportunity for free and full response. It was made clear that the evaluation was upon ways of working, not upon persons.

An Evaluation of Ways of Working in Supervision [6]
   1. When did you learn that supervisory help was available?
   2. Who first told you about it?

6 *Ibid.*, pp. 261–262.

3. Were you given an opportunity to say whether or not you wanted supervisory help?
4. What was your understanding of it?
*5. How did you feel about the supervisor's first visits to your classroom and school?
*6. (a) What did the supervisor do to make you feel comfortable and at ease (or uncomfortable)?
   (b) Can you suggest other ways in which all might have been made more comfortable?
7. What was the first assistance or encouragement you received?
8. What help did you request first from the supervisor?
*9. Does the supervisor ever suggest things to do which you do not understand how to do? If so, indicate the kind of things.
*10. Are there kinds of help which you have wanted but which the supervisor has not given? If so, what?
*11. What do you consider the most valuable help the supervisory service has contributed to the educational program in your school?
12. Have you found opportunities for and ways of working with other people which you had not experienced before?

Person   Ways of Working

Other teachers
Principal
Parents
Children

13. As a result of the supervisory program, have you used other services more extensively?
   (a) Services within the school
   (b) Services and agencies outside the school
*14. What helpful changes, if any, have you made in your teaching this year?
*15. Please evaluate the following list of ways of working as (1) very helpful, (2) helpful to some extent, (3) of little help:
   Group conferences and discussions ⸻⸻⸻⸻
   Individual conferences ⸻⸻⸻⸻⸻
   Visitations ⸻⸻⸻⸻⸻
   Receiving visitors ⸻⸻⸻⸻⸻

Reading professional books and magazines ———————
Provision of teaching materials ———————————
Demonstrations ————————————————————
Supervisor planning with children ————————————
Help of visiting consultants ———————————————
Other ways of working ————————————————

It is clear that, while the focus is on ways of working, there would be many implications for other aspects of the program. For instance, number 10, regarding kinds of help wanted but not yet received, would bear upon the scope of supervisory services in the future. Or number 14, relating to changes, would have significance for understanding attitudes toward change and for stimulation of change.

The evaluation just described took time, ingenuity, and cooperative effort on the part of teachers and instructional leaders. But by focusing on one highly significant phase of supervision and by devising an instrument and plan appropriate to the situation, they were able to carry out a manageable study. In return for their effort, all concerned had a wealth of sharpened insight and information as a basis for work in both the immediate and distant future.

Appraising the Total Program

A fifth type of evaluation relates to appraising the total program. Here the major effort is to see the program as a whole, to find relationships among parts, to gain information that will help in achieving balance in the program of supervision, and to see how different phases of the program can reinforce one another to the best advantage.

It is notoriously difficult to walk among the trees and still keep the forest in mind. The area of supervision is no exception. There are the trees of diversity and specialization among many workers, the trees of daily responsibilities and priorities of demands upon too limited time, and the trees of re-routing when obstacles and frustrations occur. It takes 20/20 vision to see the forest.

DETECTING DIRECTION. Typical of efforts to state ideal ends and appaise the status and direction of the local program is the instrument developed by Moorer, "How Good Is Your Supervisory Program?" In the introductory paragraph he states:

> A good supervisor is constantly seeking to narrow the gap between *what is* and *what might be* in the county supervisory program. This means that the supervisor often takes stock of *what is* and looks at the present program in the light of *what might be*. It is important to know where the program stands along the line of development from an *inferior program* to a *superior program*.

Ten generally agreed-upon principles and purposes are then listed as clues to *what might be:*

Reliance upon Democratic Leadership
Development of Education Leadership
Total Program of Education
Materials and Resources
Long-Range Plans
Research and Experimentation
Purposes of Education
Human Growth and Learning
Coordination of Effort
Cooperation with Other Agencies

A five-point rating scale is provided, along with contrasted examples of inferior and superior programs. The observation is made that every supervisory program makes use of these principles to some extent, but that it is important for the persons in the system to decide how far the county has advanced along the line of progress from an inferior program to a superior program. As a sample, the section on Long-Range Plans follows.[7]

LONG-RANGE PLANS. The supervisory program should provide for cooperative development of both immediate and long-range plans

---

[7] Sam H. Moorer, "How Good Is Your Supervisory Program?" An Instrument for Self-Analysis (Tallahassee, Florida: State Department of Education).

which are continuously adapted to the needs and conditions in the county.

Inferior Program

1. Activity proceeds according to the exigencies of the moment, or in response to immediate pressures. There are no cooperatively developed, comprehensive, long-range plans which serve to give direction to the program. The program is on its way, but no one knows where it is going.

2. Whatever plans exist are static and routine in nature. Plans are not subject to revision, although conditions may have changed to such an extent that they are no longer valid.

3. All county plans are made by the administrative and/or supervisory staff and handed down to teachers. Teachers do not understand these plans, or see the relationship of present activities to an over-all long-range program of improvement.

4. Activity proceeds for its own sake. Much "Busy-Work" goes on which is fleeting and fragmentary and in which there is no continuity. Passing fads and fancies are taken

Superior Program

1. There are carefully developed comprehensive long-range plans. Plans for immediate action are always made in terms of long-range goals. Specific next steps are set up for short periods of time, and achievement is evaluated in terms of accomplishments of them.

2. Plans are flexible and subject to adjustment in light of changing needs and conditions.

3. Teachers and parents know what the supervisory plans for the county are, and understand and support them because they have had a part in making them.

4. There is a balance between activity and reflection upon activity. The criteria for determining the relevance of specific activities are found in long-range plans for improve-

Inferior Program	*Superior Program*
up with no appraisal of their real significance to the county program.	ment of instruction in the county.
5. Whatever plans exist are so vague and indefinite, or so out-of-tune with the experience and ability of teachers, the social outlook of the community, and the financial status of the county school system, that there could be little likelihood of their realization.	5. Plans are concrete and specific. They are consistent with the capacities and thinking of the teaching personnel and the lay citizens. Plans for immediate action are those which are judged to have the best chance of succeeding.

1	2	3	4	5
Inferior Program	Moving Toward	Average Program	Moving Toward	Superior Program

It is important to note that while the use of rating scales has several disadvantages, among them the dangerous illusion that precision of measurement accompanies the use of figures, it also has at least one large advantage. The effort to apply a scale, rather than simply give assent or dissent to the existence of a quality, often leads an individual or group to discover the haziness of thinking that is present. Out of the necessity for reaching an agreement on "how much" of a quality is to be claimed comes (1) a more diligent search for evidence, and (2) a sharper definition of what amount is desirable.

SCOPE OF TOTAL PROGRAM. Another way of trying to appraise the total program of instructional leadership is found in the use of nationally prepared criteria, such as the statements suggested by the A.S.C.D. 1960 Yearbook Committee. Eight areas of appraisal are proposed, with several sub-items under each:

Educational Objectives
Role Perception
Organizational Structure
Group Action and Morale
Experimentation
Communication
Resources
Evaluation

Typical of the sub-items are those listed under Experimentation:

1. The climate of the school situation is conducive to creativeness, experimentation, and expression of individual skill and talent.

2. Experimentation is regularly conducted to discover better ways of using the intelligence of people in solving the problems of the schools.

3. Hypotheses which have been established for improving practices are being tested in action.

4. New ideas which seem to the instructional staff and the patrons to have promise are tested by school workers to determine their effectiveness.

5. Individuals and groups are eager to explore or experiment with suggestions which are made by the group.

6. The staff uses knowledge and data effectively in solving problems and resolving issues.

7. Provision is made so that all staff members are constantly acquiring new skills, understandings, and attitudes.

8. Although most program decisions are made at the local school level, consideration is given to a system-wide framework of common purposes, philosophy, and scope that gives unity and guidance to individual schools and staff members.

The need for flexibility of use is emphasized. "The categories are not mutually exclusive, nor are they meant to be all-inclusive. Groups or individuals wishing to appraise leadership practices should use the criteria freely—modifying, deleting, or adding other criteria in terms of locally held values and goals." [8]

Locally prepared criteria provide still another way of looking at the total program of supervision. A local staff could take a comprehensive statement of purposes, their own statement or some other, and develop the sub-items needed to reflect their concerns and the conditions of the local system at that point in its history. For instance, a group could start from the statement of general functions of supervision derived from the bases of supervision described in this text: coordination of efforts, provision of leadership, extension of experience, stimulation of creative effort, facilitating and evaluating change, analysis of learning situation, contributing to a body of knowledge, and integration of goals. Selecting one area, such as stimulation of creative effort, as a beginning point, a committee could refer to the considerations described for that area in Chapter 4, and turn some of the factors suggested there into statements of expectation (criteria) for the local school situation. Once some confidence is established and some momentum achieved, the committee would have little trouble in extending the questions in its search for evidence. It could also devise symbols for keeping a record of the present status as a marker from which to measure future progress.

BONUS BENEFITS FROM EVALUATION

In addition to helping achieve the major purposes for which it is undertaken, evaluation usually pays extra dividends. These additional values cannot be commanded or deliberately ordered to appear. Yet persons who have engaged in the evaluation process, and have watched others do likewise, find these benefits emerging.

[8] Association for Supervision and Curriculum Development, *Leadership for Improving Instruction*, Yearbook, 1960 (Washington, D.C.: National Education Association, 1960), pp. 164–168.

Self-Assurance

Typically, individuals gain in self-assurance, a quality somewhat lacking in many educators. A sturdiness of belief develops. Even though the conditions revealed by the evaluation contain many problems, individuals can move with greater confidence because they know where they are starting from and where they are headed. Their assurance is founded in reason.

Mutual Respect

As individuals come to understand the total program better, the varied ways different people are contributing to its achievement, the obstacles to be overcome, and the structure and ways of working, they greatly increase their respect for one another. Often for the first time an individual has sufficient knowledge of what his co-workers are doing, what their ultimate goals are, and some of the personal tribulations they may live with daily, to have a real basis for respect and appreciation. Since most human beings enjoy working with people they genuinely respect, the degree of satisfaction in working together is heightened.

Commitment to Change

Most individuals and groups engaging in evaluation arrive at a vivid but realistic commitment to change. Because goals have become clearer, current conditions analyzed, strengths and weaknesses detected, then the steps recommended for improvement can be formulated cooperatively. The necessity for each step can be thoroughly understood. There is an expectation of change, with the specific steps usually arranged in some kind of achievable sequence. The whole climate for the individual and group is one of carrying through on promises made to themselves and others.

Zest for Work

Out of the sustained working together in a productive, goal-centered atmosphere comes an esprit de corps. Zest for new undertakings rises as self-assurance, mutual respect, and evidence of accomplishment continue to increase.

AIDS TO STUDY AND DISCUSSION

1. Just what is a faculty in a specific school trying to accomplish through supervisory aid in a week? a year? Can you name several general goals and then some specific intermediate steps?

2. Take the statement of values and goals developed in the question above and see if you can turn it into a series of questions or criteria which could be used in appraising growth during the year, and in appraising the contribution of supervision to that growth.

3. In evaluation it is often not easy to locate evidence, or even to be sure what would constitute evidence, of a certain condition. Consult the sub-items suggested on page 250 for the appraisal of the area of Experimentation. Choose two of them and see if you can cite examples of what you would accept as evidence.

SUGGESTIONS FOR FURTHER READING

Adams, Harold P., and Frank G. Dickey, *Basic Principles of Supervision* (New York: American Book Company, 1953).

Association for Supervision and Curriculum Development, *Leadership for Improving Instruction*, Yearbook, 1960 (Washington, D.C.: National Education Association, 1960).

Dull, Floyd W., *Criteria for Evaluating the Supervision Program in School Systems,* unpublished doctoral dissertation (Columbus: Ohio State University, 1960).

Franseth, Jane, *Learning to Supervise Schools* (Washington, D.C.: Superintendent of Documents, U. S. Government Printing Office, 1951).

Greene, John, *A Study of Some Curriculum Changes of Teachers Who Participated in the Child Study Program,* unpublished doctoral dissertation (Institute for Child Study, University of Maryland, 1952).

Louisiana Supervisors Examine Their Practices, The Louisiana School Supervisors Association in Cooperation with College of Education, Louisiana State University and the State Department of Education (Baton Rouge: Louisiana School Supervisors Association, 1958).

Moorer, Sam H., "How Good Is Your Supervisory Program?" An Instrument for Self-Analysis (Tallahassee: Florida State Department of Education).

Supervisors Study Their Services, a Cooperative Research Enterprise, Department of Instruction and Guidance (Chicago: Chicago Public Schools, 1955).

CHAPTER 12

FRONTIERS OF SUPERVISION

Iᴛ is the purpose of this chapter to examine the growing edge of supervision, to see where possible what shape the pull of the future is giving to supervision. The history of supervision has helped shape present practices and principles (Chapter 2). The foundations of a need for supervision are discernible in present conditions and provide the basic dimensions or description of what supervision should be if the needs are to be met (Chapters 3 and 4). Now it is important to examine another major force—the impact of relatively new knowledge upon the concept or expectations of supervision. From much of this new knowledge, especially that concerning human potentialities for learning and for cooperation, can come a vivid sense of direction for the immediate future.

In describing the westward movement in America and the opening of new frontiers, writers sometimes distinguish between two types of pioneers: the hunter pioneers who explored new territory, sighting important objects and tracing out the general lay of the land; and second, the farmer pioneers who settled the country, beginning the arduous task of bringing new land into production, while the situation was still strange and full of novel problems. It took both types of pioneers to develop the whole country. Without the hunter pioneer, additional frontiers would have remained unopened and the first frontier would have become the last. But without the farmer pioneer, the new land, sometimes so dearly bought in terms of human effort, would have remained unutilized. Often, too, the pioneer carried both roles in the course of his lifetime. The hunter pioneer who opened up new land stayed to cultivate it; and, conversely, a farmer pioneer sometimes became the one to push the new frontier farther west.

In a similar manner, the field of education needs both types of pioneers, if new frontiers of educational advance are to be opened and if the territory thus opened is to be put to productive use. The last few decades have witnessed the discovery, exploration, and partial use of a number of significant ideas from research in education, psychology, human development, sociology, and other fields. But much remains to be done to achieve the full utilization of these ideas, and further exploration is needed to clarify numerous ramifications of the general concepts. Meanwhile tantalizing glimpses are caught of whole new frontiers to be attempted. Many educators of today, especially instructional leaders, have the privilege of serving within their lifetime both as hunter pioneers and farmer pioneers, as they deal with such matters as the nature of leadership or the role of perception in behavior.

Many of the educational explorations of the last few years are highly relevant to supervision. Seven such areas of exploration are discussed in this chapter: the study of leadership, human relations and group efforts, change and the mature individual, creativity and the classroom, new knowledge about learning processes, perception and behavior, and an interdisciplinary approach to the improvement of learning. Each of these areas is a domain in which much exploration and settlement have already occurred; but each is a domain which needs further exploration in its hidden valleys and undiscovered recesses; and each is also a domain from which new frontiers are glimpsed, with new possibilities beckoning just beyond the present horizon. Supervision needs to take part in these frontier efforts, in both the hunter and farmer pioneer roles, in order to meet its responsibilities for leadership and to make its full contribution to progress in education.

STUDY OF LEADERSHIP

In the last three or four decades, the efforts to analyze the nature of leadership have been widespread. Leadership has been of continuing interest to many people as a psychological and sociological phenomenon. It is of interest to all persons as they experience the impact of leadership in daily living. It is of great concern to those persons in industry, government, armed services, and other walks of life who are especially responsible for the education of new leaders. Several helpful generalizations can be drawn from the work so far.

Leadership Redefined

In the effort to visualize a kind of leadership truly consistent with a democratic way of life, the actual nature of leadership has come under close scrutiny. It has been examined from the standpoint of what successful leaders in democratically organized situations are perceived to do, and also from the standpoint of what, theoretically, leaders *should* do if they are acting on democratic principles. The examination has led to a considerable revision in the concept of leadership. In place of the idea of a leader as an all-knowing, all-powerful figure giving rigid directions to followers, which had been appropriate to an autocratically organized society, there has emerged a concept of a leader as one who helps a group clarify its values and organize to achieve its goals, who improves the human relationships in a group, who stimulates and releases leadership in others, who provides expertness along certain lines, and who coordinates the efforts of others (see Chapter 3).

In the 1930's, following their studies in social atmospheres, Lewin, Lippit, and White came to the conclusion that democratic leadership, in which the leader helped the group organize itself and make its own decisions, proved in the long run to produce the best results in terms of (1) things accomplished, (2) cooperative relationships, and (3) personal growth.[1] Here is the essence of both the nature and the benefits of democratic leadership. The intervening years have witnessed many efforts to analyze current procedures and to create new means for achieving cooperative relationships and personal growth through democratic leadership.

According to the Association for Supervision and Curriculum Development, certain contemporary findings in human motivation offer several insights which need to be integrated into a concept of leadership:

1. Men seek a cause for which to live—an individual is not genuinely and lastingly happy unless he has something beyond himself to care about and for which to work.

2. Desire for success often leads to conformity—some individuals gain their sense of security from conforming, but at what point does conformity become a surrender of the precious heritage of freedom?

3. Being alone or different is not easy—to be out front experimenting with novel ways of doing things, talking about ideas that are in the process of formulation is not easy for most people.

4. Feelings are important—honest recognition of emotions and their relations to the intellectual process is needed, and leaders have a long way to go in encouraging positive use for their co-workers' feelings.[2]

The concept of leadership is constantly under revision in a democracy. The basic tenet that a democratic society is always capable of improvement calls for it; new refinements in the ideals and in the means of democracy necessitate the revision; and deepened psychological insights such as those above also demand it. Each generation should expect to make its contribution to the definition of leadership.

    1 Kurt Lewin and others, "Patterns of Aggressive Behavior in Experimentally Created Social Climates," *Journal of Social Psychology*, Vol. 10, No. 3 (May, 1939), pp. 271–299.
    2 Association for Supervision and Curriculum Development, *Leadership for Improving Instruction*, 1960 Yearbook (Washington, D.C.: National Education Association, 1960), pp. 19–21.

Leadership and Personal Qualities

Much of the early consideration of leadership involved a search for a specific quality or qualities in an individual's make-up which could be identified as leadership. In general, such qualities, when identified, were expected to be rather constant, even inherent, stemming in some manner from a natural will to power, desire to dominate, persuasiveness of thinking, or dedication to some noble (or ignoble) cause. In the common view at least, leaders were regarded as primarily natural-born, with their inherent attributes causing them to become leaders in one field or another.

However, for some time it has been recognized that leadership was far more than a personal attribute, or constellation of personal attributes, possessed by a few persons. The part played by the rest of the group and by the total set of circumstances operant at the moment was too obvious to miss. But giving full recognition to the importance of the situation does not dispose of the need to consider the characteristics of an individual that fit him especially well to assume the role of leader in specific situations.

Some of the characteristics that equip an individual to carry the role of leader may well have an inherent basis, in the sense that an individual's constitutional endowments are a fundamental and continuing part of his life style. For instance, the body chemistry and physiological systems of one individual may enable him to function with a higher energy level, greater stamina, quicker reaction time, and less irritability than any of his peers. For some situations, this endowment would contribute greatly to his success as a leader. He would be a "natural" for some phases of leadership, in that nature had equipped him unusually well for the role.

Of special interest to educators is the study of characteristics stemming less from physiological endowments and more from the impact of life experiences. For instance, what experiences of childhood, adolescent and adult years can be made to yield that measure of self-confidence, trust in judgments (his own and others), and depth of conviction that enable the leader to think widely, be sensitive to needs, take calculated risks, and brook minor criticisms of a personal nature in order to continue to serve a cause?

The stimulation of leadership is often cited as a major purpose of supervision; shared leadership is a commonly used term; and the expectation prevails that every normal person has leadership potential for at least some types of situations. Therefore, it is extremely important for instructional personnel to give further thought to the kinds of experiences, in school years and later, that may reasonably be expected to nurture the personal qualities that are productive when leadership is demanded. Apparently, at the present time, many persons have undergone crippling rather than nurturing experiences, for great numbers of individuals are reluctant to make any leadership contribution or offer ideas even in small, familiar groups. Some of the human potential for cooperative problem-solving is thereby lost. Friendly, supportive supervision might prevent such loss.

Leadership Situationally Influenced

It has been obvious through the years, of course, that the success of an enterprise was dependent on more than the leadership provided. The total situation, including many chance factors, was involved. A visitor touring an historic battlefield, for instance, is often impressed with the frequency in the guide's description of such expressions as, "If the supply train had arrived an hour earlier," "If it had not rained during the night," "If the message had not been intercepted."

What has not been realized so clearly until recently is that the very nature of what constitutes adequate or "good" leadership varies from one situation to another. Leadership, instead of being a constant, almost an entity, is perceived as a function of the total situation (including earlier-mentioned qualities of the leader). Sometimes leadership is regarded as the best possible *fit* between the persons and the circumstances.

The situation evokes or creates a demand for specific emphases in the leader's behavior. For example, under combat conditions, military leaders must exhibit great speed of decision. In another situation, however, speed of decision is not highly significant, but wide-ranging imagination is crucial, as when a toy manufacturer launches a new venture. Or a teacher, leading a class into an understanding of a difficult concept in geometry, may need neither speed of decision nor eccentric imagination at the moment, but rather need extreme sensitivity to the increasingly blank look in the eyes of students, and have flexibility enough to use several analogies in explaining the concept.

What constitutes adequate or good leadership, then, is redefined in part with every situation. The size of the group, the purpose to be accomplished, the time and materials available for carrying out the project, and the cohesiveness in the group are but a few of the factors currently recognized as significant in appraising and reappraising the leadership needs in a situation.

Leader Behavior

Instead of referring to leadership almost as an entity, it is perhaps helpful to think of leader behavior or leadership behavior. There is then less tendency to regard leadership as a static personal quality, and more opportunity to focus on the interaction of persons, purposes, and situational factors.

Hemphill, in an extensive study of situational factors in leadership, found certain broad sorts of behavior required of all leaders regardless of the situations in which they functioned. A leader's behavior is characterized as follows:

1. He exhibits behavior indicative of his ability to advance the purpose of the group.

2. He exhibits behavior indicating competence in administrative functions.

3. His behavior is characterized by the ability to inspire the members of a group to greater activity, or to set the pace for a group.

4. His behavior is of a kind which seems to add to the individual member's feeling of security in his place in the group.

5. The leader's behavior is relatively free from activities serving only his own interest.

Hemphill further observes that the inter-relationships among the level of pleasantness of group membership (hedonic tone), the tendency of the group to function as a unit (viscidity), and leadership adequacy and the leader's behavior indicate that "a leader's most important function in the dynamics of group behavior may well be that of maintaining group membership as a satisfying experience for members of the group, and facilitating their acting as a unit rather than as separate individuals." [3]

Further Questions

The gains made over the past generation in both the theory and practice of democratic leadership have been remarkable. The spread of the concept of democratic leadership and decision-making beyond the civic-political area to most other aspects of living—from business and industry to church and family life—has been relatively rapid and highly significant. The very expectation that democratic leadership will be forthcoming, and that anything less is just cause for complaint, is quite recent. A full generation ago, for instance, the members of a school faculty assumed authoritarian organization and leadership to be the norm, and the appearance of any democratic tendency was merely a pleasant surprise.

But the gains made so far are not fully consolidated. There has necessarily been much stumbling and uncertainty. The means for democratic decision-making are not casually and easily achieved. In the impatience for more effective procedures, it is easy to forget how hard-won and how long in the making had been earlier advances in man's efforts toward better group living.

Meanwhile, as the 1960 A.S.C.D. Yearbook Committee pointed out, certain factors in contemporary living augment the difficulty of holding to democratic commitments about decision-making: (1)

[3] John K. Hemphill, *Situational Factors in Leadership* (Columbus: Ohio State University, 1949), pp. 99–100.

the complexity of problems to be considered; (2) the rapidity with which solutions must be found; and (3) the size of the population concerned with any given problem. Hence this generation is in a quest for desirable relationships between individuals and groups, freedom and authority.

Signs of maturity in educational leadership, of growing up to the ways of democracy, may be observed in the shift from easy generalizations about decision-making, the role of leaders, respect for individuals and cooperative procedures to more specific and searching questions such as these: Should all decisions be made by involvement of all those affected by them? Are there any decisions that may be appropriately made by officially designated leaders? What is the nature of involvement? Should it be the same for all people with regard to all decisions? Wherein does authority for decisions reside? Is it the same for all situations? Do individuals and groups always make wise decisions? When may a leader suggest, recommend or even impose? [4]

Supervision faces many hard questions with regard to the nature and techniques of leadership, and to the detecting and nurturing of leadership. Encouragingly, a number of state, regional, and national groups are giving increasing attention to the study of leadership. Helpful publications from several groups are appearing, such as *Experimentation in Preparing School Leaders* from the Cooperative Program in Educational Administration,[5] *Leadership in Action* from the National Training Laboratories,[6] and the *Your School and Staffing* series from the Cooperative Development of Public School Administration in New York State.[7] Supervision has much to contribute to, and much to learn from, the efforts to advance the frontier of effective leadership.

[4] *Op. cit.*, p. 14.
[5] Leonard E. Meece and Howard Eckel, *Experimentation in Preparing School Leaders*, Bulletin of The Bureau of School Service, University of Kentucky, Vol. 33, No. 4 (June, 1961).
[6] *Leadership in Action*, Selected Reading Series (Washington, D.C.: National Training Laboratories, National Education Association, 1961).
[7] *Your School and Staffing*, Series from the Cooperative Development of Public School Administration in New York State (Albany: New York State Teachers Association, 1956).

HUMAN RELATIONS AND GROUP EFFORT

The effort to understand human behavior is not a new phenomenon. For centuries, philosophers, historians, dramatists, and poets have attemped to describe and account for a man's actions. But the systematic, sustained study of individual and group behavior is relatively new. Furthermore, some major factors in contemporary living, such as the increasing concentration of population into large centers, the fantastic economic and cultural interdependence of an industrial society, and the extension of democratic principles to most aspects of life, make imperative a more satisfying and productive utilization of men's energies. Men *must* learn how to conduct themselves individually and interact with one another in both small and large groups in ways that are constructive rather than destructive.

Industry, business, government agencies, the military services, and civic groups are interested, along with education, in knowing more about human relations and group effort. The schools have a double stake, perhaps, in the venture of greater understanding of human relations and group effort, for the school is not only a person-to-person enterprise needing to utilize new knowledge itself; it is also the living laboratory in which members of the next generation are daily shaping some of the attitudes and habits of perception which will play a large part throughout their lives.

Supervision of instruction is vitally concerned, for human relations and group efforts are at the heart of improving teaching-learning conditions. Five aspects of the subject will be discussed briefly: primacy of feelings, self-understanding, impact of person-to-person relations, dynamics of change, and dynamics of group effort. In each area significant understandings have been achieved, but only a beginning has been made. Instructional leaders need to contribute to this field of knowledge, as well as apply to relevant situations the findings from other researchers.

Primacy of Feelings

Perhaps one of the most telling insights has been the recognition of the primary quality of feeling in a situation. Emotion, or feeling tone, has a way of carrying power and taking priority. How a person feels in a situation intrudes upon the scene and commands attention, sometimes all of it. Individuals, especially adults, have considerable control of their emotions, but this control is far from complete. Strong feeling has an involuntary quality that makes it override an individual's efforts to concentrate wholly upon the task at hand. Even when he succeeds in controlling his emotions, the toll exacted in energy loss is only partially glimpsed. Robinson, in an article with the disconcerting title, "Neurotic and Normal Discourtesy in the Classroom," pointed out that teachers and pupils both finish the day far more weary than necessary, as a result of the constant jolting from the general lack of amenities, the direct commands, and the abrupt statements which are typical of many classrooms.[8] At more intense levels, some individuals are inhibited, almost paralyzed, by high anxiety.

Feelings have great power, for good or for ill. Strong feelings of a negative nature can reduce an individual's effectiveness in at least three ways: (1) by pre-occupying his attention until there is little or no time left for the task at hand; (2) by inhibiting his actions around the persons or subjects connected with the strong feeling; and (3) by distorting his perceptions of the situation.

Conversely, strong feelings of a positive nature increase energy and well-being. The individual moves about his task with a sense of warmth and lift. His interaction with others is enhanced. He is open to his own perceptions and the views of others. In either event, feelings have a stubborn ascendency which gives them great force in the daily living of each person, child or adult. If education can learn more about the conditions that will reduce negative feel-

[8] B. B. Robinson, "Neurotic and Normal Discourtesy in the Classroom," *Understanding the Child*, Vol. 15, No. 1 (January, 1946), pp. 8–10.

ings and increase positive ones, many teaching-learning situations can become vastly more productive. Supervision is strategically located for rendering help.

Self-Understanding

Out of the study of human behavior has come another insight of great significance to educators, namely, the importance of self-understanding. All the facts of behavior, all the mechanisms for ego-defense and ego-enhancement that people have developed for engaging in the transactions of life, and which the psychologists have cleverly classified and named, are true not just for the other fellow but for educators too. Three areas are mentioned here.

PROJECTION OF FEELING. If educators can become sensitive to the ease with which they, along with all other human beings, resort to rationalizing to "explain" mistakes in judgment, or project blame upon others when failure occurs, or are irritable in their dealings when anxiety is high, then there is considerable chance for improving the quality of living and learning in the classroom and throughout the system. Jersild,[9] Witherspoon [10] and others have indicated some common danger points for teachers in such matters as handling their own hostilities and traumatic experiences, in seeing children as they really are, in showing sustained kindness toward others, and in developing self-confidence and integrity. But much remains to be learned, both at the theoretical level and in application to specific situations.

ROLE OF THE SELF-CONCEPT. The central role of the self-concept in setting a person's expectations for himself and in selecting and rejecting new experiences is only partially understood. How the concept arises, maintains some aspects tenaciously and yet is modifiable

[9] Arthur T. Jersild, *When Teachers Face Themselves* (New York: Columbia University, 1955).

[10] Ralph I. Witherspoon, "Teacher, Know Thy Self," *Childhood Education*, Vol. 35, No. 2 (October, 1958), pp. 56–59.

by new experience, has been a subject of study from the time of Meade [11] and Cooley [12] and in the last few years has received a large amount of attention. Jersild,[13] Bills,[14] Pfuetze,[15] and Combs,[16] among others, have sought to trace the etiology of the self-concept and also to emphasize the power of the concept in shaping daily behavior. Again, if an educator can understand a little better how he is controlled by his own self-expectations, he is in a better position to act rationally, i.e., to make judgments based on all the known facts relevant to a situation.

THE PHENOMENOLOGICAL WORLD. Each person lives in a world slightly different from any other person's world. The nature of perception and uniqueness of experience make this condition inevitable. To recognize this fact is important in self-understanding, human relations and cooperative effort. When people work closely together, as educators do constantly, there will be some miscuing, some misunderstandings, because of differences in perception and experience. If individuals are keenly aware of this condition, they can accept minor difficulties with good humor, not seeking to place blame or ascribe ill-will and stupidity to all concerned. If they are sensitive to the ease of possibility of misunderstanding, they can, of course, often proceed in such a way as to prevent some of it.

Impact of Person-to-Person Relations

An understanding which seems almost too self-evident to mention relates to the importance of person-to-person relations. Yet the fact that many efforts in education have moved slowly or partially

[11] George Herbert Meade, *Mind, Self, and Society* (Chicago: University of Chicago Press, 1934).

[12] C. H. Cooley, *Human Nature and the Social Order* (New York: Scribners, 1922).

[13] A. T. Jersild, *In Search of Self* (New York: Columbia University, 1952).

[14] Robert E. Bills, *About People and Teaching*. Bulletin of the Bureau of School Service, Vol. 28, No. 2 (Lexington: University of Kentucky, December, 1955).

[15] Paul E. Pfuetze, *The Social Self* (New York: Bookman Associates, 1954).

[16] Arthur W. Combs. "New Horizons in Field Research: The Self-Concept," *Educational Leadership*. Vol. 15, No. 5 (February, 1958), pp. 315–319.

failed seems to arise in part from a lack of understanding of the significance of person-to-person relations. Sometimes a change in instructional method or curriculum design has been introduced, or some new goal incorporated, as though it had feet of its own on which to move forward. Yet almost every transaction in education is a person-to-person affair: child and child, child and teacher, teacher and teacher. If ideas are to have effect, it is usually through persons. Ideas are mediated by people. Hence, the feeling tone referred to above, along with other factors, gives considerable direction to the acceptance, rejection, or modification of ideas.

Perhaps the fact that the impact of person-to-person relations is so easily overlooked is only further evidence of the dimness of understanding in this area. Supervision should be in an excellent position to contribute to knowledge in the field, and also to profit from any increased understanding which is achieved.

Dynamics of Change

Human beings find themselves in a dilemma with regard to change. In many ways it is pleasant to cling to familiar procedures and materials; but at the same time it is pleasant to encounter the new and unexpected. In any event change, which is present in some degree in all cultures, proceeds at an accelerating pace in American society. The culture conflicts and ambivalent attitudes toward change cause frequent strains within a group of people trying to work together, and indeed within any one person. There is much unevenness in the way a given change proceeds.

Why some changes are made smoothly while others are resisted, why some people tend to welcome change while others habitually shun it, and why emotion is often so easily aroused in connection with change have been the subject of considerable investigation in the last three or four decades, under the general heading of dynamics of change. A number of new insights have been achieved, but much remains to be learned. A few of the generalizations having special import for supervision are mentioned here.

KNOWLEDGE ALONE IS SELDOM ENOUGH TO STIMULATE CHANGE. New knowledge does little by itself to bring about change, especially where long-standing habits are involved. For instance, publicizing the nutritional value of soy beans was not enough to bring the relatively strange food into the eating pattern for many American families. But when it became necessary to utilize food resources economically during the war, soy bean products became more popular. In like manner, some findings from educational research have little impact, since the person who might use them does not see them as important: i.e., they don't do anything for him or meet any need of his that isn't already met to his level of satisfaction some other way.

CHANGING ATTITUDES IS A SLOW PROCESS. Occasionally a sharp change in attitude springs from one or a few dramatic experiences, but typically the change is slow and basically difficult. Not only are related changes in habits of action involved, but prior to that must come changes in perception. These changes in perception are difficult, even painful, for an individual to achieve, for his current perceptions are deeply rooted in earlier experiences (often including childhood loyalties), unquestioned assumptions, and unanalyzed beliefs. To modify attitudes takes more than exhortations by co-workers.

ATTITUDES ARE COMPLEX AFFAIRS. The present level of understanding regarding attitude formation is far greater than in former years, but still is extremely limited. Improvement in teaching-learning situations often hinges on a modification in attitude. Hence instructional leaders have every reason to try to profit from what is now known and to help seek further understanding.

RESISTANCE TO CHANGE IS NOT CONTRARINESS. Sometimes resistance to change makes persons appear stubborn, perverse, or contrary, at least to those who favor the change. Spicer points out, however, that people do not naturally resist change and that constant change is a part of living. People do resist change when:

(a) They believe their basic securities are threatened
(b) They do not understand the change
(c) They resent being forced to change.[17]

It is extremely easy for the person who already sees the usefulness of a proposed change and who feels competent enough to take the beginning steps, to assume that the other fellow perceives the situation the same way. Therefore, any reluctance in the latter tends to look like contrariness or senseless opposition. But in reality, one or more of the factors mentioned by Spicer, or still other conditions, are operating to hinder fresh perception. Instructional leaders cannot afford to dismiss resistance to change as some kind of perversity or willfulness especially strong in some individuals, when what is needed is further examination of the underlying conditions.

CHANGE IS ENCOURAGED WHERE SUPPORT IS PRESENT. As pointed out earlier, change involves a degree of risk and output of effort. This takes energy. An individual is more likely to initiate change and to carry through change if he knows that others, whom he respects, are supporting him with their interest, good wishes, and often material aid. To know that other people are engaging in a similar effort is usually helpful. To live in an atmosphere of expectation of an experimental approach to problems is conducive to change. Clearly, supervision has a strategic role to carry in providing the support which expedites change. Much remains to be learned as to how to give effective expression of that support.

Dynamics of Group Effort

The analysis of conditions that enhance or dissipate group efforts has been of great concern to a number of individuals and organizations for several decades. Further exploratory and experimental work must be continued in order to extend present insights. Four observations having special import for supervision are mentioned here.

---

[17] Edward H. Spicer, *Human Problems and Technological Change* (New York: Russell Sage Foundation, 1952), p. 18.

POWER OF HIGH MORALE. The energy-giving nature of high morale in a group has been noted informally for a long time. For instance, playing teams and military units with unusually high morale have often performed remarkable feats or broken previous records. In recent years, experimental studies involving careful controls have been made in connection with production in industry, and have documented the power effect of high morale in teamwork.[18] More seems involved than sheer efficiency springing from well-coordinated efforts, although smooth coordination undoubtedly makes for greater productivity.

Just how the feeling tone of high morale translates itself into energy for work is not clearly understood. Some interesting possibilities are suggested by the clue in the common observation that persons working with high morale seem to experience less fatigue than ordinarily. Might it be that individuals working with high confidence and trust in one another, with expectation of mutual acceptance of their efforts in a joint undertaking, expend little or no energy in self-defense mechanisms and needless anxieties, and hence have more than normal energy for the work at hand? If so, supervision has a clue for constructive work in helping develop high morale.

IMPORTANCE OF PURPOSE. Whatever other factors may be operating in a given situation, the purpose for which the group exists remains central. It is the vital core of operation. It is only when the purpose is kept sharply in focus that appropriateness of procedures can be judged adequately. Some persons, attempting to study factors in group dynamics, have found themselves investigating peripheral matters if the central purpose of the group was not kept constantly in mind. For instance, the desirable size of a group cannot be studied in isolation from the question of the purpose of that group. How a group of thirty should be seated in a room depends in part upon whether or not the purpose of the meeting is primarily discussion among members. When the purpose of a group is clear,

[18] Norman Maier, *Psychology in Industry*, 2nd Ed. (Boston: Houghton-Mifflin, 1955).

several forms of organization or structure may be found to be appropriate or at least possible.

INVOLVEMENT OF MEMBERS.   Group effort becomes effective and members willingly give themselves to it when they feel actively involved, not merely in the doing, but in the deciding of what is to be done. According to Selznick,[19] members of an organization take a genuine interest in their group when they have a chance to make significant rather than routine choices regarding the organization. Instructional leaders have much to contribute and much to learn about helping members of educational groups become involved at more than a perfunctory level.

VARIETY OF ROLES.   One of the relatively new insights gained from analysis of group efforts is the realization of the variety of roles being carried in a functioning group, and the constructive purposes served by the different roles. The interaction in a group is not all of the same piece or quality, to be charted adequately with arrows and tallied as to frequency of member responses. In a group thinking deeply about a subject, there will be, for instance, the quick suggestor or initiator of ideas, the qualifier, the negator who sees all the reasons why an idea won't work, the humorist whose comments may relieve tensions and restore perspective, the irritator who likes to startle others into new thinking. It takes many kind of reactions to move the thinking forward and arrive at decisions. It is interesting to note that while one individual may tend to carry the same role, because of personality or experience background, throughout a session or in several meetings, he is not to be regarded as uniformly carrying one role. In the course of a single meeting he may make contributions of practically every type ever categorized. Instructional leaders need to be students of the interaction in a group, in order to involve the talents of all the members and to expedite the group's efforts.

[19] Philip Selznick, *Leadership in Administration* (White Plains, N. Y.: Row, Peterson & Company, 1957), pp. 56–61.

CHANGE AND THE MATURE PERSON

The familiar statement that "as a person grows older he becomes neither better nor worse, only more like himself" has a kernel of truth in it, but is far from the whole truth. On the one hand, there are many factors which make for stability and continuity in personality and outlook. For instance, such broad qualities as sunniness of disposition or perseverance are recognizable in an individual over a period of years.[20] In fact, they may be partly rooted in constitutional conditions, factors which remain largely constant throughout an individual's lifetime. In addition, for the mature person, prior experience has built up assumptive forms which he brings as expectations to new experience, with the expectation being so rigid at times as to distort his perception of the new.[21]

Hence there are good reasons why mature people continue to be "like themselves." Indeed, it would be a chaotic world if human beings could not develop enough stability and consistency in their values and behavior to anticipate their own and others' actions.

Desire for New Experience

But that is not the whole story. Human beings also have a desire for new experience. As Murphy points out, the yen to know more, to break through the cultural mold, is part of man's humanness.[22] Even if an individual does not actively seek adventure, some new experience comes his way and alters his behavior, at least a little.

Mature people *do* change and they *do* give some direction to that change. Zirbes raises the pertinent question, "What does a mature

[20] Patricia Neilon, "Shirley's Babies After Fifteen Years," *Journal of Genetic Psychology*, Vol. 73, No. 2 (December, 1948), pp. 175–186.

[21] Hadley Cantril, *The Why of Man's Experience* (New York: The Macmillan Co., 1950).

[22] Gardner Murphy, *Human Potentialities* (New York: Basic Books, Inc., 1958).

person do who wants to keep on growing?" and offers a number of suggestions:

1. He uses his problems as challenges to go beyond the point where his habits and previous experience take him, to go beyond his habit-tracks and current know-how to find out more.
2. He turns whatever *is* in the way of resources to account in new ways to serve his needs and challenges.
3. He is open to new ideas in an exploratory, evaluative way, taking time to gain insight as to why an idea might work, and not being precipitate in his movement away from old ways.
4. He is not rigid, fixed; not willing to fall into a stereotype and turn his mind away.
5. He considers his situational realities as challenges to his own formative action, trusting himself in the process of groping, and then forming a plan.
6. In due time he aspires to try out some new action, perhaps in a small way. He acts on the realization that he can learn by trying, without expertness first, knowing that the first attempt is the starting point for further development.
7. He is not defeatist nor easily squelched. If he is blocked in one direction, he tries another, finding some new channel or new part of the field around which to polarize, or something in the circumstances to modify.
8. He does not ask someone to give him a pattern to which he just conforms. He expects his own initiative to help shape whatever he engages in.
9. He doesn't go at things blind or piecemeal. He considers the whole as he works with parts, and sees whatever he is looking at in a context of present and potential relationships.
10. He does something with hunches and ideas. He lets hunches nudge him into action.
11. He is energized by the satisfaction of the process of closure and the feed-back of creative effort. He is deeply and whole-heartedly involved, giving himself without strain or stricture.
12. He looks ahead, seeing next steps. He moves into the next phase with momentum. He doesn't so much *plant* his feet; he puts them down lightly, rhythmically, knowing there are more steps to take.

13. He likes to cooperate, is not a crank for his own ideas. He knows that second thoughts are sometimes better than first ones and that interaction of ideas leads to still further ideas.
14. He becomes increasingly aspiring, confident, trusting of new experience, and creative.[23]

There is great urgency for educators, psychologists, sociologists, and others to study the processes and conditions conducive to the continued personal growth of adults. The rapidly increasing life-span means that many more pepole have many more years of mature living than used to be the case. Meanwhile, the accelerating pace of social and technological change brings a host of major changes within the lifetime of any one individual. If human beings are to benefit from the majority of changes in their personal and professional lives, they need to learn to enjoy the process of change, instead of being thrown into frequent panic by it. Supervision has a tremendous role to play in helping teachers make transitions, and in supporting them emotionally and materially as new developments make new demands upon them.

Adult Capacity for Learning

One encouraging factor is the reassessment of the capacity to learn in adult years. Fortunately, the old assumption that mature people could learn only with difficulty is being dispelled. While it is true than an individual's sensory acuity and reaction time decline gradually during his maturity, the decline is slow and slight. Kidd reports studies indicating that in his later years a person still has, barring the effects of accident or disease, a high percentage of the acuity and reaction time which he possessed at the peak of his physical attainments. Meanwhile, some aspects, such as capacity to use vocabulary, show no loss during adult years, and for people engaged in work demanding verbal skill there is a tendency for these areas to show an increase. Kidd also makes the observation that adults

[23] Laura Zirbes, Abridged from Lecture in Conference on *Creative Leadership* (Florida State University, August, 1958).

of all ages can learn effectively, and that age has no veto power over learning.[24]

Supervision not only needs to help teachers find the growing edge of their lives and assist them in pushing back the boundaries; it needs to render this assistance in such a manner that the individual gains the self-direction, confidence, and understanding necessary to keep on growing. Stimulation of growth that leaves the individual dependent upon the instructional leader for further growth is short of the ideal. Just how this is to be accomplished needs much more attention and analysis than has been given so far. Perhaps one suggestion can be inferred from the fact that instructional leaders should not expect to be thanked by an individual for the help rendered while he was taking the next step in personal development, for unless the person sees the step as something he took by himself (and therefore no expression of thanks is called for), he cannot gain the independence needed for later steps.

Instructional leaders themselves need to keep on growing, of course. Where is their support for change and growth in mature years to come from? Part of their stimulation for growth comes from the very fact that they are working with the vanguard of ideas, and in their struggles with daily problems are constantly looking ahead. But the degree to which they can deal constructively with problems and ideas may be closely related to the quality of relationships among themselves and with all school personnel. If the atmosphere is one of trust and confidence, they can be open to one another, supportive, and concerned. Then instructional leaders too, find it not only safe, but also exciting, to explore and to grow.

CREATIVITY, ANXIETY, AND THE CLASSROOM

The basic need of human beings for creativity in their lives, and the urgent need of current society for creative individuals has been

---

[24] James R. Kidd, *How Adults Learn* (New York: Association Press, 1959), Chs. 3 and 4.

discussed in Chapters 3 and 4, dealing with foundations and major functions of supervision. One important frontier of educational effort today relates to extending an understanding of how children and teachers can live in the classroom in such a way as to encourage the development of creativity.

It is true that there are many forces in contemporary society which tend to stifle creativity. For instance, to indicate but a few, there is the loss of the geographic frontier with its demands for improvisation, initiative, and resourcefulness in daily living. There is the drive toward conformity in an industrial society which, to operate smoothly, must deal in "standard parts" and therefore has difficulty in utilizing odd sizes. There is the impact of mass media of communication in shaping a similarity in information, reaction, and opinion.

On the other hand, there are also forces in contemporary society which stimulate creativity. For instance, again to name but a few, there is the great variability in human talents exhibited in a heterogeneous population. There is the explosion of knowledge which, in its applications and in its theoretical extensions, leads to still further invention and discovery. There is the great variety of material available to man for creative use. And there are in human relations and other areas enormous problems calling for fresh and imaginative solutions. Out of this welter of conflicting forces, educators must try to clarify what it is that will help nurture creative approaches to problems.

It has been observed that young children, upon coming to school, still have a great deal of candidly expressed curiosity and explore the world with free-ranging imagination. Somewhere in the next few years these qualities seem sharply to diminish for most children. It is proper to ask whether this apparent diminishing is a natural developmental phase, or whether classroom living and other aspects of life unwittingly stifle these qualities. It is also important to look at adults who are especially creative to see what qualities distinguish them, and then to ask the proper question as to whether there is anything the schools can do to nurture those qualities.

Qualities of the Creative Individual

Spontaneity is a quality often observed in creative persons. Lowenfeld identified several qualities, including flexibility in thinking and imagination, emotional freedom and fearlessness enough to deviate from stereotype repetitions, and experimental attitudes, to be characteristic of children engaged in creative work.[25]

Taylor and his associates, in studying scientists who were outstandingly productive, found the following qualities or dimensions of the mind highly prized: flexibility, fluency of ideas, sensing a problem area, playfulness with ideas, capacity to be puzzled, depth of penetration, foresight of consequences, and tolerance of ambiguity while seeking closure of the field.[26]

All that is important about creativity cannot be encompassed by classifying qualities. Yet the effort to ascertain qualities relevant to creative persons gives school personnel some sense of direction in working with children and youth, and with one another.

Creativity and Intelligence

Taylor also points out that when productive scientists themselves were asked to rank intellectual characteristics as needed on the job, they put adaptive flexibility first. Among the twenty characteristics ranked highest, only one—verbal power—is well represented in typical tests for intelligence. The school has long been dedicated to the intellectual development of children and youth, but it may well be that intellectual development has been defined too narrowly, having been associated almost exclusively with high accomplishments in verbal and quantitative skills.

The tendency of contemporary society to equate creative talent with extremely high intelligence test scores is unfortunate. According to Taylor, reports from the three Utah conferences on the Iden-

[25] Victor Lowenfeld, *Creative and Mental Growth*, 3rd Ed. (New York: The Macmillan Co., 1957), pp. 50–59.

[26] Calvin W. Taylor, "The Creative Individual," *Educational Leadership*, Vol. 18, No. 1 (October, 1960), pp. 7–12.

tification of Creative Scientific Talent (1955, 1957, 1959) indicate that creativity scores and I Q scores are at most only lowly related. This situation should not be surprising, perhaps, since traditional intelligence tests do not reflect ability to create new ideas or things.[27]

Creativity and the Classroom

It may be argued by some that creativity is so highly individual-istic that what the schools do can have little influence, or that the influence is minor, if it exists at all, since the school is not the only place nor the ideal place for cultivating creativity. But many other people look to the school to promote creativity. An uneasy feeling prevails among many educators that not enough goes on in nu-merous classrooms to contribute to the development of qualities needed by creative people, and that too much goes on which blights the opportunities for creativity to flourish.

Far more needs to be known about what creative teachers do in the classrooms, and what conditions seem to be conducive to de-veloping in children the qualities needed by creative persons. For instance, what conditions would encourage children to be playful with ideas, to be sensitive to problem areas, to revise their own first ideas on a subject? Plainly, some practices rather commonly found in schools in the past would not encourage, but actually negate, the development of the desired qualities. For example, the rigid sched-uling of the day into small periods, the tightly structured lesson-plans, and the constant sense of haste associated with some class-rooms would preclude the opportunity for much spontaneity or adaptive flexibility on the part of either children or teachers.

Anxiety and the Classroom

Possibly one of the most destructive forces for creativity is the high degree of anxiety experienced by many children and teachers. Intense, sustained anxiety can apparently disable or cripple many persons, causing them to be less noticing and adaptive in situations

[27] Ibid.

calling for wise action and problem-solving than if they were not under strain.

Sarason found high-anxious children and youth scattered among all age levels and all ability levels. Many highly intelligent children were also highly anxious. Apparently many highly anxious children are extremely dependent on what others think of them, and the question, "Am I doing it right?" is constantly before them. When the highly anxious child is put into a problem-solving situation where he has to make choices on his own, he does not function well.[28] In like manner, it may be supposed that highly anxious teachers and other school personnel do not function well when they are in problem-solving situations: i.e., it is hard for them to risk themselves in open-ended situations where a clear answer is not already available as to whether or not they are "doing it right."

Often the highly anxious or over-stimulated person is so eager to reach the goal that he is oblivious to new ideas or nuances of meaning. It is easy to see that such a person, whether teacher or learner, would find it hard to tolerate second thoughts, revisions of ideas, and alternate routes to a goal. He would not want to take time to be creative.

There is much to be learned about how instructional leaders can help teachers and children (and one another) reduce crippling anxiety so that all may function at their best. Instructional leaders have a very real responsibility to see that, as they work for the improvement of teaching-learning situations, they themselves do not create new irrational anxieties for others.

NEW KNOWLEDGE ABOUT
THE LEARNING PROCESS

Answers to many key questions about the process of learning still elude the psychologist, psychiatrist, physiologist, educator, and

---

[28] Seymore B. Sarason, "Anxiety and Learning," *Human Variability and Learning*. Association for Supervision and Curriculum Development (Washington, D.C.: National Education Association, 1961), pp. 14–23.

other students of the subject. However, much has been learned in recent years which still needs to be incorporated more widely into the classroom, and the experimental work necessary to make wise use of research findings is a challenge to instructional leadership. Meanwhile, the general shape of several significant concepts is taking enough form to let educators know that something important is imminent. Only a few such ideas are mentioned here.

Power of Human Mentation

Kubie argues that the power of human mentation is enormous, but that much of the potential is lost or impeded through conflicts and defenses.

"Under ideal circumstances, memory and thinking are carried on neither consciously nor unconsciously but in the preconscious stream of automatic mentation, which proceeds at phenomenal speed. Of this swift stream, conscious processes provide us with tentative summaries and fragmentary samples; but conscious and, even more, unconscious processes combine to distort and delay and impede and sometimes wholly to block the processes of conscious summary and sampling by which the data from the preconscious stream can be put to work in human affairs." [29]

The role of the preconscious in creativity is a large one, according to Kubie, for it is here that a person's total experience is available to him in a free-ranging situation, not delimited by the boundaries of conscious effort and not distorted by the rigidities of the sub-conscious.[30] Apparently our senses take note of, and the nervous system records, far more than we are aware of. All these impressions are actually present in the preconscious as data or "grist for the mill," as the organism attempts to solve its problems of living. A person is richer than he knows.

If Kubie is right about the velocity and sweep of mentation, instructional leaders have an urgent need to participate in some of

[29] Lawrence S. Kubie, "Are We Educating for Maturity?" National Education Association Journal, Vol. 49, No. 1 (January, 1959), pp. 58–63.
[30] Lawrence S. Kubie, Neurotic Distortion of the Creative Process (Lawrence: University of Kansas, 1958).

the research relating to a better understanding of the process of mentation and the role of the preconscious. Also, the need is imperative for them to engage immediately in a thorough analysis of the routines and regimen of the school day, in order to find those policies and procedures, often widely accepted by educators and lay persons alike, which tend unnecessarily to augment the normal stress of living instead of offsetting some of the strain.

Subliminal Learning

The term, *subliminal learning*, has received considerable public attention in recent years, accompanied by varied feelings. The ominous quality connected with its possible use in brain-washing techniques has been felt by many. At the same time, persons have felt mixed emotions, including humor, over the advertizing world's efforts to use subliminal stimuli in television.

Apparently persons in any situation are receiving more information from their sensory reporters than they are conscious of noting and cataloging. The process is probably that of the preconscious as Kubie refers to it. Many examples have been documented through the years of persons under hypnosis being able to recall clearly what they could not remember intentionally before, and of persons under an anesthetic or other drug reciting passages in a foreign language which they had heard only once casually.

One of the most significant examples, from the standpoint of education, relates to individuals who are taken into a strange room for a few minutes and upon coming out, are asked to list all that they noticed. If they are then hypnotized and asked to describe what they observed, they list far more items than before.

The implications here are large for the importance of a rich classroom and total school environment and atmosphere. The situation lends some credence to the old observation, that some things in education "are better caught than taught." Once again there is a big role for instructional leaders in helping create conditions that assure constructive rather than destructive subliminal stimulation, and in helping the understanding of its wise, intentional use.

Uniqueness of Learning Style

Another idea now glimpsed only dimly relates to the possible connection between brain-wave patterns as revealed by the electro-encephalogram, and dependence upon a particular style of learning. Several rhythms have been noted. Walter and his associates have found distinctions based on the way a person's EEG record changes with stimulation.[31] Could it be that persons exhibiting a strong alpha rhythm are dependent primarily upon hearing or kinesthetic perceptions for their learning, while those showing little alpha rhythm are largely dependent upon visual imagery in thinking?

In the present state of knowledge, doctors and school personnel probably could not classify profitably the brain-wave patterns of all learners. But even with the present limited understanding, it is reasonable to suppose that any one classroom contains all types of learners, and therefore that it is *basic* for a variety of media and procedures to be used in every classroom if all participants are to learn efficiently. A child having prolonged difficulty in learning might conceivably be in trouble, not through any lack of desire or effort on his part, or insufficient cleverness on the part of the teacher, but largely because of extreme dependence upon a now obscure style of learning.

Body Chemistry and Learning

The idea of improving an individual's learning through changes in his nutrition, vitamin utilization, or basal metabolism is a fascinating one. Sometimes over-enthusiastic popular acclaim has greeted any finding in this area, and has led to high hopes which were soon dashed. Nevertheless a number of gains have been made, and the near future holds great promise. It is apparently still fanciful to picture a whole class of fifth-graders taking a vitamin tablet each day to improve their spelling or arithmetic computation skill, but that

[31] W. G. Walter, *The Living Brain* (New York: Norton, 1953), Ch. 8, "Intimations of Personality."

the learning of certain individuals may profit, under some conditions, from vitamin therapy is probably not unrealistic. Tyler observes, "There is some possibility that in younger children dietary deficiencies may impair mental functioning as well as personality, and that proper treatment may improve it." She then cites studies in the use of thiamin and of glutamic acid where the findings, on the surface at least, seemed flatly contradictory, with some studies indicating a positive relationship and others not. Furthermore, when gains in I.Q. scores were found, the amount was small, less than five points on the average.[32]

Nevertheless the whole field of chemotherapy is rich with promise for the future. Such basic factors in learning as the retentiveness of the nervous system and vividness of sensory impression, which are known to differ considerably from one person to another, might conceivably be related to chemical conditions, and hence persons suffering from deficiencies might benefit from treatment.

Utilization of Learning Aids

Another frontier which is still new enough to need intensive farmer pioneer work is that of the utilization of learning aids in the form of machines. While educators are still in the process of finding the best ways to use television, still another major product of the technological world is brought to a point of beginning use, namely, automated learning machines. These machines present a highly sequential program of material, and involve the individual's response, pacing, and immediate feed-back from the effort to learn.

Instructional leaders have a large job to do in helping ascertain the best ways of utilizing learning machines. The search seems to have at least three directions.

One search is in the direction of finding the conditions for optimum use, and involves such questions as the length of time, the type of subject matter, the kind of skill and understanding which is

---

[32] Leona E. Tyler, *The Psychology of Human Differences*, 2nd Ed. (New York: Appleton-Century-Crofts, Inc., 1956), pp. 433–434.

the goal, and the kind of learner who benefits most. Each question requires much experimental work. Some studies need to involve the cross-section approach, whereas others will need to be longitudinal in nature.

A second direction is that of preventing abuse. Perhaps because children and teachers alike are under considerable pressure to learn rapidly, there is a tendency for many persons to regard any new learning aid as a panacea with almost magical powers. Under those conditions the aid may be used indiscriminately, without proper regard for its appropriateness for the situation, the individual, or the point at which diminishing returns set in. Then sometimes the same persons who were over-enthusiastic to begin with, cry out in disillusionment and denounce the aid entirely. Educators need to help themselves, as well as parents and children, be discriminating in their use of machines and realistic in their expectations of outcomes.

A third direction of search is perhaps the most challenging of all for instructional leaders: that is, the most constructive use of the time and effort saved through incorporating machines into the supply of learning materials. Theoretically, the machine helps children learn efficiently (i.e., maximum learning increment per units of time and energy expended) that which is already known in the world.

Theoretically too, the machine frees teachers from many of the repetitive tasks of teaching. What constructive ends can this saved time and energy be made to serve? Are classrooms ready to make creative use of the precious human potential thus made available?

PERCEPTION AND BEHAVIOR

Throughout the chapters of this book it has been important to take note frequently of the significance of perception as related to behavior, especially in making changes in behavior. The field is mentioned here simply because it is a frontier where much remains to be learned, where what has already been learned needs wider utilization, where the findings, both old and new, are so central to the daily work of supervision, and where instructional leaders have such a vital part to play in the pursuit of new knowledge. Five general areas, each calling for further work, are mentioned.

Role of Previous Experience

The role of prior experience is crucial in perception of new situations. The viewer makes the best sense he can out of the new event or object, according to what possible meanings are available to him from his previous encountering of similar situations. Thus a first-grade child who is familiar with the concept and word *trashbasket*, but not *trespasses*, may be heard to repeat earnestly, "Forgive us our trashbaskets as we forgive others." Adults, too, will usually try to bring to bear all they have upon a new situation. Hence, to see a problem afresh often requires an extension of experience. The fixity or rigidity with which a person assigns meaning to a situation which, at first glance, resembles familiar ones has also been recognized. Studies from such laboratories as the Hanover Institute for Associated Research and the Visual Demonstration Center at the Ohio State University, have greatly enlarged understanding as to how hard it is for human beings to form new perceptions that go counter to prior experience. Here again, there are implications for supervision.

Uniqueness of Perception

The extent to which a person assumes that what is obvious to him is obvious to others, and remains unaware that he and the other fellow are not (cannot be) seeing the same event exactly alike, is highly significant in supervision. Personal misunderstandings, strained human relations, and what appears to be professional indifference or antagonism are often traceable to differences in perception springing from uniqueness of experience. This frequently documented fact needs to be remembered more widely as people try to work together closely.

Impact of Emotion

The extent to which emotion enters into perception, making a person highly selective of what he notices, is of concern in supervision. Feelings of fear or anxiety, for instance, often create an expectation of threat, and what a person expects to see, he tends to find or read into the next situation. Hence, such a person may find threat or disapproval of himself in the most innocent of suggestions or, sometimes, even in routine announcements.

Role of the Self-Concept

The role of the self-concept in shaping a person's expectations for himself, and therefore the way he perceives his response to new situations, is significant in supervision. Of great importance too is the finding, from the work of Bills and others,[33] of the relationship between the way a person sees himself as an adequate or inadequate individual, and the way that person sees others, and the way he assumes others see themselves and others. Evidently, a person not only tends to read his own evaluation of himself into the estimate he thinks others are making of him, but he also assumes that they estimate themselves and others in like manner.

Perception, Belief, and Behavior

Perception gives the basis for believing, and believing is the basis for taking action. Hence behavior follows as naturally as day follows night, water runs downhill, or rain falls when the atmospheric conditions are in a certain relationship. Seeing is believing, as

[33] Robert Bills, *About People and Teaching*, Bulletin of the Bureau of School Service, Vol. 28, No. 2 (Lexington: University of Kentucky, December 1959), p. 20.

Combs and Snygg have observed, and the behaving that follows the seeing-believing of a situation is extremely rational and logical in the eyes of the behaver.[34] All the conditions being what they are at the time of perception—such as physical status, prior experience, value system, purposes and emotional involvement—the individual is convinced of the reailty of his seeing and therefore acts with conviction.

The extremely important point for supervision, for teaching in the classroom, and for other human relations undertakings is the increasingly clear realization that persons seldom act out of whimsy or intentional contrariness. What a person does is usually plausible and right to him. If his action appears unwise to others, nothing is gained by their assigning his actions to undesirable motives and then complaining about the limitations and fallabilities of human beings. But much can be gained by a sympathetic effort to analyze the situation to find out what he sees, and therefore that on which he must believe and act.

AN INTERDISCIPLINARY APPROACH:
TRANSLATING AND INTEGRATING KNOWLEDGE

It has become almost commonplace to speak of the explosion of knowledge in the mid-twentieth century. But while busy marveling at the products of this knowledge, many persons find it easy to overlook an important problem arising from its vastness and complexity: namely, the increasing difficulty of communication among disciplines.

Need for Integration of Knowledge

The extent of man's knowledge led him long ago to try to systematize his findings into areas for logical arrangement, storing, and

---

[34] Arthur W. Combs and Donald Snygg, *Individual Behavior*, Rev. Ed. (New York: Harper & Brothers, 1959), Ch. 2.

further extension of the boundaries of understanding. The last few years have seen the addition of whole new disciplines and the frequent sub-dividing of familiar ones. The amount of specialization has necessarily increased. But a point of compartmentalization and fragmentation has been reached in many situations, which is so great that even workers within the same discipline have difficulty communicating with one another. The old observation that a specialist is one who knows everything about his subject except its relation to the rest of the world, threatens to take on intense meaning.

There is great need for integration of new knowledge both into its own discipline and into related fields. New knowledge won at the growing edge of a discipline, has to be incorporated into the logic of that discipline. This is not always easy, for it involves re-evaluation of existing knowledge, and frequently a drastic reorganization and even rejection of former beliefs.

Meanwhile the new knowledge can also be utilized in other situations and disciplines, but only if helpful variations and implications are noted. The ability to grasp the principle involved in a new idea, rather than being fixated upon its present form and derivation, is essential as individuals try to use new ideas. Yet there is sometimes serious difficulty in grasping the principle, for the complexity of the process by which the new knowledge was won encrusts the idea and obscures the core of its meaning. There needs to be a kind of translation before the essence is discernible.

Double Role of Education

Education has a double role with regard to new knowledge. First, education is an avid user of research from its own field and from the many disciplines relevant to learning processes, human development, and social ideals. Hence it is constantly concerned with seeking new understandings and integrating them into the body of knowledge and techniques available to the profession in fulfilling its purposes.

Second, education has a vital role to play in the translation act referred to above. Here is a frontier brought into existence by the great need to get at the essence of ideas so that many persons can benefit from them. How it is to be accomplished is not fully understood. But it is clear that specialists and educators need to work together in the translating process,[35] in at least three types of situations: (1) with children, for apparently children and youth can grasp significant and difficult ideas earlier than sometimes supposed, if the ideas are not encumbered with complicated forms and rituals; (2) with adults retraining for new types of complex work; and (3) with specialists who need to understand one another's worlds.

Supervision and the Integration of Knowledge

Supervision, involved as it is with the continuous improvement of teaching-learning situations, is at the heart of the effort to extend and to utilize interdisciplinary approaches. In the first place, instructional leaders constantly seek new information, for they are aware of the urgency of problems and frustration points in the teaching-learning act. Second, they need to engage in contemplation, and in collaboration with specialists, to strip away obscuring details in order to let the essence of ideas shine through. Third, they need to hypothesize and test relationships, for they are often in the best position to see implications and to speculate upon the possible significance of findings from many fields. Fourth, instructional leaders need to help integrate the new findings with one another and with older knowledge, so that a self-consistent whole emerges, rather than a tangled eclecticism. Here indeed is a frontier for supervision.

From a study of the frontiers of supervision can come a sharpened sense of direction for both long-range goals and immediate objectives. Careful consideration of the nature of the frontiers can also yield deepened convictions as to the profound worth of the educational enterprise and the full significance of the contributions of supervision to that enterprise. In turn, clear purposes and deep convictions help provide energy for the still greater realization of the dimensions of supervision.

[35] Jerome S. Bruner, *The Process of Education* (Cambridge: Harvard University Press, 1960).

AIDS TO STUDY AND DISCUSSION

1. Select one of the suggested frontiers, and go to professional periodicals for the current year in search of further findings in the area.

2. Go to the literature on group dynamics for an analysis of such activities as buzz sessions and brain storming. What underlying principles are actually involved? What is the difference between group dynamics as a social science and as a technique or gadget?

3. Using as a starting point Zirbes' description of mature persons who want to keep on growing, devise questions or a check-list for an instructional leader to use in finding out whether he is helping or hindering teachers as they try to grow in their mature years. Analyze your list for implications as to what a leader should do in order to be helpful.

SUGGESTIONS FOR FURTHER READING

Association for Supervision and Curriculum Development, *Leadership for Improving Instruction*, 1960 Yearbook (Washington, D.C.: National Education Association).

Bills, Robert E., *About People and Teaching*. Bulletin of the Bureau of School Service, Vol. 28, No. 2 (Lexington: University of Kentucky, December, 1955).

Brown, C. G., and Thomas S. Cohn, *The Study of Leadership* (Danville, Ill.: The Interstate Printers and Publishers, Inc., 1958).

Bruner, Jerome S., *The Process of Education* (Cambridge: Harvard University Press, 1960).

Cantril, Hadley, *The Why of Man's Experience* (New York: The Macmillan Co., 1950).

Combs, Arthur W., "New Horizons in Field Research: The Self-Concept," *Educational Leadership*, Vol. 15, No. 5 (February, 1958), pp. 315–319.

Combs, Arthur W., and Donald Snygg, *Individual Behavior*, Rev. Ed. (New York: Harper & Brothers, 1959), Ch. 2.

Cooley, Charles Horton, *Human Nature and the Social Order* (New York: Scribner's, 1922).

The Dynamics of Instructional Groups, Fifty-ninth Yearbook, Part 2, Nelson B. Henry, Editor (Chicago: National Society for the Study of Education, 1960).

Hemphill, John K., *Situational Factors in Leadership* (Columbus: Ohio State University, 1949), pp. 99–100.

Jersild, A. T., *In Search of Self* (New York: Columbia University, 1952).

———, *When Teachers Face Themselves* (New York: Columbia University, 1955).

Kidd, James R., *How Adults Learn* (New York: Association Press, 1959), Ch. 4.

Kubie, Lawrence S., "Are We Educating for Maturity?" National Education Association Journal, Vol. 48, No. 1 (January, 1959), pp. 58–63.

———, *Neurotic Distortion of the Creative Process* (Lawrence: University of Kansas, 1958).

Learning and the Teacher, 1959 Yearbook, Association for Supervision and Curriculum Development (Washington, D.C.: National Education Association, 1959).

Lewin, Kurt, and others, "Patterns of Aggressive Behavior in Experimentally Created Social Climates," *Journal of Social Psychology*, Vol. 10, No. 3 (May, 1939), pp. 271–299.

Lowenfeld, Victor, *Creative and Mental Growth*, 3rd Ed. (New York: The Macmillan Co., 1957), pp. 50–59.

Maier, Norman, *Psychology in Industry*, 2nd Ed. (Boston: Houghton Mifflin Company, 1955).

Meade, George Herbert, *Mind, Self, and Society* (Chicago: University of Chicago Press, 1934).

Meece, Leonard E., and Howard Eckel, *Experimentation in Preparing School Leaders*, Bulletin of the Bureau of School Service, University of Kentucky, Vol. 33, No. 4 (June, 1961).

Murphy, Gardner, *Human Potentialities* (New York: Basic Books, Inc., 1958).

National Training Laboratories, *Selected Reading Series*: One, "Group Development"; Two, "Leadership in Action"; Three, "Forces in Learning"; Four, "Community Development" (Washington, D.C.: National Education Association, 1961).

Neilon, Patricia, "Shirley's Babies After Fifteen Years," *Journal of Genetic Psychology*, Vol. 73, No. 2 (December, 1948), pp. 175–186.

Pfuetze, Paul E., *The Social Self* (New York: Bookman Associates, 1954).

Robinson, B. B., "Neurotic and Normal Discourtesy in the Classroom," *Understanding the Child*, Vol. 15, No. 1 (January, 1946), pp. 8–10.

Rokeach, Milton, *The Open and Closed Mind* (New York: Basic Books, Inc., 1960).

Sarason, Seymore B., "Anxiety and Learning," *Human Variability and Learning*, Association for Supervision and Curriculum Development (Washington, D.C.: National Education Association, 1961), pp. 14–23.

Selznick, Phillip, *Leadership in Administration* (White Plains, N. Y.: Row, Peterson & Co., 1957), pp. 56–61.

Spicer, Edward H., *Human Problems and Technological Change* (New York: Russell Sage Foundation, 1952).

Taylor, Calvin W., "The Creative Individual," *Educational Leadership*, Vol. 18, No. 1 (October, 1960), pp. 7–12.

Tyler, Leona E., *The Psychology of Human Differences*, 2nd Ed. (New York: Appleton-Century-Crofts, Inc., 1956), pp. 433–434.

Walter, W. G., *The Living Brain* (New York: W. W. Norton & Company, Inc., 1953).

Williams, R. J., *Biochemical Individuality* (New York: John Wiley & Sons, Inc., 1956).

Witherspoon, Ralph I., "Teacher, Know Thy Self," *Childhood Education*, Vol. 35, No. 2 (October, 1958).

Your School and Staffing, Series from the Cooperative Development of Public School Administration in New York State (Albany: New York State Teachers Association, 1956).

Zirbes, Laura, Lecture in Conference on Creative Leadership (Tallahassee: Florida State University, August, 1958).

APPENDIX A

SUPERVISION AS EXPERIENCED BY TEACHERS

EACH of the following incidents is described in the teacher's own words.

INDUCTION OF A NEW STAFF MEMBER

During the fall, I accepted a half-time position as a county test analyst. In this position the majority of my duties were psychometric in nature; however, I was also to work with principals on a type of minor in-service training program in measurement, and to encourage and assist teachers in doing action research. In order to do this it would be necessary for me to make myself known to the teachers and the principals in the county. Since I had never had any experience in the public school system nor worked in a professional capacity before, I felt very insecure in the role in which I had been cast.

I am certain that I would have been reluctant to visit schools, and too insecure to describe fluently my services to the school personnel. Fortunately this was a responsibility from which I was relieved. The county supervisor accompanied me on initial school visits, introduced me, and did a far better job of selling me than I could have done myself. I believe that by helping me in this way to overcome my initial insecurity, the supervisor helped me and the county. She helped me by supplying needed confidence, and this confidence helped me to perform my county duties more effectively.[1]

INTERPRETING A CHANGE IN PROGRAM

A young, enthusiastic kindergarten teacher fresh from college replaced an older woman who was teaching kindergarten "just because no one else would take it." She had no degree in anything and made it clear that she would no longer teach kindergarten, that the children just couldn't learn to read and write as well as she thought five-year-olds should.

The new teacher feared the harm which might arise if she immediately replaced formal reading and writing with other forms of activities. She thought that the parents would not consider that she was teaching reading, science, arithmetic or English if she did not have definite periods and texts, in some cases, for teaching her subjects.

The young teacher, new in the community, had through visits and pre-school conferences found out that the parents were greatly concerned as to how much reading and writing their children were going to learn in kindergarten. The teacher put sole trust in her supervisor. Together they decided on a plan through which the supervisor would simply tell the true objectives of kindergartens to the parents. Through informal personal contacts, at club meet-

---

[1] Contributed by Mrs. Joan Bashaw, Tallahassee, Fla.

ings, and at various places and opportunities, she purposely, but without announcement of her purpose, quietly sold the new teacher and her program to the community.[2]

THE PRINCIPAL SAVES A BEGINNING TEACHER

CAST OF CHARACTERS: a new teacher
                        an old-timer teacher
                        a principal

SETTING: An elementary school during the first week of classes in the fall.

SITUATION: A new teacher, fresh out of college with zealous idealism, is employed as a first grade teacher in a modern-looking elementary school in the United States. Flashback: Unbeknownst to the young teacher, three previous new teachers have left this very school after one year of teaching because of a common experience. The common experience for all three teachers was confronting a certain "old timer." This teacher, equipped with dogmatic ideas, unshakable self-confidence, and permanent tenure, constituted a traumatic encounter for each of the soft-shelled newcomers. The situation of employing and holding new teachers at this school was becoming a crucial one to the principal.

PRESENT ACTION: The principal decides definite action must be taken to avoid such a surprising, traumatic encounter again. He must provide an atmosphere conducive for attracting young, idealistic teachers, for he believes this is necessary leaven for the sagging doughy "old-timers" (of which he has many). He also must uphold the reputation of the school.

Up to this point, the principal has never forewarned a new

2 Contributed by Mr. Ben Eubanks, Bristol, Fla.

teacher. This time he decides to "talk it over" with the new teacher. How does he go about this? He calls the new teacher into his office during the pre-planning sessions prior to the opening of school. He explains, confidentially, to the new teacher that she will have to work with a woman who has been thought by some as "difficult to deal with." He assures her, however, that because of certain factors in this woman's life she has had to develop a hardness to people. He enumerates the older teacher's good points and suggests ways the young teacher might call upon the older one for assistance. He suggests other initial approaches: be friendly but impervious to brusque remarks; be independent but willing to accept some suggestions from a more experienced teacher; seek advice from several different teachers, so that no one teacher feels "responsible" for the success or failure of the new teacher.

FOLLOW-UP: Teacher followed suggestions of principal. Teacher stayed on a second year. Her staying seemed to inspire—gave confidence and tact to the older teacher. Other teachers noticed the change in her.[3]

HELPING A TRANSPLANTED TEACHER

As a transplanted sixth grade teacher, whose specialization was in the area of biological sciences, I felt insecure about teaching sixth grade English. The principal suggested taking this problem to the school's language arts supervisor. The supervisor was contacted, and a few days later she slipped quietly into the back of the room during the latter part of the English class. Having made this appointment with the supervisor myself, I was fully aware of a specific reason for her visit and looked forward to getting some specific help on my problem.

After the children left, the supervisor stayed to discuss with me the program of language arts in the sixth grade. She answered my

[3] Contributed by Mrs. Catherine Fixx Davis, Verona, N. J.

questions which were of a general nature. Then the supervisor and I began to discuss the children and their general problem of communication. We attempted to ascertain their needs in the area of language arts and discussed them in regard to what our sixth grade language arts curriculum had to offer. Thus she helped me to isolate and analyze my problems. During the course of this conference I felt a growing wish to help these children with difficulties and problems in the area of language arts. I felt a wish to challenge them to a new interest in their native language. The supervisor had succeeded in motivating me to action.

The supervisor put at my disposal some instructional aids for sixth grade English, made suggestions for planning units of study which would include a wide range of materials suited to the heterogeneous group in this class, and made available some solutions to the problems which had been used successfully with similar groups of sixth graders.

This supervisor created a favorable attitude toward her role in the school program. This helped me develop professionally and gave me self-confidence toward supervisory experiences.[4]

4 Contributed by Mrs. Catherine Gretch, Tallahassee, Fla.

APPENDIX B

CURRICULUM COUNCIL ORGANIZATION[1]

THE Elementary Principals' Association, in recognition of the ever-changing needs in the elementary program, recommended that a curriculum council be formed with representatives of all persons concerned with the development and continuation of a good school program.

During the school year 1957–58, the Director of Elementary Education and a planning committee of eight elementary principals made plans for the formation of such a council. It soon became evident that in order to solve our own local problems, it was necessary to develop a tailor-made plan to meet our own needs.

From time to time, the work of the committee was evaluated and revised by the elementary principals, elementary teachers and administrative staff of Pinellas County.

The cooperative plans herein are presented, as revised in July, 1960, to be used as guidelines as the councils continue in actual operation. These plans will be continuously evaluated and adjusted as determined by emerging needs.

[1] Excerpts from "A Cooperative Approach to Curriculum Development in Pinellas County," Floyd Christian, Superintendent, Clearwater, Florida, Revised, July, 1960.

CURRICULUM COUNCIL

We Believe:

That continuous planning, development and evaluation of the curriculum are essential

That curriculum should be defined as including those experiences of children for which the school accepts responsibility

That the individual school is the basic unit for curriculum planning

That the principal is responsible for the instructional leadership in his school

That the classroom teacher is the key person responsible for effecting desirable growth of children under her guidance

That children should be provided with opportunities to participate cooperatively with the teacher in planning and evaluating experiences

That the effectiveness of the curriculum should be measured by desired growth in the behavior of children, i.e., in appreciations, attitudes, skills, self-discipline, self-confidence, respect for the worth and dignity of the individual, critical thinking, value judgments, creative thinking, study habits, concepts, intellectual curiosity, moral and spiritual values, respect for authority, citizenship, safety and health habits, and respect for the dignity of work

That it should be the responsibility of all school personnel to interpret the curriculum to the public, and to give due consideration to its critical thinking.

Function:

This council should have regularly scheduled meetings and be a continuous part of the school program

This council should provide a two-way channel of communication

This council should have representation from all personnel that influence the experience of the learner

The work of this council should include recommendations of policy regarding any part of the total school program

This council should recommend in-service education in terms of expressed needs

This council should determine needs in the area of special services and work for maximum coordination in the use of these services

This council should determine the needs for the development of curriculum guides and organize special committees to work in these areas

This council should provide for vertical (continuity from grade to grade) as well as horizontal (experiences within the grades) articulation of the curriculum.

Organization:

The county elementary schools are divided into eight geographic areas, each with an area curriculum council.

Area Curriculum Councils:

A. COMPOSITION

1. One classroom teacher from each school

2. One elementary principal from each area

3. One music consultant from each area

4. One art consultant from each area

5. One reading consultant from each area

6. One visiting teacher from each area

B. Tenure

1. Classroom teachers, three years (one-third to be appointed for one year; one-third for two years, and one-third for three years— for the first year only, in order to establish a rotating membership)

2. Elementary principals one year

3. Music consultants permanent

4. Art consultants permanent

5. Reading consultants, three years (same as classroom teachers)

6. Visiting teachers permanent

C. Duties of members of area curriculum councils

1. To present problems which the groups whom they represent have discussed and have directed them to take to the area council

2. To decide which of these problems are of county-wide importance. Concerns sent to the area council by one group or school should, if not solved or explained in the meeting of the area council, be directed to all schools in the area for consideration and recommendation

3. To discuss, analyze and make recommendations to the Central Curriculum Council upon which the majority of schools in an area have agreed

4. To record and duplicate, in sufficient quantity for each member of the area and central council, the minutes of each Area Curriculum Council meeting as follows:

   a. Problems presented and discussed

   b. Problems directed to all schools in the area for consideration

   c. Recommendations to the central council,—such recommendations to be made when the majority of schools in an area have considered the recommendation and are in agreement that the problem is one of concern to the area as a whole

5. To discuss the minutes of the Area Curriculum Councils' meetings with members of the organizations which they represent

6. To select one member to represent the Area Council on the Central Curriculum Council for a two-year term

D. MEETINGS

1. To be held four or five times annually at one of the schools in the area

2. Each to last approximately one and one-half hours—from 3:30 to 5:00 p.m.

3. To follow Central Council meetings by approximately six weeks

E. STEPS IN THE CONSIDERATION OF A PROBLEM RAISED BY A LOCAL FACULTY

1. The local school faculty or group concerned about a problem directs its representative to the Curriculum Council to present the problem to the Area Council

2. The Area Council considers the problem. If the solution or explanation cannot be effected in this meeting, the problem is directed to the faculties of all the schools in this area:

   a. To discover the nature and extent of the problem

   b. To make recommendations for the solution of the problem

3. The representative from each school or group in the area takes the recommendations to the next Area Curriculum Council meeting

4. If, after careful consideration by the members of the Area Council, it is felt that the problem is one of area-wide concern, the group makes a recommendation to the Central Council for the solution of the problem, or refers the problem to the Central Council for study.

Central Curriculum Council

A. COMPOSITION

1. Eight classroom teachers (one from each Area Curriculum Council)

2. One representative from Instructional Materials

3. One representative from the Elementary Librarians' group

4. One representative from Educational Services

5. One representative from Special Education

6. One representative from Area Art

7. One representative from Area Music

8. One representative from Administrative Services

9. One representative from the Elementary Principals' Association (chairman of the elementary principals or his selected representative)

10. One representative from Educational Television

11. One representative from Elementary Supervision

12. One representative from School Lunch

13. Chairman of the Central Curriculum Council—Director of Elementary Curriculum

14. Director of Secondary Curriculum or his representative

15. One elementary principal from the Administrative Council

16. Assistant Superintendent for Instruction or his representative

B. TENURE

1. All permanent appointments, with the exception of the classroom teachers and elementary principals

2. Classroom teachers appointed for two years (½ appointed for one year; ½ appointed for two years for the first year, to establish rotating membership)

C. Duties of members of the central curriculum council

1. To present problems

2. To decide which of these problems are of county-wide importance

3. To consider problems, discussions and recommendations presented from the Area Curriculum Councils

4. To discuss, analyze and make recommendations to the elementary curriculum councils and the county administration

5. To recommend and appoint special committees as needed (to develop curriculum guides; to do research; and to work on related problems)

6. To dismiss special committees upon completion of work

7. To record and duplicate for each member the minutes of all curriculum council meetings as follows:

   a. Problems presented

   b. Discussion

   c. Recommendations

8. To discuss the minutes of the Central Curriculum Council meetings with members of the organizations which they represent

D. Meetings

1. To be held approximately four times annually

2. Sessions to last from approximately 2:30 to 5:00 p.m.

3. To follow the area council meetings by approximately two weeks

Area Council recorders are requested to use the following form for reporting meetings. Use of this form will greatly facilitate the organization of material sent from all area councils. Sufficient copies of these minutes should be duplicated so that each member of the Area and Central Council can have a copy. Two copies should be forwarded immediately to the Director of Elementary Curriculum.

Minutes of Area ——————— Curriculum Council

Date ——————————— Place of Meeting ———————————

   I. Members present:

  II. Problems, if any, directed to schools or groups in this area for further study and/or recommendations:

      1.

      2.

 III. Recommendations, if any, to the Central Curriculum Council:

      1.

      2.

 IV. Notes from the meeting concerning the problems presented or studies undertaken:

———————————————————

Secretary

INDEX